Project Success

To my family, Mary Anne, Rebecca and Roxanne

Project Success

Critical Factors and Behaviours

EMANUEL CAMILLERI
Visiting Senior Lecturer,
Faculty of Economics, Management and Accountancy,
University of Malta

Routledge
Taylor & Francis Group

LONDON AND NEW YORK

First published in paperback 2024

First published 2011 by Gower Publishing

Published 2016 by Routledge
4 Park Square, Milton Park, Abingdon, Oxon OX14 4RN

and by Routledge
605 Third Avenue, New York, NY 10158

Routledge is an imprint of the Taylor & Francis Group, an informa business

British Library Cataloguing in Publication Data
Camilleri, Emanuel.
   Project success : critical factors and behaviours.
   1. Project management.
   I. Title
   658.4'04–dc22

Library of Congress Cataloging-in-Publication Data
Camilleri, Emanuel.
  Project success : critical factors and behaviours / Emanuel Camilleri.
     p. cm.
  Includes bibliographical references and index.
  ISBN 978-0-566-09228-2 (hbk. : alk. paper)
 1. Project management –Evaluation. I. Title.

  HD69.P75C362 2010
  658.4'04–dc22

           2010033177

ISBN: 978-0-566-09228-2 (hbk)
ISBN: 978-1-03-283840-3 (pbk)
ISBN: 978-1-315-60249-3 (ebk)

DOI: 10.4324/9781315602493

Contents

PART V   ORGANIZATIONAL PROJECT DIAGNOSTIC MODEL

List of Figures and Table

Table

Foreword

Project management has become an important way of managing tasks in modern organizations in all sectors, private, public, and not-for-profit. Research demonstrates, however, that most projects fail to deliver on time, within the allocated budget and with the expected quality of performance. Because of this paradox, the book *Project Success: Critical Factors and Behaviours* is timely. Dr Emanuel Camilleri defines in a very structured way what project management is, and what kind of interventions might contribute to achieve a higher success rate.

According to Camilleri, successful project management is obtained if three basic categories of project management factors are optimized: the project hygiene support factors (strategic fit, project scope, project organization, project team, project planning and control), the informational support factors (information flow and knowledge management, project risk management, project competency development) and the behavioural and managerial support factors (management and leadership, employee commitment and participation, internal and external communication). Dr Camilleri brings these three main categories of factors, each with its subparts, together in one single model for project success and discusses every component in detail. He also offers a methodology to help assess the maturity of an organization to undertake projects and determine whether it has the mechanisms in place to implement its projects.

The book is not only well structured, it is also illustrated with examples and figures that facilitate a reader's comprehension. Students will undoubtedly find this book an interesting text because of its completeness. Practitioners will enjoy the book because of the many examples of factors one has to keep in mind in managing projects. Finally, scholars will appreciate reading this book because the author pays a lot of attention to the scientific context and gives many references for further reading.

This successful combination of teaching, practical and scientific value is due to the experiences and competencies of Dr Emanuel Camilleri. In addition to his long experience as a lecturer and researcher, he had a long career in banking (Commonwealth Banking Corporation) and public service (Australian Public Service, Maltese Public Service) in which he applied the fundamentals of project management repeatedly. This has certainly contributed to the success of this book project.

We recommend this book to all who want to enhance their knowledge, skills and abilities in project management.

Prof. Dr Annie Hondeghem,
Public Management Institute,
K.U. Leuven (Belgium)

Prof. Dr James Perry,
School for Public and Environmental Affairs,
Indiana University (USA)

Preface and Acknowledgements

This book, entitled *Project Success: Critical Factors and Behaviours* goes beyond merely discussing and examining the concept of project management. The book is inspired by over 40 years of experience and is supported by extensive research into what makes projects truly successful.

My first involvement with a project was in the late 1960s when I was an employee with the Commonwealth Savings Bank of Australia. The project involved the computerization of the head office branch in Melbourne. More specifically, the project, which was to be conducted during the Easter long weekend holiday period, had the objective of converting about 1.5 million ledger accounts (hard copies) into a format that could be read by a mainframe computer. I was just one person of several hundred who played a role in what was considered to be a daunting undertaking. What made the undertaking a daunting one was the demand for an extremely high level of accuracy and the short time period involved for the data conversion process. However, with the proper level of planning and the appropriate application of resources, the assignment was achieved and the bank opened for normal business on the Tuesday following Easter Friday. The transition that took place in those several days was to enable the bank to change over from an entirely manual process to a computerized system. Later, I came to appreciate that project management is just one phase of a much longer delicate process.

However, it was not until I joined the Commonwealth of Australia, Department of Supply (later known as Department of Defence Support) in the beginning of the 1970s that projects became an integral part of my working life and have remained so since then. The Department of Supply was responsible for the production of munitions, small arms, ordnance, and aircraft production. In this type of industrial environment, projects were never lacking, however the necessary tools to define and manage projects were still at an embryonic stage. It was during this period that Sidney Silk, Industrial Engineering Divisional Head, inspired and encouraged me to apply Operations Research (OR) techniques at the Ammunition Factory, namely, using Project Evaluation Review Technique (PERT) for managing projects, simulation of production lines using General Purpose Simulation System (GPSS) and solving various linear programming problems using LP500. PERT was extensively used, particularly in the establishment of new production lines and in managing the development of accounting and production control computer systems. In fact, I view this book as a tribute to my colleagues at the Ammunition Factory, particularly Sidney Silk. One must understand that this was an era of experimentation and development in what was considered as a pioneering undertaking in using OR techniques, particularly the integration of management information systems, such as accounting and production control systems with project management using PERT.

In 1980 I was seconded to the Australian Development Assistance Bureau (ADAB) as an aid expert to establish the Malta Government Computer Centre (GCC). This was also a pioneering undertaking because it was the birth of the extensive application of information technology and management information systems development in Malta.

During my headship tenure at GCC, my team managed to establish a professional computer centre and undertake the development of over one hundred major Government computer systems. Although extensive development in the field of computer technology has taken place since that period, the databases generated by these pioneering systems were fundamental for some of the major modern systems that are in place today. In the mid-1980s, I joined the Maltese Public Service at the Ministry of Finance, and have worked on numerous change-management projects in preparation for Malta's accession as a member of the European Union. The major projects undertaken during this period included, the establishment of the Value Added Tax (VAT) Department; the business process reengineering of the Inland Revenue Department (IRD); the establishment of the Tax Compliance Unit (TCU); the introduction of Accrual Accounting across Government Ministries; defining the strategy for implementing eProcurement across Government; and defining the strategy for the amalgamation of the Customs, VAT, IRD and TCU Departments as a single revenue collecting Department.

However, during these many years of involvement in managing projects, two questions have always intrigued me. Why are some projects perceived as failures when they have met all the traditional standards of success, namely, completed on time, completed within budget and meeting all the technical specifications? Why are some projects perceived to be successful when they have failed to meet two important criteria that are traditionally associated with success, namely, not completed on time and not completed within budget? It is these questions that are the fundamental basis of my research on project success. In this book I have tried to combine experience with research. This combination of knowledge from experience and research highlight that project success depends not only on the traditional project management characteristics, particularly, project planning and control, but also on behavioural and informational support factors.

It must also be recognized that the value added from both experience and research are often incremental. For instance, the lessons learnt through experience are cumulative, because each project tends to be unique and has its own individual concerns and successes. A major lesson that I have learnt in managing projects is that technical issues are normally resolved without too much fuss. However, human behavioural related issues tend to be the most troublesome. Furthermore, knowledge from research tends to build on the research of others. My research is no exception. Therefore, I would like to formally acknowledge the work of other researchers, particularly Brian Sutton for the work related to his model regarding assessing project success; James Antill and Ronald Woodhead for their explicit work regarding Project Planning and Control; and the Project Management Institute for the compilation of the Project Management Body of Knowledge, covering every aspect of project management.

Finally, I would like to acknowledge the effort of all the staff at Gower publishing, namely Martin West who provided his invaluable and professional advice regarding the development of the general concept of this book and its specific focus; Donna Shanks who assisted me with formatting the book and ensuring that I followed the established Gower publishing standards; Anthea Lockley who meticulously carried out the proofreading; Emily Ruskell for her valuable assistance in the production process; and Sue White and her marketing team for the professional way they promoted this book.

Emanuel Camilleri

List of Abbreviations

CBS	Cost Breakdown Structure
CEO	Chief Executive Officer
CPM	Critical Path Method
CSF	Critical Success Factors
DSS	Decision Support Systems
EFT	Earliest Finish Time
EIS	Executive Information Systems
EST	Earliest Start Time
FF	Free float
HR	Human Resource
ICT	Information and Communications Technology
IRM	Information Resource Management
LFT	Latest Finish Time
LST	Latest Start Time
MIS	Management Information System
MOST	Mission, Objectives, Strategic Direction and Tactics
MRP	Material Requirement Planning
NASA	National Aeronautics and Space Administration
PERT	Project Evaluation Review Technique
PMI	Project Management Institute
PPS	Project Planning and Scheduling
TF	Total float
WBS	Work Breakdown Structure
Y2K	Millennium bug (computer malfunction on 1 January 2000 at 12 a.m.)

In Search of Factors That Facilitate Project Success

The chapters in Part I have the objective of setting the scene and identifying the factors that facilitate project success. They illustrate the importance of the application of project management in organizations and why organizations are motivated to develop project management competencies. Furthermore they provide details of what constitutes a project thus distinguishing project management from operations management. A brief history of project management is also provided so that the reader may appreciate the need for this important organizational tool and how it has developed and evolved through the different industrial development periods.

Finally, project management research studies are examined with the aim of identifying the reasons why some projects succeed and others fail. The various project success and failure reasons are then classified into what is referred to as project success factors. The aim is to offer applied research findings to both the practitioner and the academic researcher. A project success model is proposed which will provide the basis for the remaining chapters, where each project success factor category is examined and discussed in detail.

CHAPTER 1

Introduction

The secret to getting ahead is getting started. The secret of getting started is breaking your complex, overwhelming tasks into small manageable tasks and then starting on the first one.

Mark Twain, writer (1835–1910)

Project management is an important topic because all organizations, be they small or large at one time or other are involved in implementing new undertakings. These undertakings may be diverse, such as the development of a new product or service; the establishment of a new production line in a manufacturing enterprise; a public relations promotion campaign; or the construction of major building programmes. Whilst the 1980s were about *quality* and the 1990s were all about *globalization*, the 2000s are about *velocity*. That is, to keep ahead of their competitors, organizations are continually faced with the development of complex products, services and processes with very short time-to-market windows combined with the need for cross-functional expertise. In this scenario, project management becomes a very important and powerful tool in the hands of organizations that understand its use and have the competencies to apply it.

The development of project management capabilities in organizations, simultaneously with the application of management information systems allows enterprise teams to work in partnership in defining plans and managing take-to-market projects by synchronizing team-oriented tasks, schedules and resource allocations. This allows cross-functional teams to create and share project information. However, this is not sufficient; management information systems have the potential to allow project management practices to take place in a real-time environment. As a consequence of this potential project management proficiency, locally, nationally or globally dispersed users are able to view and interact concurrently with the same updated project information immediately, including project schedules, threaded discussions and other relevant documentation. In this scenario the term *dispersed user* takes on a wider meaning. It not only includes the cross-functional management teams but also experts drawn from the organization's supply chain and business partners.

On a macro level, organizations are motivated to implement project management techniques to ensure that their undertakings (small or major) are delivered on time, within the cost budget and to the stipulated quality. On a micro level, project management, combined with an appropriate management information system, has the objectives of reducing project overhead costs; customizing the project workplace to fit the operational style of the project teams and respective team members; proactively informing the executive management strata of the strategic projects on a real-time basis; ensuring that project team members share accurate, meaningful and timely project documents; and ensuring that critical task deadlines are met. However, whilst the motivation and objectives to apply project management in organizations is commendable, they do not assure project success.

Why are some projects perceived as failures when they have met all the traditional standards of success, namely, completed on time, completed within budget and meeting all the technical specifications? Why are some projects perceived to be successful when they have failed to meet two important criteria that are traditionally associated with success, namely, not completed on time and not completed within budget? The question regarding what constitutes project success is a complex and illusive issue because it depends a great deal on the perceptions of different stakeholders. To reduce this complexity, it is imperative that a critical set of project management success factors are identified and explored. Adherence to these identified project success factors would minimize project risk and maximize the probability of project success in terms of stakeholder perceptions. Therefore, a primary objective of this book is to examine project management research studies so that key factors that affect perceived project success and failure are identified. By doing this, a number of measures that need to be adopted to influence and develop a project success mind-set within the various stakeholders may be prescribed.

What Constitutes a Project?

A close inspection of organizations reveals one obvious common factor between them, they all perform work. However, a closer scrutiny of the work that organizations perform reveals a very important distinction, in that work can generally be classified into two primary categories, routine tasks (or operations) and projects. In some instances these two categories of work may overlap.

A major function of an organization is to be able to manage its work, be it operations or project related. For instance, the management of operations focuses on carefully supervising the processes to produce and distribute products and services. Operations management also refers to all the operations within the organization. Related operational activities include managing purchases, inventory control, quality control, storage, logistics and evaluations. The primary focus of operations management is on efficiency and effectiveness of processes. Hence, operations management is often comprised of considerable measurement and analysis of internal processes. Ultimately, the nature of how operations management is carried out in an organization depends very much on the nature of products or services rendered by the organization. For example, retail, manufacturing, wholesale and a variety of others. Therefore, a primary attribute of operational work includes the repetitiveness of processes over a period of time.

In contrast, a project is seen as a finite (temporary) piece of work that has a beginning and an end (Butterick, 2000). For instance, a factory manufacturing components is predominantly conducting a series of operations or processes on an ongoing and repetitive basis until all customer orders have been completed. However, the same factory may want to establish a new production line to manufacture a completely different component. Hence, the tasks to establish this new production line may be considered as a project since it is temporary. Note that it is the task of setting up the new production line that is temporary. Once the new production line is established, the new components will be manufactured by a series of processes on a repetitive basis until no more orders are received from customers (these process become the core functions of the organization).

However, projects and operations do have some common attributes. They are both performed by people, are confined by limited resources and are planned, executed and controlled. The important element that differentiates projects from operations is the level of uniqueness. The spectrum of human undertakings spans from totally repetitive to totally unique. Therefore, at one extreme is the production of commodities such as beer and at the other extreme is the construction of structures such as the San Francisco Golden Gate Bridge or Channel Tunnel linking the United Kingdom with France. In between, there is a mixture of other undertakings, such as the construction of roads, erection of dwellings, the development of new products, such as a new variety of beer and the development of new services in banking, retail or tourism. The Project Management Institute Standards Committee (1996, p. 4) defines a project as a temporary endeavour undertaken to create a unique product or service. The word *temporary* means that every project has a definite beginning and a definite end; whereas *unique* signifies that the product or service is different in some distinguishing way from all similar products or services.

When referring to projects, there is often the connotation of something major or grand. However, it must be emphasized that projects may be undertaken at all levels of the organization and may involve only one person or numerous persons; may require relatively few hours to complete or thousands of hours; may involve a single unit of an organization or may cross organizational boundaries as for instance in private–public partnerships. Other examples of projects include developing a new product design; preparing and delivering a report; the installation of new equipment; a new marketing campaign; moving to a new office block; and organizing a conference or a reception. Projects may also be viewed as an agent of change. Thomsett and Thomsett (2000) view this attribute as the key to the difference between process and project work.

What is Project Management?

Projects are not reserved for a particular profession, such as engineers or architects. Everyone at sometime or other has to coordinate tasks. Frequently, there is the need to coordinate numerous collections of related tasks that result in the carrying out of a number of projects concurrently. In addition, these concurrent projects require bringing together suitable people for the appropriate reason, with the proper resources, at the fitting place and at the appropriate time. This is what project management is all about.

Project management is often viewed as the application of knowledge, competencies, methods and tools to achieve the defined project tasks in order to satisfy stakeholder requirements and expectations from a project. However, this view of project management is too generic; the terms used may equally be applicable to operations management. Turner (1993) highlights four major differences between projects and operations:

1. The operations environment is relatively stable, whereas the project environment is very flexible and may change from day-to-day;
2. Operations become increasingly more efficient through a variety of work study methods. However, it is more difficult to attain efficiency gains with projects because being unique they have no precedent. Hence, the project team must be effective in achieving its objectives;
3. Operations personnel have predefined roles, whereas the role of project teams are constantly changing and at times require individuals to fulfil several roles concurrently;

4. Projects are prone to considerable risk depending on their level of uniqueness. Having no precedence, the project team is constantly uncertain whether the targets may be achieved. Once operational processes have been functioning for some time delivery targets are predictable.

These differences suggest that projects and operations are very different and therefore require a different managerial emphasis and approach. Traditionally, project management has been viewed as the mechanism by which a project is brought to a successful conclusion within the constraints of time, cost and quality. However, the most important consideration is whether or not the project achieves its objective; that is, has the project achieved it purpose, does it do what it is supposed to do.

Therefore, project management may be seen as a formalized and structured method of managing change in a meticulous manner. It focuses on developing specifically defined outputs that are to be delivered by a certain time, to a defined quality and with a given level of resources so that planned outcomes and benefits are achieved. However, the application of any general project management methodology requires an appropriate consideration of the corporate, business and sometimes social and political culture that forms a particular project's environment. As stated previously, whether a project is considered successful ultimately depends on the perceptions of different stakeholders that have an interest in the project.

A Brief History of Project Management

Project management has been practised for thousands of years dating back to the Egyptian epoch. However, it was in the mid-1950s that organizations commenced applying formal project management tools and techniques to complex projects. Modern project management techniques had their origins in two parallel but different problems of planning and control in projects in the United States. The first case involved the US Navy which at that time was concerned with the control of contracts for its Polaris Missile project. These contracts consisted of research, development work and manufacturing of parts that were unique and had never been previously undertaken. This particular project was characterized by high uncertainty, since neither cost nor time could be accurately estimated. Hence, completion times were based on probabilities. Duration estimates were based on optimistic, pessimistic and most likely times. These three time scenarios were mathematically assessed to determine the probable completion date. This procedure was called Project Evaluation Review Technique (PERT). Initially, PERT did not take cost into consideration. However, the cost feature was later included using the same estimating approach as with time. Due to the three estimation scenarios, PERT was found to be best suited for projects with a high degree of uncertainty reflecting their level of uniqueness.

The second case, involved the private sector, namely, E.I. du Pont de Nemours Company, which had undertaken to construct major chemical plants in the USA. Unlike the Navy Polaris project, these construction undertakings required accurate time and cost estimates. The methodology developed by this company was originally referred to as Project Planning and Scheduling (PPS). PPS required realistic estimates of cost and time, which makes it a more definitive approach than PERT. The PPS technique was later developed into the Critical Path Method (CPM) that became very popular with the construction industry. During the

1960s and 1970s, both PERT and CPM increased their popularity within the private and public sectors. Defence Departments of various countries, NASA and large engineering and construction companies world wide applied project management principles and tools to manage large budget, schedule-driven projects.

The popularity in the use of these project management tools during this period coincided with the development of computers and the associated packages that specialized in project management. However, initially these computer packages were very costly and executed only on mainframe or mini-computers. The use of project management techniques in the 1980s was facilitated with the advent of the personal computer and associated low cost project management software. Hence, during this period, manufacturing and software development sectors started to adopt and implement sophisticated project management practices as well. By the 1990s, project management theories, tools and techniques were widely received by different industries and organizations. Carayannis, Kwak and Anhari (2005) identify four periods in the development of modern project management:

1. Prior to 1958 – Craft system to human relations;
2. 1958 to 1979 – Application of Management Science;
3. 1980 to 1994 – Production Centre to Human Resources;
4. 1995 to Present – Creating a New Environment.

PRIOR TO 1958 – CRAFT SYSTEM TO HUMAN RELATIONS

During this time, the evolution of technology, such as automobiles and telecommunications shortened the project schedule. For instance, automobiles allowed effective resource allocation and mobility, whilst the telecommunication system increased the speed of communication. Similarly, the job specification that later became the basis of developing the Work Breakdown Structure (WBS) was widely used and Henry Gantt invented the Gantt chart. Examples of projects undertaken during this period as supported by documented evidence include:

1. Building the pacific railroad in the 1850s;
2. Construction of the Hoover Dam in 1931–1936, that employed approximately 5,200 workers and is still one of the highest gravity dams in the USA generating more than four billion kilowatt-hours a year;
3. The Manhattan Project in 1942–1945 which was the pioneer research and development project that designed and built the atomic bomb, involving 125,000 workers and costing nearly US$2 billion.

1958 TO 1979 – APPLICATION OF MANAGEMENT SCIENCE

Significant technology advancement took place between 1958 and 1979, such as the first automatic plain-paper copier by Xerox in 1959. Between 1956 and 1958 several core project management tools including CPM and PERT were introduced. However, this period was characterized by the rapid development of computer technology. The progression from the mainframe computer to the mini-computer in the 1970s made computers affordable to medium sized companies. In 1975, Bill Gates and Paul Allen founded Microsoft. What is more, the evolution of computer technology encouraged the emergence of several project management software companies, including Artemis and Oracle in 1977, and Scitor Corporation in 1979. In the 1970s other project management tools such as Material Requirement Planning (MRP) were introduced. Examples of projects undertaken during this period and which influenced the development of modern project management as we know it today include:

1. The Polaris missile project initiated in 1956 that had the objective of delivering nuclear missiles carried by submarines, known as Fleet Ballistic Missile for the US Navy. The first Polaris missile was successfully launched in 1961;
2. The Apollo project initiated in 1960 with the aim of sending man to the moon;
3. E.I. du Pont de Nemours chemical plant project commencing in 1958, that had the goal of building major chemical production plants across the USA.

1980 TO 1994 – PRODUCTION CENTRE TO HUMAN RESOURCES

The 1980s and 1990s are characterized by the revolutionary development in the information management sector with the introduction of the personal computer (PC) and associated computer communications networking facilities. This development resulted in having low cost multitasking PCs that had high efficiency in managing and controlling complex project schedules. During this period relatively low cost project management software for PCs became widely available that made project management techniques more easily accessible. Examples of major projects undertaken during this period that illustrate the application of high technology, and project management tools and practices include:

1. The England–France Channel project, 1989 to 1991. This project was an international project that involved two governments, several financial institutions, engineering construction companies and many other organizations from the two countries. The language, use of standard metrics and other communication differences needed to be closely coordinated;
2. The Space Shuttle Challenger project, 1983 to 1986. The disaster of the Challenger space shuttle focused attention on risk management, group dynamics and quality management;
3. The XV Calgary Winter Olympic of 1988 which successfully applied project management practices to event management.

1995 TO PRESENT – CREATING A NEW ENVIRONMENT

This period is dominated by the developments related to the internet that dramatically changed business practices in the mid-1990s. The internet has provided a fast, interactive and customized new medium that allows people to browse, purchase and track products and services online instantly. This has resulted in making organizations more productive, more efficient and more customer-oriented. Moreover, many of today's project management software have an internet connectivity feature. This allows automatic uploading of data so that anyone around the globe with a standard browser may:

1. Input the most recent status of their assigned tasks;
2. Find out how the overall project is doing;

3. Be informed of any delays or advances in the schedule;
4. Stay "in the loop" for their project role while working independently at a remote site.

An example of a major project undertaken during this period is the Year 2000 (Y2K) project. The Y2K Project, known as the millennium bug referred to the problem that computers may not function correctly on 1 January 2000 at 12 a.m. This was a global phenomenon and was highly problematic because resolving the problem at one's organization did not guarantee immunity, since a breakdown in the organization's supply chain could affect the organization's operating capability. Many organizations set up a project office to control and comply with their stakeholders regarding the Y2K issue.

Furthermore, use of the Internet was common practice that led to the establishment of the virtual project office. The goal of this virtual project office was to deliver uninterrupted turn-of-the-century monitoring of the Y2K project efforts. It was also to provide coordination; develop a risk management plan and communicate Y2K compliance efforts with various stakeholders. Thus, the virtual project office was a focal point for all the project works. It increased the awareness and importance of risk management practices to numerous organizations.

Why Project Management?

There is no doubt that organizations today face more aggressive competition than in the past and the business environment they operate in is a highly turbulent one. This scenario has increased the need for organizational accountability for the private and public sectors, leading to a greater focus and demand for operational effectiveness and efficiency. Effectiveness and efficiency may be facilitated through the introduction of best practices that are able to optimize the management of organizational resources. It has been shown that operations and projects are dissimilar with each requiring different management techniques. Hence, in a project environment, project management can support the achievement of project and organizational goals; and provide a greater assurance to stakeholders that resources are being managed effectively.

Research by Roberts and Furlonger (2000) in a study of information systems projects show that using a reasonably detailed project management methodology, as compared to a loose methodology, improves productivity by 20 to 30 per cent. The use of a formalized project management structure to projects can facilitate:

1. Clarification of project scope;
2. Agreement of objectives and goals;
3. Identifying resources needed;
4. Ensuring accountability for results and performance;
5. Encouraging the project team to focus on the final benefits to be achieved.

Moreover, the research indicates that 85 to 90 per cent of projects fail to deliver on time, on budget and to the quality of performance expected. The major causes identified for this situation include:

1. Lack of a valid business case justifying the project;
2. Objectives not properly defined and agreed;
3. Lack of communication and stakeholder management;
4. Outcomes and/or benefits not properly defined in measurable terms;
5. Lack of quality control;
6. Poor estimation of duration and cost;
7. Inadequate definition and acceptance of roles (governance);
8. Insufficient planning and coordination of resources.

It should be emphasized that the causes for the failure to deliver on time, on budget and to the quality of performance expected could be addressed by the application of project management practices. However, the failure to deliver on time, on budget and to the quality of performance expected does not necessarily mean that the project was itself a failure. At this stage what is being discussed is the effectiveness and efficiency of project execution and not whether a project is a success or failure. It is stressed that project management should be viewed as a tool that helps organizations to execute designated projects effectively and efficiently. However, the use of this project management tool does not automatically guarantee project success. Project success is a complex issue that will be discussed in subsequent chapters.

Conclusion

Project management is an important issue because all organizations irrespective of their size and industry are involved in initiating new undertakings during their life cycle. These endeavours can be straightforward, such as organizing a conference, to being quite intricate, such as the development of new products and services. Project management practices permit an organization to keep ahead of competition by decreasing the time-to-market windows for the development of new products and services through the synchronization of tasks, defining plans and schedules, and resource allocation. Moreover, project management in conjunction with information systems allows the integration of an organization's resources with its supply chain, by sharing project information in a real-time environment to a diverse and dispersed user base irrespective of their physical location. Organizations have an urgent need for project management practices due to:

1. A more aggressive competitive and turbulent business environment;
2. An increased demand for organizational accountability;
3. An insistent requirement for a greater focus on operational effectiveness.

References

Butterick, R. 2000. *The Interactive Project Workout* (2nd Edition). London: Pearson Education Limited (FT Prentice Hall).

Carayannis, E.G., Kwak, Y.H. and Anbari, F.T. 2005. *The Story of Managing Projects. An Interdisciplinary Approach*. Westport: Greenwood Publishing Group.

Project Management Institute Standards Committee. 1996. *A Guide to the Project Management Body of Knowledge.* Upper Darby: Project Management Institute.

Roberts, J.P. and Furlonger, J. 2000. *Successful IS Project Management.* Gartner [ID No. TU-09-2012]: 2

Thomsett, R. and Thomsett, C. 2000. *The Busy Person's Project Management Book.* [Online] Available at: http://www.thomsett.com.au/main/projectbook/book.htm [accessed: 24 May 2009].

Turner, J.R. 1993. *The Handbook of Project-Based Management.* Maidenhead: McGraw-Hill.

2 *The Perception of Project Success*

> *Managing is like holding a dove in your hand. Squeeze too hard and you kill it, not hard enough and it flies away.*
>
> *Tommy LaSorda, American baseball player and coach*

In the previous chapter, two questions were posed:

1. Why are some projects perceived as failures when they have met all the traditional standards of success, namely, completed on time, completed within budget and meeting all the technical specifications?
2. Why are some projects perceived to be successful when they have failed to meet two important criteria that are traditionally associated with success, namely, not completed on time and not completed within budget?

Some practitioners advocate that a project is successful if it satisfies all three legs of the triple constraint, namely, performance (specification), cost and time. This is viewed as the most basic level of project success (Greer, 1999). Thomsett (2002) in an extensive examination of 20 failing projects over a period of 18 years expands this criteria of success as: "satisfies stakeholder groups, meets functional requirements, meets quality expectations and requirements, within cost, within deadline, delivers sustained and actual benefits and provides the team with professional satisfaction and learning".

However, extensive as it may appear, this definition does not seem to fully embrace the meaning of project success. An example that comes to mind is the Sydney Opera House in Australia. The Sydney Opera House is one of the most recognizable images of the modern world. Not only is it recognizable, it has come to represent Australia. However, it cost about sixteen times as much to build and took four times as long to complete as the original estimates commencing in the 1950s and finally opening in 1973. A project management disaster with the resignation of its designer almost brought the project to a halt in the 1960s. However, was this project really a failure?

Although the causes for project success and failure have been the focus of numerous research studies, there has been no consensus on the issue. Pinto and Slevin (1987) argue that in spite of extensive research there has been limited convergence on the components and causes of project success.

A Different View of Projects

Shenhar et al. (2002) contend that one criticism regarding project management research concerns the assumption that a general theory of project management can be applied to all types of projects. They refer to researchers, such as Dewar and Dutton (1986), Pinto and Covin (1989), Damanpour (1991) and Shenhar (1993) who argue that the search for a universal theory may not be appropriate given the fundamental differences that exist across innovation and across project types. In addition, they contend that many project management enthusiasts make the assumption that all projects are made up of a universal set of functions and activities.

Shenhar et al. (2002) argue that simplistic measures have often equated success with meeting the objectives of project budget and schedule, and achieving an acceptable level of performance. However, all such measures are at best partial and misleading. For example, these types of measures may consider as successful, projects that resulted in a product which was difficult to market. Shenhar et al. (2002) contend that project success may also differ according to the assessor; thus success means different things to different people. For instance, they argue that an architect may consider success in terms of aesthetic appearance, an engineer in terms of technical competence, an accountant in terms of expenditure under budget, and a human resources manager in terms of employee satisfaction. Therefore, they argue that a comprehensive success criterion must reflect different views and interests.

From information collected about 127 projects undertaken in Israel, Shenhar et al. (2002) found that project success factors were contingent upon the specific type of project. Their analysis also indicates that the list of project success factors varies with project type and that project managers must carefully identify those factors that are critical to their particular project. They classify projects by degree of technological uncertainty and degree of system scope (complexity). They view technological uncertainty as having four dimensions with each dimension having its own characteristics. The technological uncertainty dimensions include:

1. *Low-tech projects*. These types of projects rely on well-established technology that is widely and equally available to all industries. These projects may be large in magnitude but no new technology is utilized at any stage of the project. Therefore, technology uncertainty is almost zero. Examples of these types of projects include most construction and road building projects;
2. *Medium-tech projects*. These types of projects mainly use existing technology but may utilize some new technological features. Therefore, these projects have a low level of technological uncertainty. Furthermore, the new technology feature is normally the basis of the project's advantage. Examples include improvements or enhancements to existing products;
3. *High-tech projects*. These types of projects use technologies that are mainly new but have already been developed and utilized. For example, projects utilizing the integration of technologies for the first time would be characterized by a high level of uncertainty;
4. *Super high-tech projects*. These are based entirely on new technologies that may need to be developed. Hence, the anticipated new technologies may still be at the research and development stage, and therefore involve exceedingly high levels of uncertainty. These types of projects are rather exceptional and are normally undertaken by large organizations such as governments. An example of this type of project is the Polaris missile project undertaken in the late 1950s.

Shenhar et al. (2002) view the degree of system scope as having three dimensions that measures the breadth, complexity and number of hierarchical levels of a product or a system. These dimensions include:

1. *An assembly*. This is a collection of components and modules combined into a single unit to perform a well-defined function as part of a larger system or as an independent self-contained unit. For example, a hard disk drive is an assembly that works as part of a larger system such as a computer or a CD player which is an independent self-contained unit;
2. *A system*. This is classified as being a complex collection of interactive components or assemblies within a single product collectively performing a diverse range of independent tasks or functions to achieve a particular operational requirement. Examples include a computer application system, a computer network or a motor vehicle;
3. *An array*. An array is a large, widely diffused assortment of diverse systems that function collectively to achieve a common objective. Arrays are normally spread over a wide geographical area and consist of a mixture of systems such as a national railway network.

Shenhar et al. (2002) show that project management is an extensive domain and that projects are different and share limited common features. Their analysis suggests that high-uncertainty projects must be managed differently from low-uncertainty projects. They illustrate that high-uncertainty projects demand special focus on project definition; project milestones; design considerations; documentation; policy; and customer participation.

However, low-uncertainty projects require focus on formal and structured selection of contractors; budget monitoring; early design freeze; design for manufacturability; quality objectives; statistical quality control; and project manager autonomy. Projects that are broad in scope are more sensitive to formal proposal and bid preparations; identification of project milestones at initiation; project manager autonomy; formal contracts; and formalization of various other documents (formal methodology).

The concept of regarding projects as being different, based on specific attributes has a lot of merit. However, in Shenhar et al. (2002) the taxonomy of projects by technological uncertainty (four dimensions) and degree of system scope (three dimensions) appear to be too complex and is not easily applied in practice. Sutton (2005a) has a similar view to Shenhar et al. (2002) in terms of distinguishing projects but tends to simplify the project type differentiation. Sutton (2005a) posits that all projects are different and that different projects experience different points of failure. However, unlike Shenhar et al. (2002), he contends that projects are not as dissimilar as they seem and can generally be grouped under two major categories:

1. *Type One Projects*. Sutton views these projects as being involved with the delivery of a manufactured structure such as a construction project, for example, an office block, a bridge or ship. This type of projects may be characterized as having:
   a) Consensus at the beginning of the project regarding the required output and outcome;
   b) An output and outcome that are normally indistinguishable and concurrent;

c) A tangible end product at the point of project closure with an intrinsic value;

d) An end product that can be depicted in some detail at the project commencement stage and is commonly illustrated by an accurate model. Moreover, some of these projects may be considered as being complex, but their complexity tends to be easily manageable;

2. *Type Two Projects*. Sutton views these projects as typically dealing with non-physical objects. For instance, projects that are intended to bring about some form of societal or organizational change, such as initiating traffic congestion fees, a new performance incentive scheme and practically all information system developments. This type of projects normally have multiple and powerful stakeholders, often with rival agendas. Under these conditions securing agreement on project output is a possibility, however, project purpose or intended outcome may be more ambiguous and even contentious, and acquiring agreement on how to measure project success may be difficult to achieve. Other factors that characterize this type of projects include:

a) Output may not have an intrinsic value;

b) Outputs and outcomes may not occur concurrently, since value will normally accrue as a result of the outcomes that come about through the usage of the output;

c) Ownership will often change during the project life, with every new champion having a different interpretation of project purpose;

d) Will always exhibit dynamic and political complexity, but may or may not display detail complexity;

e) Represent the greatest strategic value by having consequences that go beyond the boundaries of the organization in which they are envisioned;

f) Experience far greater levels of failure than Type One projects.

Sutton (2005a) identifies five major reasons for project failure, these include unclear scope; initiating projects without the full agreement between sponsors; inappropriate steering arrangements and without tolerances being set; no change control; and no exception reporting structures being in place. Unclear scope, that is, the extent to which the functional requirements can be accurately specified at the outset of the project, is the most fundamental failure factor identified. What is more, he maintains that being aware of the project attributes at the beginning (being Type One or Type Two projects) will indicate their probable behaviour and thus can help management in anticipating and addressing difficulties.

Classifying projects using the project uncertainty and complexity matrix whilst helpful, does not explain the observable fact that stakeholders may perceive the project differently. For instance, even though a project may be classified as Type One (delivery of some kind of manufactured structure) there may be circumstances that destine a project to be a failure. For example, controversial designs of buildings or monuments, where there may be a wide variation of perception of those viewing from those using the delivered object. In such an example, the news media may have an important influence on perceptions even though it is neither an owner nor user. It is suggested that although projects may be broadly classified into two distinct categories, with one category being more difficult to achieve success than the other, the perception of stakeholders is fundamental to success.

The Perception of a Successful Project

The word success when applied to projects is very illusive. De Wit (1988) and many other researchers make a distinction between project success and project management success. For instance, they contend that project success is measured by comparing the project outcomes to the overall objectives of the project; whereas project management success tends to be measured against the traditional measures of performance, namely, cost, time and quality. Moreover, a further distinction is made between project success criteria and project success factors. In De Wit's (1988) view, success criteria refer to the measures by which success or failure of a project or business will be evaluated; whereas success factors are those inputs to the management system that lead directly or indirectly to the success of the project or business. According to Cooke-Davies (2002) it requires answering three questions, not one, to answer the question: "What are the critical factors that 'really' lead to successful projects?" These three questions are:

1. "What factors are critical to project management success?"
2. "What factors are critical to the success of an individual project?"
3. "What factors lead to consistently successful projects?"

Cooke-Davies (2002) in a study of 136 European projects executed between 1994 and 2000 by a total of 23 organizations found that there was a strong correlation between schedule delay and cost escalation. However, cost escalation was not primarily caused by simply a schedule delay but due to a lack of a mature scope change process. Furthermore, Cooke-Davies (2002) found that an analysis of six project management bodies of knowledge suggested that anticipated benefits was a major criterion for formal and informal assessment of project success by senior management. Moreover, it was found that benefits are not delivered or realized by the project manager and project team, but require actions from operations management and close cooperation between the project team on the one hand and the sponsor or customer on the other.

It was also found that delivering project success is more difficult than delivering project management success, because it predictably involves aspects which may be beyond the control of the project team. With these second order controls, both goals and methods are prone to change; whereas project management success may be achieved by holding goals constant but changing practices to meet the predetermined goals. Cooke-Davies (2002) argues that the ultimate aim of an organization should be to introduce practices that allow the enterprise to resource fully a portfolio of projects that are rationally and dynamically matched to the corporate strategy and business objectives.

This view is further enhanced by Sutton (2005b) who contends that projects are not dichotomous, it is not a matter of success or failure, but that there are degrees of success and failure. He identifies four distinct levels of success, each having its own discipline, tools and techniques. Thus, excellence at each level is critical for absolute success. These four levels are similar to those of Cooke-Davies (2002) and consist of the following:

1. Project management success;
2. Repeatable project management success;
3. Project success;
4. Corporate success.

It is important to note that there is a definite distinction between the four success levels. Project management success refers to whether a particular project has produced the desired outputs (deliverables), while project success refers to whether a particular project has produced the desired outcomes (project purpose or objective). Hence, project outputs and outcomes are distinct. Repeatable project management success refers to the organization's ability to consistently execute projects that have produced the desired outputs. Corporate success refers to whether the outcomes produced have the intended impact on the business strategy of the organization.

Sutton's (2005b) model takes a holistic corporate approach by linking project delivery to corporate strategy. These levels of success may also be viewed as addressing different stakeholders ranging from the owners, users and corporate management. Moreover, both classes of owners and users may also be diverse depending on the nature of the project. Figure 2.1 illustrates this concept by showing the relationship between the major project success levels, their respective project affect and the possible stakeholders.

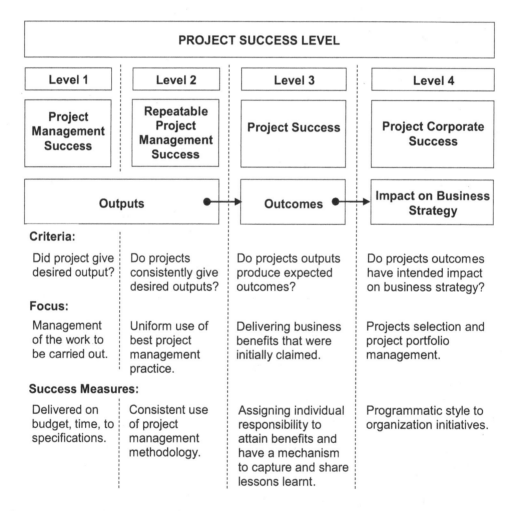

Figure 2.1   Project success framework

For instance, in a building construction project, the output is the building itself, and whether it has been built within the time and cost constraint and specifications. However, the outcomes are more related to the users of the building. Is the building functional for the purpose it was built for? Does it accommodate different individuals' general needs? For example, does the building design cater for individuals with special needs? From a corporate success aspect one would need to assess whether the finished building and its design is promoting the business strategy of the organization. For instance a building designed for financial services will need to project an image differently from one that functions as a medical clinic.

Sutton (2005b) maintains that project failure could occur at any one of the four levels. Therefore, managers should understand where and how they are failing and then target the measures that produce the greatest likelihood of success. According to Sutton (2005b), each project success level has a specific project success criterion, focus, discipline, success measure and a set of corrective interventions for concerns that may arise from time-to-time. Sutton's propositions are summarized below.

LEVEL 1: PROJECT MANAGEMENT SUCCESS

Project Success Criteria: Did the project produce the desired deliverables (outputs)?
Focus on: The management of the work to be done.
Discipline, Tools and Techniques:

1. Unambiguous scope and deliverable definition;
2. Thorough and continuous risk assessment;
3. Business case monitoring;
4. Plan project to an appropriate level of detail;
5. Good estimating practices;
6. Appropriate scheduling and resource usage;
7. Cost and schedule tracking;

Project Success Measures: Delivered on time, to budget and specifications.
Interventions to concerns:

1. Apply product based planning to facilitate agreement regarding the nature of the required deliverable and the quality criteria to be applied;
2. Improve on-time delivery by applying risk management practices;
3. Decrease cost with rigorous change control procedures;
4. Lower cost through earned value analysis;
5. Apply good project reporting practices;
6. Ensure that the project is truly in control;
7. Foster a project culture that rewards not penalizes;
8. Improve cost and time scheduling by having fault reporting procedures;
9. Focus on the management of outputs with the aim of preventing rework;
10. Apply a method that helps to eliminate ambiguity of outputs, such as conducting stakeholder workshops to attain scope definition consensus;
11. Know the likely benefits and the time profile in which benefits can be attained by using simulations or pilot implementation;

12. Have project control boards to ensure continuity of purpose, should significant stakeholders change;
13. Identify interim deliverables to ensure that powerful stakeholders benefit early from the project.

LEVEL 2: REPEATABLE PROJECT MANAGEMENT SUCCESS

Project Success Criteria: Do projects undertaken by the organization consistently produce the desired deliverables?
Focus on: Consistent application of good project management practice, such as a standard project management methodology.
Discipline, Tools and Techniques: Having appropriate organizational structures that are designed to share and support best project management practice and ensure predictability of outcome.
Success Measure: Use a standard project management methodology throughout the organization.
Interventions to concerns: Implementation of a standard project management method that is consistently applied throughout the organization. Where practical, establish a project support office that supports a mechanism for learning from experience.

LEVEL 3: PROJECT SUCCESS

Project Success Criteria: Have the deliverables from the projects undertaken by the organization produced the desired outcomes?
Focus on: Ensuring that projects deliver business benefits that were initially claimed.
Discipline, Tools and Techniques: The integration of project outputs into business operations and the concurrent development of process change and people skills.
Success Measure: Understanding of benefits logic, assigning individual responsibility for attainment of benefits and incorporating a mechanism to capture and share lessons learned.
Interventions to concerns:

1. Proactive management of project benefits through the identification of benefits in the business case and conducting a business case review when a major change request is requested or applied;
2. Clear ownership for the attainment of benefits;
3. Rigorous post-implementation review processes that hold people accountable for the delivery of benefits;
4. A clear knowledge management mechanism for the capture of lessons learned from projects undertaken by the organization.

LEVEL 4: CORPORATE SUCCESS

Project Success Criteria: Do the project outcomes have the intended impact on the organization's business strategy?
Focus on: Project selection and portfolio management.

Discipline, Tools and Techniques: Choosing the optimum mix of projects that collectively will most effectively contribute to defined business strategy.
Success Measure: Programmatic approach to organizational initiatives.
Interventions to concerns:

1. Introducing portfolio management to ensure that approved projects complement the desired strategic direction of the organization;
2. Implementing programme management tools, particularly if projects are managed as a financial portfolio;
3. Implementing a *balanced scorecard* approach to measure organizational performance and as an enabler for organizational learning.

Conclusion

Sutton's (2005a) dual classification of projects appears to be a simple and practical approach for ascertaining the particular characteristics of a specific project in terms of complexity and uncertainty. Type One projects are regarded as having tangible outputs with an inherent value and possessing general consensus about their purpose; whilst Type Two projects are characterized by having ambiguity of purpose, a lack of tangible outputs with no specific intrinsic value, and tend to have frequent change of ownership and momentum.

Furthermore, Sutton's (2005b) multi-dimensional project success model takes a holistic view of the project lifecycle by articulating the project impact on the project outputs and outcomes, and the organization's business strategy. Hence, this project success framework takes an overall corporate view by linking project delivery to corporate strategy. There is also a definite distinction and particular focus between the four success levels. Sutton's project success framework enables project managers to understand where and how they are failing and then target the measures that produce the greatest likelihood of success.

References

Cooke-Davies, T. 2002. The "real" success factors on projects. *International Journal of Project Management*, 20, 185–90.

Damanpour, F. 1991. Organizational innovation: a meta-analysis of effects of determinants and moderators. *Academy of Management Journal*, 34, 555–90.

Dewar, R.D. and Dutton, J.E. 1986. The adoption of radical and incremental innovations: an empirical analysis. *Management Science*, 32, 1422–33.

De Wit, A. 1988. Measurement of project success. *International Journal of Project Management*, 6(3), 164–70.

Greer, M. 1999. *Handbook of Human Performance Technology*. San Francisco: Jossey-Bass.

Pinto, J.K. and Covin, J.G. 1989. Critical factors in project implementation: a comparison of construction and R&D projects. *Technovation*, 9, 49–62.

—— and Slevin, D.S. 1987. Critical factors in successful project implementation. *IEEE Transactions on Engineering Management*, EM-34(1), 22–7.

Shenhar, A.J. 1993. From low to high-tech project management. *R&D Management*, 23(3), 199–214.

——, Tishler, A., Dvir, D., Lipovetsky, S. and Lechler, T. 2002. Refining the search for project success factors: a multivariate, typological approach. *R&D Management*, 32(2), 111–26.

Sutton, B. 2005a. *Why Projects Fail – Mastering the Monster (Part 1)*. [Online] Available at: http://www.itarchitect.co.uk/articles/display.asp?id=203 [accessed: 1 October 2007].

Sutton, B. 2005b. *Why Projects Fail – Mastering the Monster (Part 2)*. [Online] Available at: http://www.itarchitect.co.uk/articles/display.asp?id=224 [accessed: 1 October 2007].

Thomsett, R. 2002. Project Pathology, Causes, patterns and symptoms of project failure. [Online] Available at: http://www.thomsett.com.au/main/articles/path/toc.htm [accessed: 1 October 2007].

3 *Why Some Projects Succeed and Others Fail*

Success and failure. We think of them as opposites, but they're really not. They're companions – the hero and the sidekick.

Laurence Shames, author

The previous chapter addressed the issue of what is meant by project success. Sutton's (2005) project success framework took a holistic corporate view by linking project outputs (deliverables) and outcomes (objectives) to corporate strategy. Sutton's project success framework defined four project success levels which enable project mangers to understand where and how they are failing within each level. However, this project success framework takes a macro view of project success it does not specifically identify the success and failure factors within each of the four project success levels.

This chapter will take a micro view of project success by addressing the issue of why some projects succeed and others fail in the normal course of events. These project success and failure factors are applicable to all environments, irrespective of whether a project is being conducted in a multi-project environment or an international setting. Furthermore, the various identified success and failure factors will be categorized into a number of universal project success–failure dimensions, with the objective of enabling the organization to appraise its competency in the field of managing project behaviour.

These project success–failure dimensions together with Sutton's (2005) project success framework will be used to formulate a Project Success Model. The Project Success Model will become the basis for the major part of this manuscript. Extensive literature research was conducted to identify the project success–failure dimensions. The objective was to confer with the many existing project related research literature for the purpose of determining the actual reasons why projects succeed or fail.

What May Go Right and Wrong with Projects

A detailed examination of the literature research reveals what may go right and wrong with projects. The literature research consisted of studies related to various industries that included construction, engineering, information systems and consultancy assignments, thus providing a wide range of project types.

LITERATURE RESEARCH FINDINGS: POSSIBLE REASONS WHY PROJECTS SUCCEED

This section itemizes the research findings from each literature source which were examined. This provided what the researchers considered to be the reasons why the projects under investigation were successful.

Findings from Appelbaum (2004)

- Emphasis on client results (outcomes) rather than deliverables (outputs);
- Clear and well-communicated expectations and outcomes;
- Visible executive support;
- Adaptation to client readiness;
- Investment up-front in learning the clients' environment;
- Incremental successes;
- Real partnership between client and project implementers.

Findings from Boadle (2004)

- Adequate planning and regular plan reviews;
- Level of planning to reflect the complexity of the project;
- Deliverables that meet the business need;
- Change request process in place;
- Well-defined project scope;
- Management of risk;
- Appropriate relationship between project manager and sponsor (owner);
- Managers to inspire a shared vision;
- Managers to communicate with people at all levels;
- Managers to demonstrate integrity by embracing ethical practices;
- Managers to lead with enthusiasm and exhibit exceptional energy levels;
- Managers to display consideration towards project team members;
- Competent managers who delegate tasks, are cool under pressure, possess team building skills and have excellent problem-solving skills;
- Managers to be results-driven and have phenomenal political skills;
- Project team to display focus and enthusiasm for the tasks at hand.

Findings from CERF (2004)

- Appropriate project team structure;
- Effective project director;
- Project managers having the necessary technical and leadership skills;
- Robust front-end planning and risk assessment;
- Management skills of the project team;
- Best practices in schedule and cost control;
- Regular and periodic project reviews by internal and external parties;
- Project tracking by regular and periodic project reviews by external parties;
- Develop a procurement strategy at the conceptual design stage of the project;
- Integrate procurement strategy with the risk management programme;
- Tailor procurement approaches to project needs;
- Link contractor performance to desired business results;
- Use of performance metrics and incentives;
- Require peer reviews for first-of-a-kind and technically complex projects;
- Phase funding by linking to the critical decision points.

Findings from Kanter and Walsh (2004)

- Define and promulgate functional requirements;
- Implement control changes procedures;
- Develop realistic project schedules;
- Match skills to needs at the proper time;
- Know and respond to the real status of the project;
- Honest feedback and communication;
- Establish and control the performance of the contractors.

Findings from Mengesha (2004)

- Suitable project organization;
- Formulating a contract strategy;
- Having a proper project planning and control process in place;
- Stakeholder management;
- Ensuring that the technology being implemented works well;
- Having an objective management orientation;
- Top management support;
- Interface with surrounding projects;
- Management of the design process.

Findings from Sturdivant (2004)

- Clear statement of requirements;
- Proper planning;
- Clear vision and objectives;
- Hard working and focused staff;
- Competent staff;
- User involvement;
- Realistic expectations;
- Executive management support;
- Project ownership (ensuring that a project champion is present);
- Smaller project milestones.

Findings from Frese and Sauter (2003)

- User involvement;
- Executive management support;
- Clear statement of requirements;
- Proper planning and realistic expectations;
- Clear responsibility and accountability;
- Adequate schedule control;
- Clearly defined goals;
- Competent project manager;
- Competent project team members;
- Sufficient resource allocation;

- Adequate communication channels;
- Project control mechanisms in place;
- Feedback capabilities;
- Responsiveness to client and proper client consultation;
- Ensure that the technology being implemented works well;
- Client acceptance;
- Adequate troubleshooting;
- User involvement;
- Experienced project manager;
- Clear business objectives;
- Minimized scope (Don't allow scope to grow).

Findings from Charvat (2002)

- Assess the impact of change by having a change control process in place;
- Project documentation to serve as a clear communication channel;
- Develop testing and quality assurance process at the time of project launching.

Findings from Cooke-Davies (2002)

- Adequate company-wide education on concepts of risk management;
- Maturity of an organization's processes for assigning ownership of risks;
- Adequacy with which a visible risk register is maintained;
- Adequate and up-to-date risk management plan;
- Adequate documentation of organizational responsibilities on the project;
- Keep project (or stage duration) below three years if possible at one year;
- Allow changes to scope only through a scope change control process;
- Maintain the integrity of the performance measurement baseline;
- Cooperation of project management and line management functions;
- Effective benefits delivery and management process;
- Portfolio and programme management practices matched to corporate strategy and business objectives;
- A suite of project, programme and portfolio metrics that provide direct line of sight feedback on current project performance;
- Continuous improvement of project management processes and practices through learning from experience.

Findings from Belassi and Tukul (1996)

- Competent project manager and the team members;
- Suitable project organization;
- Monitor external environment.

Findings from Pinto and Kharbanda (1995)

- Keep organization mission at the forefront;
- Early and continuous client consultation;

- Use of suitable technology;
- Have a proper scheduling system;
- Competent project team members and team structure;
- Top management support;
- Continual "What if?" approach.

Findings from Tukel and Rom (1995)

- Top management support;
- Client consultation;
- Adequate preliminary estimates;
- Availability of resources;
- Monitor project manager's performance.

Findings from Morris and Hughes (1987)

- Clear project objectives;
- Mitigate technical innovation uncertainty;
- Community involvement;
- Clear financial contract to avoid legal problems.

Findings from Pinto and Slevin (1987)

- Clear project objectives;
- Top management support;
- Adequate project planning;
- Communication with client;
- Suitable human relations practices;
- Client acceptance of project scope and deliverables;
- Proper level of project control;
- Adequate communication channels with stakeholders;
- Ensure that a problem handling process is in place.

Findings from Morris (1986)

- Ensure adequate risk assessment is conducted;
- Have the appropriate project organization structure;
- Establish a clear and comprehensive project organization;
- Simplify project organization reporting mechanism;
- Evaluate impact of project on environment and people;
- Prevent both hurried and competitive bidding;
- Exclude rushed preliminary project definition, design and development;
- Explain project schedules;
- Examine the possibility of appointing contractors on the project earlier;
- Consider other bids even though they may not be the cheapest offer;
- Ensure the appropriate level planning in terms of detail and precision;
- Devise support strategies to cater for unforeseen events;

- Divide project into manageable parts with clear and minimum interfaces;
- Ensure adequate funding;
- Ensure that legal arrangements are clear, simple and equitable;
- Ensure the commitment of project sponsors;
- Establish government commitment (for public sector projects);
- Forecast important events and risky situations;
- Government to allow flexible management (for public sector projects);
- Government to give clear objectives (for public sector projects);
- Minimize conflict of participants' objectives;
- Minimize the number of contracts;
- Minimize technical uncertainty by using tested and proven products;
- Ensure continuity and frequent monitoring of progress;
- Acquire motivated and experienced project team members;
- Ensure the client participation by considering their suggestions;
- Encourage a flexible project design (avoid rigidity);
- Foster good internal and external communication practices;
- Promote positive attitudes and relationships;
- Need for the fair allocation of risk;
- Need for unrushed project commitment;
- Ensure that one person or group has overall authority;
- Encourage participative decision making with socially orientated leadership;
- Endeavour to execute long-term projects in phases;
- Ensure that the project scope is well investigated, communicated and agreed;
- Simplify design and avoid late project design changes;
- Streamline financial arrangements;
- Rationalize specifications through simplification;
- Take strategic action when currency exchange rates change;
- Terminate project if necessary.

Findings from Baker, Murphy and Fisher (1983)

- Ensure clear project goals;
- Espouse goal commitment from project team;
- Have an on-site project manager;
- Ensure adequate project funding to completion;
- Have adequate project team capability;
- Ensure the accuracy of initial project cost estimates;
- Minimize project start-up difficulties;
- Ensure that planning and control techniques are in place;
- Have a balanced task–social orientation;
- Eliminate bureaucracy.

Findings from Cleland and King (1983)

- Provide an adequate project summary and defined operational concept;
- Acquire top management support;
- Obtain financial support;

- Focus on logistic requirements and facility support;
- Gather market intelligence related to proposed project;
- Ensure an adequate level of detail for project scheduling;
- Establish an executive development and training programme;
- Have a suitable project organization and an adequate manpower plan;
- Have appropriate information and communication channels;
- Conduct continuous and regular project reviews.

Findings from Martin (1976)

- Have clear goals;
- Establish the appropriate project organizational philosophy;
- Attain general management support;
- Organize and delegate authority;
- Ensure the careful selection of project team members.

Findings from Sayles and Chandler (1971)

- Ensure the recruitment of a competent project manager;
- Have an adequate level of project scheduling;
- Ensure that control systems are in place and responsibilities defined;
- Have regular and continuous project monitoring and feedback;
- Have continuous involvement in the project.

LITERATURE RESEARCH FINDINGS: POSSIBLE REASONS WHY PROJECTS FAILURE

This section itemizes research findings from each literature source that were examined, regarding what the researchers considered to be the reasons why projects fail.

Findings from Appelbaum (2004)

- Failure to identify the real problem (requirement definition);
- Promising too much, too soon;
- Failure to specify roles and responsibilities;
- Recommending unfeasible actions;
- Ineffective communication.

Findings from Boadle (2004)

- Inadequate planning;
- Project manager lacking appropriate management skills and experience;
- Over-ambitious or impossible project requirements;
- An inappropriate degree of executive sponsorship;
- Poor enterprise management role alignment, particularly responsibility.

Findings from CERF (2004)

- Excessive reliance on *earned value systems* to monitor projects;
- Not using tools such as critical path scheduling methods;
- Frequent re-base-lining masking the true state of some projects;
- Unpredictability of funding.

Findings from Kanter and Walsh (2004)

- Lack of communication;
- Unreasonable project schedules;
- Lack of the right skills at the right time;
- Inadequate project definition (requirements);
- Incomplete or unstable requirements;
- Ineffective project leadership;
- Inadequate initial plan as baseline;
- Inconsistent application of resources;
- Incomplete testing plan and/or environment;
- Inadequate monitoring and control system.

Findings from Sturdivant (2004)

- Incomplete requirements and specifications;
- Lack of user involvement;
- Changing of project requirements and specifications;
- Lack of (or insufficient) project documentation;
- Unclear project objectives;
- Infrequent project reviews;
- Unrealistic expectations;
- Lack of executive support;
- Insufficient testing and lack of testing procedures;
- Lack of resources and unrealistic time frames;
- Lack of independent quality assurance group;
- Inadequate competence regarding the technology being used;
- Use of new or unproven technology;
- High amount of rework (poor quality).

Findings from Frese and Sauter (2003)

- Project scope not fully appreciated and/or needs not fully understood;
- Lack of management continuity;
- Incentive system that encourages overly optimistic benefits estimates;
- High user expectations;
- Poor alignment between IT departments and business users;
- Loss of sight of project requirements;
- Lack of user involvement;
- Incomplete project requirements and specifications;

- Changing project requirements and specifications;
- Lack of executive support;
- Technical incompetence and technical illiteracy;
- Lack of resources and unrealistic expectations;
- Lack of planning;
- Lack of IT management;
- Lack of communication (internal and external).

Findings from Charvat (2002)

- Poor communications;
- Projects poorly estimated and planned;
- Minimal project documentation;
- Poor project management procedures;
- Poor executive buy-in;
- Poor user requirements;
- User requirements not firmly agreed prior to undertaking project work;
- Dates and deliverables not aggressively monitored and tracked;
- Issues left unresolved for days, leading to schedule overruns;
- Continuous project budget overruns;
- Not keeping stakeholders aware of any planned deviation;
- Project scope creep;
- Inadequate project documentation and cutting off communication channel;
- Use of untried or new technology;
- Poor decision making;
- Project manager lacks appropriate skills and experience;
- Poor project design testing (too little testing or testing too late).

Findings from Shenhar et al. (2002)

- Lack of focus in the scope (design) process in high risk technology projects;
- Lack of adequate project definition for high risk projects;
- Lack of proper project milestones for high risk projects;
- Lack of communication through a well-documented process;
- Lack of high skill level of project team members for high risk projects;
- Lack of policy for client participation;
- Lack of focus on formal and structural selection of contractor;
- Inadequate budget monitoring;
- Lack of an early scope (design) freeze procedure;
- Project deliverables are not adequately designed for the operational stage;
- Lack of quality objectives and statistical quality control;
- Lack of project manager autonomy;
- Inadequate identification of project milestones.

Classification of Reasons for Project Success and Failure into Dimensions

The assortment of possible reasons for the success and failure of projects, which were identified in the previous section, were examined to establish whether they may be classified into a manageable set of dimensions. This process, using a face validity approach, yielded 11 categories:

1. Project Strategic Fit;
2. Project Scope;
3. Project Organization Structure;
4. Project Team Structure;
5. Project Planning and Control;
6. Management and Leadership;
7. Employee Commitment and Participation;
8. Internal and External Communication;
9. Information Flow and Knowledge Management;
10. Project Risk Management;
11. Project Competency Development.

The identified possible reasons for projects success and failure were assessed, with the objective of producing a streamlined set of projects success and failure influencing factors, for each of the project success–failure dimensions. The findings from this normalization process are itemized below.

NORMALIZED PROJECT SUCCESS FACTORS BY CATEGORY

Project strategic fit success influencing factors

- Strategic alignment of projects with the business objectives;
- Clear business mission, vision and objectives;
- Clear project objectives;
- Deliverables that meet business needs;
- Transparent procurement strategy at the conceptual design phase of project;
- Realistic project schedules;
- Divide project into manageable parts with minimum and clear interfaces;
- Effective benefits delivery and management process;
- Emphasis on client results;
- Reflect on and monitor external factors, particularly environmental changes;
- Understand and learn the clients' environment;
- Link contractor performance to desired business results;
- Link project to business strategy, products, markets, environment and trends;
- Phase the implementation of long-term projects;
- Gather market intelligence about the proposed project;
- Minimize conflict of participants' project objectives;
- Establish project prioritization;

- Establish realistic expectations;
- Define smaller project milestones.

Project scope success influencing factors

- Well-defined project scope;
- Clear statement of client requirements;
- Client scope definition acceptance;
- Minimized scope (avoid scope creep);
- Project definition to be well investigated, communicated and agreed;
- Provide a clear project summary;
- Simplify project design and specifications;
- Avoid rushed initial project definition, design and development;
- Avoid late project design changes;
- Clear and well-communicated expectations and outcomes;
- Clearly defined goals;
- Clear, equitable and simple legal arrangements.

Project organization structure success influencing factors

- Responsibilities integrated with existing organizational structures;
- Stable organizational framework conditions;
- Selection of project organizational philosophy;
- Simplify project organization structure;
- Clear and comprehensive project organization;
- Establish a project support office;
- Entrust overall project authority to one person or group;
- Have on-site project manager.

Project team structure success influencing factors

- Appropriate project team structure;
- Careful selection of project team;
- Ensure technical and team leadership skills of project managers;
- Adequate project team capability;
- Competent project team members;
- Enthusiastic, hard-working, and focused team members;
- Management skills of the project team;
- Motivated and experienced team members.

Project planning and control success influencing factors

- Keep project (or stage duration) below three years, if possible one year;
- Minimize number of contracts;
- Minimize start-up difficulties;
- Level of planning should reflect the complexity of the project;
- Acquire a feel for client project readiness status;

- Robust front-end planning;
- Forecast important events and risky situations;
- Streamline financial arrangements;
- Accurate initial cost estimates;
- Phase funding by linking it to the critical project decision points;
- Clear and transparent financial contract to avoid litigation;
- Ensure adequate funding to completion;
- Ensure availability of resources;
- Define clear project schedule;
- Clarify schedules and assign responsibilities;
- Avoid rushed bidding;
- Focus on logistic requirements particularly the acquisition of materials;
- Match skills to needs at the proper time;
- Division and assignment of resources among projects;
- Continual "What if?" approach;
- Know and respond to the *real* status of the project;
- Ensure adequate troubleshooting;
- Monitor progress and ensure continuity;
- Regular project tracking;
- Implement project control mechanisms;
- Regular project reviews by internal and external parties;
- Require peer reviews for first-of-a-kind and technically complex projects;
- Use of performance metrics and incentives;
- Establish and control contractor performance.

Management and leadership success influencing factors

- Engage experienced project managers;
- Clear responsibility and accountability;
- Competent and effective project manager;
- Managers able to organize and delegate authority;
- Managers to be cool under pressure;
- Managers to possess team building skills;
- Managers to have excellent problem-solving skills;
- Managers to have good attitudes and build human relations;
- Managers to be results-driven and have phenomenal political skills;
- Managers to demonstrate integrity by embracing ethical practices;
- Managers to display consideration towards those involved in the project;
- Managers to lead with enthusiasm and exhibit exceptional energy levels;
- Managers to possess traditional skills of leadership, motivation and planning;
- Flexible customization of management to the specific project type;
- Able to terminate project if necessary.

Employee commitment and participation success influencing factors

- Visible executive support;
- Top management involvement through transparency across projects;

- User involvement;
- Collaboration between project management and line management functions;
- Unrushed project commitment;
- Organizational ownership of the project and its deliverables;
- Ensure sponsors are truly committed to the project;
- Goal commitment of project team;
- Financial support;
- Foster partnership and collaboration between client and project agents;
- Participative decision making with socially orientated leadership.

Internal and external communication success influencing factors

- Managers to inspire a shared vision;
- Ensure information and communication channels are in place;
- Adequate stakeholder management;
- Where applicable ensure community involvement;
- Assess project impact on stakeholders and interfacing parties;
- Appropriate relationship between project managers and sponsor (owner);
- Early, regular and continual communication and consultation with client;
- Ensure honest feedback and communication with stakeholders;
- Managers to communicate with people at all levels;
- Increase horizontal and vertical communication;
- Project documentation to serve as a clear communication channel;
- Feedback and learning from project product effectiveness in operations.

Information flow and knowledge management success influencing factors

- Project metrics that provide direct *line-of-sight* view on project performance;
- Absence of bureaucracy;
- Adequate and up-to-date risk management plan;
- Maturity of organizational processes for assigning ownership of risks;
- Adequate maintenance of a visible risk register (risk inventory);
- Adequate documentation of organizational responsibilities on project;
- Maintain the integrity of the performance measurement baseline;
- Implement change control procedures;
- Change control process to assess the impact and cost of change on project;
- Changes to scope permitted only through a scope change control process;
- Best practices in schedule and cost control;
- Maintain the integrity of the performance measurement baseline;
- Adequate problem handling procedures;
- Deliver relevant information to support decision-making process;
- Tailor procurement approaches to project needs.

Project risk management success influencing factors

- Assess impact of project on environment and people;
- Assess market conditions for project outcomes;

- Adequate risk assessment procedures;
- Devise back-up strategies;
- Integrate procurement strategy with risk management programme;
- Fair allocation of risk;
- Ensure proactive management of risk;
- Minimize technical uncertainty;
- Ensure that the technology being implemented works well.

Project competency development success influencing factors

- Adequacy of company-wide education on concepts of risk management;
- Constant upgrade of project management processes and practices through *learning from experience*;
- Cross-trained staff to allow flexible and multiple roles;
- Executive development and training.

NORMALIZED PROJECT FAILURE FACTORS BY CATEGORY

Project strategic fit failure influencing factors

- High user expectations;
- Promising too much, too soon;
- Unrealistic expectations;
- Unreasonable or unrealistic time frames and schedules;
- Lack of project milestones identification, particularly for high risk projects;
- Incentive system that encourages overly optimistic benefits estimates;
- Lack of interaction between projects;
- Lack of or inadequate project methodology standards;
- Poor alignment between project implementers and business users;
- Poor enterprise management role alignment, particularly accountability.

Project scope failure influencing factors

- Lack of project definition;
- Project scope not fully appreciated and/or needs not fully understood;
- Impractical design for desired operational outcomes;
- Recommending unfeasible actions;
- Overambitious or impossible requirements;
- Inadequate design or poor user requirements definition;
- User requirements not firmly agreed prior to undertaking work;
- Incomplete or unstable requirements and specifications;
- Losing sight of project requirements;
- Questionable economic feasibility of the project;
- Unclear objectives;
- Failure to identify the real problem;
- Lack of focus on design process in technology high risk projects;
- Lack of quality objectives.

Project organization structure failure influencing factors

- Lack of project manager autonomy in low risk projects;
- Lack of management continuity;
- Failure to specify roles and responsibilities;
- Lack of independent quality assurance group.

Project team structure failure influencing factors

- Project team members lack the required skills level;
- Technical or technological incompetence.

Project planning and control failure influencing factors

- Poor estimation and lack of adequate planning;
- Inadequate initial plan as baseline;
- Frequent re-base-lining masking the true state of project;
- Unpredictability of funding;
- Lack of budget monitoring and budget overruns;
- Lack of adequate resources;
- Lack of right skills at the right time;
- Inconsistent application of resources;
- No project scope reviews;
- Infrequent project reviews;
- Dates and deliverables not aggressively monitored and tracked;
- Inadequate monitoring and control system in place;
- Not using tools such as critical path scheduling methods;
- Too much rework or rescheduled work;
- Schedule overruns due to leaving issues unresolved for days;
- Excessive reliance on earned value systems to monitor projects;
- Inadequate focus on formal and structural selection of contractor;
- Insufficient testing and lack of testing procedures;
- Inadequate statistical quality control process in place.

Management and leadership failure influencing factors

- Inadequate management by project sponsor/project management agency;
- Ineffective project leadership;
- Poor decision making;
- Poor management of the project;
- Project manager lacks appropriate skills and experience.

Employee commitment and participation failure influencing factors

- Lack of executive support or poor buy-in;
- An inappropriate degree of executive sponsorship;
- Lack of user involvement.

Internal and external communication failure influencing factors

- Lack of communication through well-documented process;
- Poor or ineffective communication;
- Lack of internal and external communication;
- Lack of or insufficient documentation;
- Not keeping stakeholders aware of any planned deviation.

Information flow and knowledge management failure influencing factors

- Lack of processes that control changing requirements and specifications;
- Lack of processes that prevent project scope creep.

Project risk management failure influencing factors

- New technology (untried or lack of experience with new technology);
- Conflict with established environmental regulations;
- Lack of transparency and regulatory institutions;
- Bribery and corruption;
- Legal instability;
- National cultural factors;
- National political instability;
- Physical factors, such as, heritage artefacts, natural disasters or hostilities;
- Social environment, for example, ethnic hostility and religious fragmentation;
- Technical factors (unavailability of expertise).

Summary of Research Findings – Project Success–Failure Dimensions

Table 3.1 provides a summary of the literature research findings. It shows the frequency that a particular category of project success–failure dimension was cited in the various literature sources. For instance, Project Planning and Control was cited 84 times in the literature as being the cause for project success or failure, followed by Project Strategic Fit with 48 occurrences. Therefore, Table 3.1 provides an indication of the ranking of each project success–failure dimension. Note that the most important dimensions for ensuring the successful implementation of projects, in order of priority, include:

1. Project Planning and Control;
2. Project Strategic Fit;
3. Project Scope;
4. Employee Commitment and Participation.

Between them, these four project success–failure dimensions, account for over 60 per cent of the literature research citations, therefore signifying the areas on which executive managers should particularly focus their attention.

Table 3.1   Summary – Number of literature citations by factor category

Factors	Failure	Success	Total	%
Project Planning and Control	26	58	84	**23.60**
Project Strategic Fit	13	35	48	**13.48**
Project Scope	19	24	43	**12.08**
Commitment and Participation	7	32	39	**10.96**
Communication	10	21	31	8.71
Management and Leadership	8	19	27	7.58
Project Risk Management	10	15	25	7.02
Project Organization Structure	4	16	20	5.62
Information Flow and Knowledge Management	3	15	18	5.06
Project Team Structure	4	13	17	4.78
Project Competency Development	0	4	4	1.12
Total:	**104**	**252**	**356**	**100.00**

The identified project management success–failure dimensions will be examined in detail in the chapters to follow.

Project Success Model Development

This section has the objective of developing a project success model by merging the literature research findings and the knowledge gained from the previous chapters, particularly, the Project Success Framework (see Figure 2.1, p. 18).

It should be recalled that the Project Success Framework based on Sutton (2005) identified four distinct project success levels. These success levels included project management success, repeatable project management success, project success and corporate success. The project management success and repeatable project management success levels focused on the project outputs, in other words, the project deliverables. However, the project success level concentrated on project outcomes, that is, the project objectives or purpose. Finally, the corporate success level refers to whether the resultant project outcomes have the intended impact on the organization's business strategy. Therefore, the four success levels have provided a macro view of project success and in fact have provided an explicit meaning of what is meant by the term *project success*.

In addition, the project success–failure dimensions identified through the literature research provided a micro view of the factors that determine whether a project will succeed or fail. Moreover, these eleven project success–failure dimensions may be further classified into three broad managerial segments, with each segment having a distinct objective in supporting the undertaking of a project. The three broad managerial segments are as follows:

1. Project hygiene support factors consisting of :
    a) Project strategic fit;
    b) Project scope;
    c) Project organization structure;
    d) Project team structure;
    e) Project planning and control.
2. Project informational support factors consisting of:
    a) Information flow and knowledge management;
    b) Project risk management;
    c) Project competency development.
3. Project behavioural and management support factors consisting of:
    a) Management and leadership;
    b) Employee commitment and participation;
    c) Internal and external communication.

What is needed now is to link the project success–failure dimensions to the four project success levels. In other words, this linkage will provide a clear picture of how the eleven project success-failure dimensions contribute to the four project success levels. The relationship between the project success–failure dimensions and four project success levels is shown in Figure 3.1.

Figure 3.1   Project success–failure dimensions and project success levels

Figure 3.1 illustrates that the project hygiene support factors contribute towards the traditional project management aspects, with the focus on the outputs and therefore have the goal to ensure project management success. The only exception within hygiene support factors that is not aimed at the project management success level is project strategic fit. Project strategic fit contributes towards the corporate success level by ensuring that the project has a positive impact on the business strategy of the organization. The project hygiene support factors are considered fundamental for good project management practice.

The project informational support factors are typically applicable for project oriented organizations, in other words, a multi-project environment. These factors together with a standard project management methodology aim for repeatable project management success. The emphasis here is still on the project outputs or the deliverables. Finally, the project behavioural and managerial support factors are viewed as influencing project success, with the focus being the project outcomes. The project behavioural and managerial support factors are applicable to all types of projects. For instance, internal and external communication would aim to satisfy the behavioural implications, such as fostering consensus amongst the various stakeholders to achieve their respective requirements and mitigate their concerns.

The resultant project success model that emerges from the linkage of the project success–failure dimensions and the four project success levels is depicted at Figure 3.2.

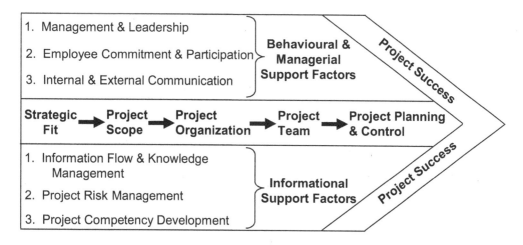

Figure 3.2   Model for project success

Note that the project hygiene support factors which represent the traditional project management aspects are central to the model. The model depicts a forward flow. It illustrates that the project hygiene support factors are being continuously and concurrently supported by both the informational support factors and the behavioural and managerial support factors, throughout the duration of the project life cycle, with the sole objective of achieving project success and ultimately corporate success.

Conclusion

The purpose of this chapter was to develop a Project Success Model by merging two sets of project behavioural knowledge. The first set refers to the project success framework. This identified the four project success levels that holistically aim for corporate success, by ensuring that the project has the appropriate positive impact on the business strategy of the organization. The second set of project behaviour knowledge was obtained from the literature research findings, which identified at a micro level the project success–failure dimensions.

It was shown that the eleven project management success–failure dimensions may be further classified into three broad managerial segments. A summary of these three broad managerial segments and their respective the project success–failure dimensions are provided below.

PROJECT HYGIENE SUPPORT FACTORS

Project strategic fit

All projects undertaken by an organization must be aligned with the organization's strategic direction and also support the project recipient's strategic goals. Projects that do not support the organization's strategic direction are consuming resources that could be utilized for other useful purposes. In other words, projects that lack strategic fit result in the under utilization of the organization's resources.

Project scope

Project scope basically defines what needs to be done. Its purpose is to ensure that the project includes all (and only) the work required (no more, no less) by sub-dividing major project deliverables into smaller more manageable components. In defining what needs to be done, it is important to also define the constraints and assumptions being made. Furthermore, project scope must be formally accepted by the relevant stakeholders. The literature suggests that the inability to freeze project scope and to close-out the project effort were two major causes contributing to project failure.

Project organization structure

The project organization structure establishes the reporting lines of communications. It defines the authority, roles and responsibilities of the project work team. The literature indicates that poor coordination with both the client and the parent organization are associated with project failure. On the other hand, a suitable organization structure that is complimentary to the project team, contributes to project success.

Project team structure

The composition of the project team will depend on the nature of the project. However, it is important that the project team members are competent in their respective field. Furthermore, whilst project team members must be flexible in their roles, they should be fully aware of the level of their authority in relation to certain critical decisions, approvals, works acceptance and communication, particularly with those who are external to the project team. The project manager must instil the necessary group discipline to avoid stressful role states, such as role conflict and ambiguity. The literature suggests that excessive structuring and insecurity within the project team contribute to project failure.

Project planning and control

Project planning is the process of arranging the tasks to be carried out in a way that commits resources in the most economic fashion. This definition implies the optimum application of resources, in terms of both time and cost. On the other hand, project control is the process of coordinating the activities of the organization in line with the accepted plan and resultant schedules for the accomplishment of the identified goals. The extent of uniqueness and resultant project risk may make the planning and control process very complex. The literature suggests that unrealistic project schedules contribute to project failure, while the judicious use of project networking techniques and adequate control procedures contribute to project success.

PROJECT INFORMATIONAL SUPPORT FACTORS

Information flow and knowledge management

The information flow and knowledge management aspect is a complex issue and is closely dependent on the project organization structure adopted. The basic issues include having an appropriate change management procedure, an information flow process with supporting reports and a detailed data set that identifies the information which should be maintained to manage the project. The change management procedure has the objective of ensuring that the proposed change is necessary and beneficial; determines that a change has occurred; and manages the actual changes when and if they occur. The change management procedure includes the paperwork, tracking systems and the approval levels necessary for authorizing changes. The information flow process and supporting reports must be timely, accurate and meaningful. The literature suggests that an inadequate project change procedure and insufficient use of status and progress reports are all associated with project failure.

Project risk management

Risk is a basic feature of projects. Risk management consists of:

1. Identifying the risks that may affect a project and documenting their attributes;
2. Evaluating the risks and assessing different scenarios;
3. Defining a strategy for responding to the identified risks where possible;
4. Executing the strategy if the risk materializes.

However, identifying all the risks that the project may encounter is very difficult. Therefore, risk needs to be continuously monitored and evaluated. The literature suggests that the availability of contingency strategies is associated with project success.

Project competency development

It is important to continually maintain the project team's knowledge with the latest technical and managerial techniques related to the activities undertaken. Once the project team is established, it is desirable that a team building programme is conducted, with repeated sessions undertaken at appropriate intervals. It is essential that an appropriate project management methodology is selected as a standard and is applied across the organization. This implies that the project team members are extensively trained in the selected project management standard. The literature indicates that the probability of project failure may be minimized if the project team is suitably trained in the relevant methodologies. Having the desire to build up internal capabilities is therefore strongly associated with project success.

PROJECT BEHAVIOURAL AND MANAGEMENT SUPPORT FACTORS

Management and leadership

A project is not likely to succeed without having strong leadership and the appropriate management skills. The normal managerial attributes of planning, controlling, organizing and leading are essential, particularly in an environment that is characterized by instability. The literature suggests that inadequate administrative, human and technical skills, and insufficient project manager influence and authority strongly contribute to project failure.

Employee commitment and participation

Commitment and participation go hand in hand. First and foremost, unless there is commitment from top management the project will fail because sufficient resources will not be allocated. Research shows that commitment increases when those involved in the project are allowed to influence decisions through their input and suggestions. In a project oriented environment, commitment takes a wider meaning. It also refers to stakeholder commitment. The major stakeholders are the project team, executive management, client and in certain cases, the public.

Employee commitment is valued because research indicates that it reduces withdrawal behaviours, such as lateness, absenteeism and turnover. The literature indicates that a lack of project team participation in the decision-making process and major problem solving; and lack of team spirit and sense of mission within the project team, all contribute to project failure. However, project team participation in determining schedules and budgets; and project manager, parent organization and client commitment to defined schedules, budgets and technical performance goals, were all associated with project success.

Internal and external communication

Project managers must continually maintain communication links with all stakeholders, whether they are within or outside the project. Admittedly, this takes a lot of time and energy but it is essential to the achievement of project success. The literature suggests that a lack of affinity and poor relations with the client, parent organization, public officials and a poor public opinion are seen as factors leading to project failure. Regular communication with employees, however, regarding the project and their performance, including how well they are doing on their assigned tasks was found to increase employee commitment to the project, with a resultant increase in individual and organizational performance.

The above have provided a general definition of each project success–failure dimension and their respective impact on a project. Subsequent chapters will discuss the three broad managerial segments and their particular project success–failure dimensions in more detail.

References

Appelbaum, S.H. 2004. Critical success factors in the client-consulting relationship. *The Journal of American Academy of Business*, Cambridge, March, 184–91.

Baker, B.N., Murphy, D.C. and Fisher, D. 1983. Factors affecting project success, in: *Project Management Handbook*, D.I. Cleland and W.R. King (eds). New York: Van Nostrand Reinhold.

Belassi, W. and Tukul, O.I. 1996. A new framework for determining critical success and failure factors in project management. *International Journal of Project Management*, 14(3), 141–51.

Boadle, M. 2004. *Project Failure and Success Factors*. [Online] Available at: http://www.acs.org.au/ Certification/Documents/PMgt/2003PM1-ProjectFailure2.pdf [accessed: 1 October 2007].

CERF – Civil Engineering Research Foundation. 2004. *Independent Research Assessment of Project Management Factors Affecting Department of Energy Project Success – Final Report*. Office of Engineering and Construction Management U.S. Department of Energy.

Charvat, J.P. 2002. *How to identify a failing project*. [Online] Available at: http://www.uk.builder.com/ manage/project/0,39026588,20269989,00.htm [accessed: 1 June 2009].

Cleland, D.I. and King, W.R. 1983. *Systems Analysis and Project Management*. New York: McGraw-Hill.

Cooke-Davies, T. 2002. The "real" success factors on projects. *International Journal of Project Management*, 20, 185–90.

Frese, R. and Sauter, V. 2003. *Project Success and Failure: What is success, what is failure, and how can you improve your odds for success?* [Online] Available at: http://www.umsl.edu/~sauterv/analysis/6840_ f03_papers/frese/ [accessed: 1 June 2009].

Kanter, J. and Walsh, J.J. 2004. Toward more successful project management. *Information System Management*, Spring 2004, 16–21.

Martin, C.C. 1976. *Project Management*. New York: Amaco.

Mengesha, W.J. 2004. *Performances for Public Construction Projects in Developing Countries: Federal Road & Educational Building Projects in Ethiopia*, Norwegian University of Science and Technology: Doctoral Thesis 2004:45.

Morris, P.W. 1986. Project management: a view from Oxford. *International Journal of Construction Management and Technology*, 1, 36–52.

Morris, P.W. and Hugh, G.H. 1987. *The Anatomy of Major Projects: A Study of the Reality of Project Management*. Chichester: John Wiley and Sons, 21–38 and 193–270.

Pinto, J.K and Kharbanda, O.P. 1995. *Successful Project Managers: Leading your Team to Success*. New York: Van Nostrand Reinhold.

Pinto, J.K. and Slevin, D.S. 1987. Critical factors in successful project implementation. *IEEE Transactions on Engineering Management*, EM-34, 1, 22–7.

Sayles, L.R. and Chandler, M.K. 1971. *Managing Large Systems: Organization for the Future*. New York: Harper & Row.

Shenhar, A.J., Tishler, A., Dvir, D., Lipovetsky, S. and Lechler, T. 2002. Refining the search for project success factors: a multivariate, typological approach. *R&D Management*, 32(2), 111–26.

Skitmore, R.M., Stradling, S.G. and Tuohy, A.P. 1989. Project management under uncertainty. *Construction Management and Economics*, 7, 103–13.

Sturdivant, J. 2004. The CNSI Requirements Analysis Process. [Online] Available at: http://www.CNS-INC.com [accessed: 11 January 2006].

Sutton, B. 2005. *Why Projects Fail – Mastering the Monster (Part 2)*. [Online] Available at: http://www.itarchitect.co.uk/articles/display.asp?id=224 [accessed: 1 October 2007].

Tukel, O.I. and Rom, W.O. 1995. *Analysis of the Characteristics of Projects in Diverse Industries,* Working Paper. Cleveland State University, Cleveland, Ohio.

Project Hygiene Support Factors

The chapters in Part II will examine in detail the project hygiene support factors that consist of the following project success–failure dimensions:

- Project strategic fit;
- Project scope;
- Project organization structure;
- Project team structure;
- Project planning and control.

The project hygiene support factors embrace the traditional project management process. The meticulous and transparent completion of these project success–failure dimensions collectively lead to best project management practice. The first chapter illustrates that *project strategic fit* has the goal of ensuring corporate success. Any undertaking carried out by an organization must have the desired impact on its business strategy. Any undertaking that does not achieve the desired impact on the strategic direction of the organization results in the under utilization of resources.

The other four project success–failure dimensions within the project hygiene support factors category have the specific objective of achieving project management success. These project success–failure dimensions are applicable to all types of projects, irrespective of the industry type, complexity and size. If project managers want to complete their assigned projects on schedule, within budget and to specifications, then these project success–failure dimensions must be conducted with care and precision.

4 *Project Strategic Fit*

*Perception is strong and sight weak. In strategy it is important to see distant
things as if they were close and to take a distanced view of close things.*
Miyamoto Musashi (1584–1645), legendary Japanese swordsman

It is important to recognize that organizations have a personality. Normally, an
organization's personality is determined by examining its strategy, which typically
consists of its mission, objectives, strategic direction and tactics. A fundamental principle
in management is that everything undertaken within the organization must be in
support of the organization's strategy. Otherwise, the utility value of the application of its
resources is not maximized and hence the organization's performance potential cannot
be achieved. Therefore, it is essential that projects are aligned with the organization's
strategic direction to facilitate the achievement of the organization's business objectives.

Business entities must have a clearly defined mission and strategic objectives
else it would be difficult for management to determine precisely whether a proposed
undertaking is aligned with the strategic direction of the organization. In the absence
of a clearly defined business strategy, managers will tend to assume what the strategy is,
and therefore their undertakings are based not on a realistic strategy but on an assumed
one. It is important that the deliverables from the undertaken projects meet the business
needs and are linked to the desired long term organizational results.

Organizational Strategic Framework

Strategy is generally viewed as being a set of decision-making rules to guide organizational
behaviour. However, objectives are seen as representing the targets the organization
is endeavouring to accomplish. The organization's strategy and its objectives are
interconnected, with strategy being the means or road map to achieve the defined
targets. Furthermore, strategy is greatly influenced by both the internal and external
environments the organization is operating in. Therefore, the concept of strategy is a
complex phenomenon, because apart from addressing the current internal functional
operations, it must also address the current and future prospects of the national economy,
the industry it is operating in, the competition and many other factors, including a whole
host of stakeholders.

It is commonly assumed that every organization has a strategy. However, this
assumption is erroneous. There are many small- and medium-sized companies that set
aside strategy since they see it as either being unsuitable for their type of business or
they simply cannot afford to dedicate resources to its formal definition. Hence, these
companies simply exist from week to week, reacting to occurring market situations in
the very short term. These companies in reality do not know where they want to be in x
years' time and just drift with the economic current. Another erroneous conception that

is often made is to view strategy as being equivalent to planning, where often planning has connotations with excessive rules, red tape and paperwork, which is only appropriate for large organizations that have the resources to support these processes.

Some organizations that have a strategy, do not communicate it to their employees in a clearly defined and easily understood manner. What is more, at times, the communication of the strategy is limited to certain hierarchical management levels. These organizational concerns need to be examined and addressed. If employees do not know the strategy of their organization, it is unlikely that they will be pulling the rope in a perpendicular direction that the organization is heading for. Hence, having a strategy and conveying it in an effective manner becomes essential if the undertaken projects are to be aligned with the organization's strategic direction.

Basically, taking into consideration the internal and external environment, a strategy defines where the organization wants to be; how it is going to get there; and when it intends to get there. For small- to medium-sized companies this process need not require vast resources. What is required is a cyclic review of the business environment, particularly if there has been, or is anticipated to be, a major change. This will allow management to appraise where the business is going and reflect on the organization's ability to compete within the market place. The objective for management in the context of undertaking projects is to ensure that a proposed project is aligned with the defined strategy, thus making certain that the organization's resources are utilized in the most suitable manner.

Characteristics of Strategic Decisions

The characteristics of strategic decisions are the unique features of the decisions that are normally carried out at a strategic level whose attributes distinguish them from other organizational functional decisions. These strategic decision attributes include:

1. *Domain of the organization's business activities.* This, basically, determines the boundary of the organization's undertakings, that is, its line of business. For instance, a fundamental issue in undertaking a project is for management to determine whether the proposed project fits within the organization's activity boundary;
2. *Harmonization of the activities undertaken by the organization with its operating environment.* This requires knowledge about the needs of the client and how these may be satisfied, the local market conditions, environmental issues and the economic situation;
3. *Equilibrium between the activities undertaken by the organization and its resource potential.* This determines whether the resources required are available or could be made available. There is no point in undertaking a proposed project if the resources required to pursue this project opportunity are not available;
4. *Resource implications of the activities undertaken by the organization.* This issue is related to risk. For example, undertaking a major project may require the entity to increase its long-term and short-term debt, thus exposing the organization to the threat of economic non-sustainability and failure;
5. *Implication of the activities undertaken by the organization on the operational decisions.* Undertaking a major project may result in key changes in the human resource policies of the organization or the financial control mechanisms. It is important to

assess the consequences of a proposed project on the operational mechanisms of the organization;

6. *Stakeholder values and expectations.* The project achievements must be aligned to the expectations of those who have the influence inside and outside the organization. Hence, stakeholder expectations must be managed in such a way that they are established on a realistic basis. Raising expectations by promising too much too soon in terms of project schedules, time frames and deliverables often leads to unsuccessful outcomes;

7. *Long-term influence on the organization.* Management must determine the long-term influence of a project on the organization's future activities. For instance, undertaking a major project that requires the organization to increase its long-term and short-term debt may restrict the organization from undertaking other concurrent projects, thus directly influencing the organization's potential future growth.

Most of what has been discussed in the above paragraphs implies corporate strategy. However, in practice, strategies exist at a number of levels within an organization. Figure 4.1 illustrates the existence of three strategic levels within an organization and provides examples of projects associated with each strategic level.

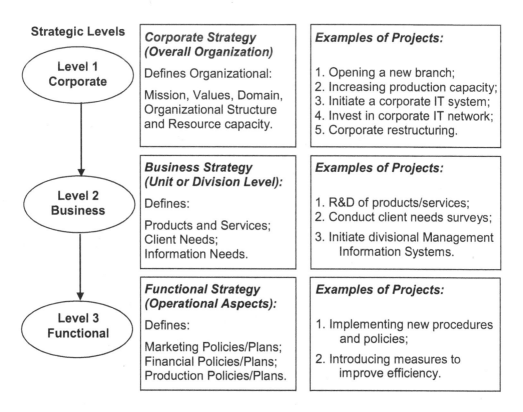

Figure 4.1   Strategic levels within an organization

At the corporate level, the main extent of the strategy revolves around the organization's business domain, with projects undertaken being in support of the organization as a whole. The business strategy is the next level and mainly deals with a division or department within the entire organization. The business strategy is linked to the corporate strategy. For instance, the corporate strategy provides a common approach; for example, aspects of the management information systems may be standardized for the organization as a whole. However, there may be specific management information systems requirements that are applicable or customized for a particular division, for example, a production control system. The functional strategies are the third and final level. These strategies are related to the operational aspects of the divisions. Normally, there is a strategy for each functional area, such as marketing, finance, production, and human resources. These functional strategies are linked to the business strategies. Many of the projects undertaken within this level may be related to organizational change associated with implementing new policies or procedures.

Strategy and the Organizational Environment

As stated previously, strategy has connotations of bureaucracy, implying heaps of paperwork and the application of costly human resources for its maintenance. This may be true for very large organizations, but need not be the case for medium and small entities. The approach used in defining strategy depends on the organizational environment, particularly, the organization type and size. Figure 4.2 illustrates the normal visualization of an organization.

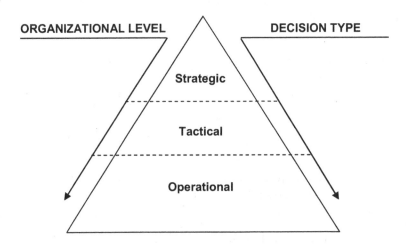

Figure 4.2   Management decision-making stratum

The top management layer is typically associated with strategic management where decisions are related to the future, taking into consideration both the internal and external environment. The information required at this level is vital for making forecasts, for example, predicting production capacity or market growth. At the second management layer is the general management team, who are required to monitor the current organizational performance with the specified objectives and targets, established at the strategic level. At this level the information is fundamentally internally generated. Finally, at the third layer reside the operations managers, who are responsible for the day-to-day running of the organizational units. Their decisions are current and usually immediate, for example, replacing an employee who reports sick on the night shift with another employee who possesses the same skill competencies.

The diagram conveys the perception of a strict delineation of management authority and responsibility. However, this delineation is theoretical and depends on the organization size and corporate management style. Often, the larger the organization the greater is the delineation. In small- and medium-sized business organizations, the owner could also be the manager, and will wear different managerial hats at different times. In one instance this individual could be making a strategic decision, in another, an operational decision. Therefore, organization size will determine the delineation of the strategic–tactical–operational decision mix.

In addition, in large organizations, top management may have the sole domain for defining organizational strategy. These individuals would define the general direction and issue the relevant directives to the other management layers, for the execution and deployment of the strategy. This is the traditional top-down approach. However, the other extreme is the bottom-up approach, where all employees at different organizational levels are requested and encouraged to contribute to the formulation of the strategy. In practice, many organizations adopt a mixture of styles, where the top corporate management define the general direction but request proposals from the other management layers. Therefore, the organizational management style will also determine the strategic–tactical–operational decision mix.

Another consideration in the formulation of the organizational strategy is whether the strategy is formally or informally defined. Large organizations may need to have a highly formalized process that is linked to the organizational budgeting process. However, in small and medium organizations the strategy may be informal. An informal strategy definition procedure minimizes the bureaucratic process. Once again, the organization size and corporate management style will influence the degree of formalization. However, communicating the strategy becomes even more critical when an informal strategy definition procedure is adopted.

The final aspect is the strategy definition horizon. Should the strategy define a short- or long-term planning spectrum? This basically depends on the industry type the organization is involved in. For example, an electrical power generation entity requires a long term strategy related to the future power generation obligation, taking into consideration regional demographics, economic growth, technological developments and many other factors. Long-term projections are required because it takes very high capital and more importantly it takes years to construct or even enhance electrical power generation capacity. On the other hand, small and medium organizations, particularly if operating in fragmented industries, where more market turbulence is experienced, may require very short planning horizons. In general, as highlighted above an organization's strategy definition approach will depend on its size, its corporate management style and the type of industry it operates in.

In reality, the defined organizational strategy is spelling out in general terms the projects that are to be undertaken by the organization in the long term and immediate future. The organizational strategy is establishing a benchmark by which management will be able to assess whether to embark on an undertaking or not.

Terminology Used in Defining the Strategy

Before the strategic fit of a particular project may be assessed it is important to be familiar with the terminology that is used in defining strategy. The basic meaning of the various terms used in the strategy definition process includes:

1. *Mission.* Prevailing idea supporting stakeholder values and expectations consisting of three elements: Aspiration or purpose (that is, describes business scope); Vision (that is, where does the entity see itself in "x" years time?); Values (that is, specifies business philosophy or principles). An example of an organization's mission is: "Having a cost effective organization".
2. *Objectives.* Objectives flow from the mission statement. Ideally, objectives should be quantified and measurable against consequent targets within a specified time period. For example: "Increase operational efficiency by 30 per cent by year 2012".
3. *Strategy.* Whilst there is a lack of consensus as to the definition of the word strategy, it may be stated that a strategy consists of a number of general statements of intent. For example: "Implement eCommerce mechanisms for the procurement process".
4. *Tactics.* Tactics include all matters within the operations of an organization that transform the overall strategy into series of actions, such as the use of milestones and critical path analysis in project management to implement the strategy. For example: "Eliminate paper transactions in the procurement process by 50 per cent through the implementation of eCommerce mechanisms by having eProcurement, eSales, eQueries and ePayments by 2012".
5. *Monitor.* Controlling and monitoring the actions defined in tactical plans to determine the progress in achieving the objectives. For example: "Measure the weekly electronic and paper transaction volume in the eCommerce mechanism; if the progress in switching to electronic transactions is acceptable do nothing, otherwise review strategies and tactics".
6. *Incentive.* An incentive is a reward or pay-off for achieving the objectives. For example: "Paying a bonus to a Project Manager who delivers ahead of schedule". Another example is to offer a discount to clients who use an eCommerce ordering facility.

Having described the strategic process and its importance to the organization, it is now appropriate to address the issue of how managers, individually and collectively, decide whether a proposed project is aligned with the organization's strategy.

Strategic Fit Appraisal of Projects

This section provides a general appraisal process to determine whether a particular project supports the business objectives of the organization and its defined business strategy, to ensure the optimum utilization of the organization's available resources. The strategic fit appraisal of a project consists of four stages described below.

STAGE 1 – TIME HORIZON ALIGNMENT AND STRATEGY FORMULATION APPROACH

Stage 1 has two objectives, namely, to determine whether the project is aligned with the time horizon of the organization's strategy and whether the organization's strategy formulation approach is a formal or informal one (see Figure 4.3).

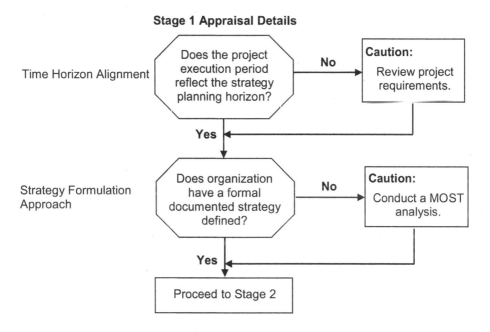

Figure 4.3   Project strategic fit – general assessment

If the organization has an informal strategy then a Mission, Objectives, Strategic Direction and Tactics (MOST) analysis is to be conducted to ensure that the organization has a defined mission, objectives, strategic direction and tactics. Without these definitions it is difficult, if not impossible, to determine whether the project has strategic fit. This stage is critical for project strategic fit process.

STAGE 2 – ORGANIZATION MISSION APPRAISAL

This stage determines whether the project supports the defined organization mission in terms of the organization's purpose, business scope, future positioning and the defined organizational values and principles (refer to Figure 4.4). Undertaking a project that does not support the organization's mission is simply wasting the organization's resources.

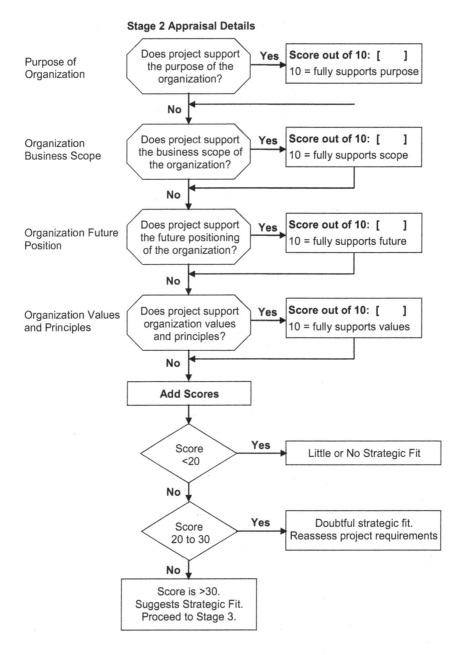

Figure 4.4   Project strategic fit – organization mission assessment

STAGE 3 – ORGANIZATION STRATEGIC OBJECTIVES APPRAISAL

Stage 3 determines whether the organization's strategic objectives have been defined in a way that allows them to be subsequently measured and compared with the established targets (refer to Figure 4.5). If the objectives have been appropriately defined, an assessment is made to determine whether the project supports the organization's strategic objectives.

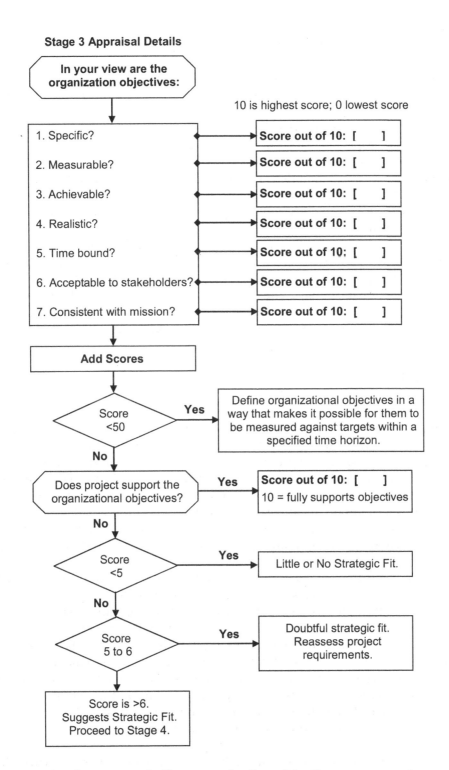

Stage 3 Appraisal Details

In your view are the organization objectives:

10 is highest score; 0 lowest score

1. Specific? — Score out of 10: [ ]

2. Measurable? — Score out of 10: [ ]

3. Achievable? — Score out of 10: [ ]

4. Realistic? — Score out of 10: [ ]

5. Time bound? — Score out of 10; [ ]

6. Acceptable to stakeholders? — Score out of 10: [ ]

7. Consistent with mission? — Score out of 10: [ ]

Add Scores

Score <50 — Yes → Define organizational objectives in a way that makes it possible for them to be measured against targets within a specified time horizon.

No

Does project support the organizational objectives? — Yes → Score out of 10: [ ] 10 = fully supports objectives

No

Score <5 — Yes → Little or No Strategic Fit.

No

Score 5 to 6 — Yes → Doubtful strategic fit. Reassess project requirements.

Score is >6. Suggests Strategic Fit. Proceed to Stage 4.

Figure 4.5 Project strategic fit – organization objectives assessment

STAGE 4 – ORGANIZATION BUSINESS DOMAIN APPRAISAL

Stage 4 is the final phase for appraising project strategic fit (refer to Figure 4.6). This stage determines whether the project to be undertaken is in line with the business activities of the organization. It also assesses whether the project is congruent with the organization's operating environment and whether the organization has the available resources (or could have) in terms of experience and competencies to undertake the project. In addition, this stage appraises whether there are likely to be any negative implications in terms of resources and future long term influences that may expose the organization to economic non-sustainability or hinder future growth potential. Finally, Stage 4 assesses whether the project supports the expectations of the major stakeholders since this is viewed as being critical to project success.

The above general appraisal process helps management to determine whether a particular proposed project is aligned with the defined strategy. Note that the scoring limits, within the appraisal process for each stage to decide strategic fit, may be changed to suit individual organizations. The project strategic fit process will ensure that the organization's resources are utilized in the most suitable manner to make certain that the organization's effort is aimed at achieving its business objectives.

Conclusion

Strategy is generally viewed as being a set of decision-making rules to guide organizational behaviour, where objectives are seen as representing the targets the organization is trying to accomplish, and with strategy being the means or road map to achieve these defined targets. Hence, it is important to ensure that everything undertaken within an organization supports its strategy. In this context it is essential that proposed projects are aligned with the organization's strategic direction to facilitate the achievement of the business objectives. It is also important to ensure that deliverables from a particular project are linked to the desired long-term organizational results. An organization's strategy may generally be determined by examining its mission, objectives, strategic direction and tactics.

Communicating the organization's strategy in an effective and easily understood manner is vital to the successful management of an enterprise and the projects undertaken by it. If employees do not know what their organization's strategy is about, it is unlikely that the activities undertaken by them will be fully aligned with the intended strategic direction and therefore the organization's resources will not be utilized in the most opportune manner. For this reason, it is essential that management has a simple process to help it determine whether a particular project supports the business objectives of the organization and its defined strategy. This will ensure the optimization of the organization's available resources. In the previous section, it was illustrated that the project strategic fit appraisal process consists of four stages:

1. Stage 1 is a general assessment to verify whether a project is aligned with the organization's strategy time horizon and whether the organization has a formal or informal strategy. Having an informal strategy means that a MOST analysis must be conducted to ensure that the organization's mission, objectives, strategic direction

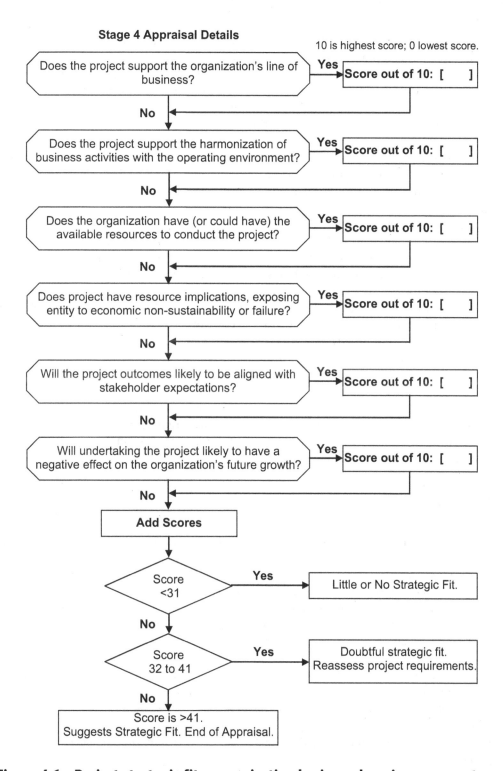

Stage 4 Appraisal Details

10 is highest score; 0 lowest score.

Does the project support the organization's line of business? **Yes** → Score out of 10: [   ]

No

Does the project support the harmonization of business activities with the operating environment? **Yes** → Score out of 10: [   ]

No

Does the organization have (or could have) the available resources to conduct the project? **Yes** → Score out of 10: [   ]

No

Does project have resource implications, exposing entity to economic non-sustainability or failure? **Yes** → Score out of 10: [   ]

No

Will the project outcomes likely to be aligned with stakeholder expectations? **Yes** → Score out of 10: [   ]

No

Will undertaking the project likely to have a negative effect on the organization's future growth? **Yes** → Score out of 10: [   ]

No

Add Scores

Score <31 **Yes** → Little or No Strategic Fit.

No

Score 32 to 41 **Yes** → Doubtful strategic fit. Reassess project requirements.

No

Score is >41. Suggests Strategic Fit. End of Appraisal.

Figure 4.6 Project strategic fit – organization business domain assessment

and tactics are defined and documented. Without these definitions it is not possible to complete the appraisal process.

2. Stage 2 determines whether the project supports the defined organization mission in terms of the organization's purpose, business scope, future positioning and the defined organizational values and principles. Taking on a project that does not support the organization's mission is simply not utilizing the organization's resources in the best possible manner.

3. Stage 3 determines whether the organization's strategic objectives have been defined in a way that allows them to be measured and compared with established targets. If the objectives are properly defined, an assessment is made to decide whether the project,supports the strategic objectives.

4. Stage 4 verifies whether:
   - Project is aligned with the business activities of the organization;
   - Project is compatible with the organization's operating environment;
   - Organization has the available resources (or could have) in terms of experience and competencies to carry out the proposed project;
   - There are likely to be any damaging repercussions in terms of resources and future long-term influences that may expose the organization to economic failure or hinder its future growth potential;
   - Project supports stakeholder expectations. This is seen as being critical to project success.

The full appraisal process helps management to determine whether a particular proposed project has strategic fit to ensure that the organization's limited resources are utilized in the most suitable manner and that all organizational effort is aimed at achieving the business objectives of the enterprise.

References

Ansoff, H.I. 1987. The emerging paradigm of strategic behaviour. *Strategic Management Journal*, 8, 501–15.

—— 1988. *Corporate Strategy* (Revised Edition). London: Penguin Books.

Bakir, A. 2001. *Understanding Organizational Strategy*. Faculty of Leisure and Tourism, Buckinghamshire Chilterns University College. [Online] Available at: http://www.mngt.waikato.ac.nz/ejrot/cmsconference/2001/Papers/Strategy/Bakir.pdf [accessed: 8 June 2009].

Feurer, R. and Chaharbaghi, K. 1995. Strategy development: past, present and future. *Management Decision*, 33(6), 11–21.

Gopinath, C. and Hoffman, R.C. 1995. The relevance of strategy research: practitioner and academic viewpoints. *Journal of Management Studies*, 32(5), 575–94.

Hardy, C. 1996. Understanding power: bringing about strategic change. *British Journal of Management*, 7, S1–S16.

Hendry, J. 1995. Strategy formation and the policy context. *Journal of General Management*, 20(4), 54–64.

Johnson, G. and Scholes, K. 1993. *Exploring Corporate Strategy* (3rd Edition). New York: Prentice Hall.

Mintzberg, H. 1994. *The Rise and Fall of Strategic Planning*. New York: Free Press.

Rowe, A.J., Mason, R.O., Dickel, K.E., Mann, R.B. and Mockler, R.J. 1994. *Strategic management: a methodological approach* (4th edition). USA: Addison-Wesley.

5 *Project Scope*

*To the person who does not know where he wants to go there is no favorable
wind.*

Seneca (5 BC–65 AD)

The first question that normally comes to mind when someone is given a project is, "How does one go about defining what needs to be accomplished?" The literature research suggests that many projects encounter difficulties primarily because they are not well defined. Despite this lack of adequate definition, project managers still undertake a project with a sense of anticipation and enthusiasm, hopeful that matters will become clearer as work progresses. Frequently, matters do become more concrete as the work being performed proceeds, however, difficulties usually arise because the work being conducted may not necessarily be what should be done nor does it lead to the owner's intended outcome. This may result in the abandonment of the project or undertaking extensive rescheduled work when project implementation is at an advanced stage.

Right from the outset, the project manager must understand the holistic view of the project being undertaken. For instance, the project manager should know:

- How the project was initiated;
- Why it is needed;
- The expected project outcomes;
- Have an understanding of the project vision from the point of view of the project sponsor.

In other words, project managers must have a complete knowledge about the purpose of the project and incorporate this as part of their formal and documented mission statement. Furthermore, project managers must keep in mind that a project must have a champion or sponsor. Research suggests that projects that lack a sponsor are doomed and therefore in this situation, the project manager must have the courage to formally renounce the project, unless this major deficiency is rectified. When defining the project scope, the project manager is developing a common understanding as to what is included and excluded from a project. In simple terms, the project scope definition deals with the "what" and "why" the project is being undertaken.

What is Project Scope?

Project scope basically defines what needs to be done. According to the Project Management Institute Standards Committee (2004), scope planning is the process of developing a written scope statement as the basis for future project decisions, including the criteria used to determine if the project or phase of a project has been completed successfully.

Its purpose is to ensure that the project embraces all the work that is required, by subdividing project outputs into smaller more manageable components, thus increasing the probability that the project will be successfully completed.

Irrespective of the project magnitude, a clear definition and statement of the impacted areas and the project domain must be determined and provided. The project scope defines the deliverables, client, work packages, outcomes, and human and financial resources. The degree of detail of the project scope depends on the project magnitude. The larger and more complex the project is, the more detail the definition. Project scope should also take into account the timeframe and resource constraints.

An ideal situation is where the project scope does not change, however, this not a realistic proposition. It should be recognized that the project scope definition is not a static process but a dynamic one. There may be a need for project scope to be reviewed a number of times over the life cycle of the project. However, it is important that the project manager endeavours to keep scope changes to a minimum and obtains a clear sign-off for any scope change that is required. The project scope change aspect will be discussed in Chapter 9 related to information flow and knowledge management.

The project scope stage is critical because it lays the foundation for the eventual project success. It should be recognized that if the project is inadequately defined and not suitably linked with organizational strategy, then there is a high probability of project failure. Therefore, ample time should be allocated for the project scope definition phase. Project managers should not be pressured or compelled into finishing the project scope unless they are fully satisfied that they have documented the fundamental nature of the project. Research shows that an inadequate project scope will haunt a project throughout its life cycle. Therefore, project scope needs to be planned and defined in a way that is clear and unambiguous and does not lead to conflicts.

How Does Project Scope Fit in the Core Planning Process?

Figure 5.1 illustrates the relationship between project scope and the core planning process. The rationale in proposing a particular project and its direct link with the corporate strategy must be established. It is essential that any project undertaken is aligned with the corporate strategic direction. It is also essential to identify the project users or those who will utilize the end product. Once management is satisfied that there is strategic fit and that the project users are identified, the project may be defined in terms of the outputs and outcomes that the end project deliverable is to accomplish.

It should be noted that it is the clients who utilize the end project product and as a result, generate the project outcomes or benefits. It is emphasized that outputs are normally under the full control of the project manager, while outcomes are normally determined by user perceptions. Although project outcomes are more difficult to deal with, project managers should actively aim to influence user perceptions. This initial phase is depicted in Figure 5.1 as being part of the strategic alignment process and is viewed as being essential to project success.

The work or effort required to produce the outputs also needs to be examined, so that the resources in human and financial terms may generally be determined. The result from this process becomes the basis for the project scope definition. The project scope is to be defined as a clear statement, which describes the project domain and the impact on the

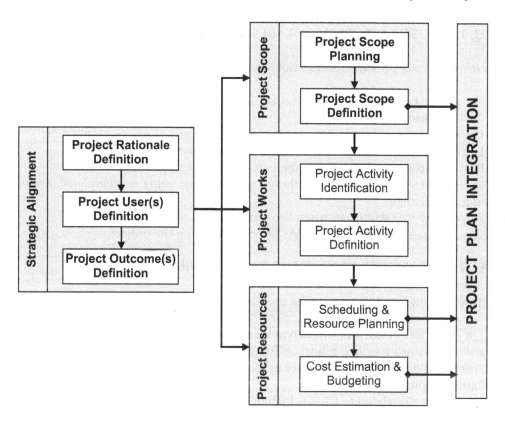

Figure 5.1   Relationship between project scope and core planning process

affected organizational sectors. Once project scope is formally agreed upon, the project manager may:

- Identify and define the activities that make up the work effort;
- Undertake the project schedule and resource plan;
- Determine the cost estimates and project budget.

The result of this process is an integrated project plan that provides a road map for project implementation. However, it must be emphasized that the process is not static. The resultant plan must be reviewed on a regular basis and must always reflect the agreed project scope.

Defining Project Scope

The project scope definition seeks to provide information on three levels:

1. Holistic information about the project;
2. Information about the project objectives;
3. Information about the project domain.

LEVEL 1: HOLISTIC INFORMATION ABOUT THE PROJECT

This level basically provides information on the following project scope aspects:

- The project background by identifying the need and the explicit agreement to explore the identified need;
- The main or overall goal of the project, in other words, the general outcome;
- The opportunity or concern that the project will resolve;
- How the project fits or supports the corporate strategic goals;
- The project's relationship with other projects that are being contemplated, evaluated or implemented;
- The change that will occur when the project is completed;
- The acceptance or rejection criteria for implementing the project.

LEVEL 2: INFORMATION ABOUT THE PROJECT OBJECTIVES

The information details regarding the project objectives include the following aspects:

- The objectives of the project, such as increasing efficiency, reducing operational costs and achieving a specified return on investment;
- Specific deliverables and outcomes in measurable terms;
- Particular project priorities;
- Explicit details related to what is included and excluded from the project;
- Specific details regarding the various options for project execution;
- Precise details about assumptions being made, with each assumption being documented and followed up at a later date to validate the scope;
- Definition and documentation of the project critical success factors including the respective key performance indicators.

LEVEL 3: INFORMATION ABOUT THE PROJECT DOMAIN

The information details regarding the project domain include the following aspects:

- Identification and documentation of the major constraints, including the information about the authority that established them and the reason for their establishment;
- Identification and documentation of all stakeholders, giving particular attention to the active stakeholders;
- Identification and documentation of those stakeholders that may be against or holding back their support for the project, including how these stakeholders may influence the project outcome;
- Identification and documentation of the project drivers, particularly outside influences, such as regulations, legislation, standards, security and safety concerns;
- Developing and documenting the operational concepts of the project deliverables;
- Identification and documentation of the external interfaces to the project that are outside the control of those managing the project, such as, technical interfaces, issuance of relevant permits and linkage to infrastructure facilities of third parties (for example, state electricity grid).

COMPLETING THE PROJECT SCOPE DEFINITION TEMPLATE

Figure 5.2 provides a sample template for defining project scope. It should be noted that very large projects may be subdivided into a number of major project components, with each component having its own project scope definition.

PROJECT DESCRIPTION:

PROJECT DETAILS:

Total Project Estimated Cost: ....   Date: /   /

Department: ....   Telephone: ....

Project Requestor: ....   e-mail: ....

Project Name: ....

EXECUTIVE SUMMARY:

PROJECT ACCEPTANCE/REJECTION CRITERIA:

BUSINESS OBJECTIVES OF PROJECT:

PROJECT DOMAIN:

INITIAL PROJECT SCOPE ESTIMATES:

Figure 5.2   Template for defining project scope

INITIAL IMPLEMENTATION PLANS:
INITIAL PROJECT SCHEDULE:
PROJECT TEAM:
POTENTIAL RISKS:

APPROVAL AND AUTHORITY TO PROCEED:

We approve the project component as described above and authorize the team to proceed.

....

....

....

....

Name & Signature   **Title**   **Date**

PREPARED BY:

....

Name & Signature   **Title**   **Date**

Figure 5.2   Template for defining project scope (continued)

The templates would be completed by the project initiator for each project and contain the following information:

1. *Project description.* This would provide the project background, including the identified need for the project and a general description of what the project is to achieve.
2. *Project Details.* The project details provides information regarding the overall estimated

cost of the project to completion, the date of the estimate, initiating department, project initiator and contact details, and project title.

3. *Executive Summary*. This section explains the overall goal of the project, the opportunity or concern that the project will resolve and how the project supports the strategic direction of the organization.

4. *Project Acceptance (or Rejection) Criteria*. This provides a brief description of the project's linkage with other projects that are either being proposed, evaluated or implemented. An explanation is also provided regarding the anticipated change that will occur when the project is completed. The project initiator is to define the acceptance (or rejection) criteria for implementing the project.

5. *Business Objectives of the Project*. This section itemizes the business objectives details, including:
   a) Specific project objectives. For example, a project may have the objective of increasing efficiency and reducing operational costs;
   b) Deliverables in measurable terms and their specific priorities;
   c) Details of how the project will be supported in terms of finance, human resources, logistics, and so on;
   d) The project critical success factors and their respective key performance indicators.

6. *Project Domain*. The section is to briefly describe the:
   a) Details related to what is included and excluded from the project, the options for project execution and a definition of the assumptions made;
   b) Major constraints, who established them and why were they established;
   c) Active stakeholders, particularly those who are against the project, including their influence on the project outcome;
   d) Project drivers, particularly outside influences such as regulations, legal issues, standards, security and safety concerns;
   e) Project deliverables operational concepts catering for the full life cycle of the end product;
   f) External interfaces to the project that are outside the control of those managing the project, such as technical interfaces and issuance of permits.

7. *Initial Project Scope Estimates*. This section describes the overall project review process, such as the titles (and names if possible) of those who are required to sign-off or review the project at various milestones. Relevant scope information is to be provided from each affected department.

8. *Initial Implementation Plans*. This section briefly describes the initial plans for the project and the general implementation strategy.

9. *Initial Project Schedule*. This section would contain a preliminary project schedule showing at minimum the project's major milestones.

10. *Project Team*. This section provides a list of the project team members assigned to the project, including their name, title, role, skills prerequisites and contact details.

11. *Potential Risks*. This section would itemize any known issues or risks to the project schedule, for example, the approval chain, suppliers, specialist skills and expertise, partner relationships, technology, regulatory requirements and so on;

12. *Approval and Authority to Proceed*. This would contain a brief statement approving the project component as described in the project scope and authorize the project team to proceed. This section is signed off by all relevant stakeholders that have a direct interest in the project.

13. *Prepared By*. This section is signed off and dated by individual(s) who prepared the project scope document. Their full name and title are to be clearly displayed on the document.

As stated previously, the level of detail of the project scope depends on the project magnitude. Therefore, larger and more complex projects require more detailed information. It should be noted that the project scope templates take into account the time frame and resource constraints, since the project originator is to provide the initial estimates, implementation plan and schedule, composition of project team, and the potential risk factors.

Appraising the Project Scope Definition

Project scope is essential to project management success. A lack of an adequate project scope is equivalent to having a weak project foundation; hence if it is not immediately rectified, it will eventually lead to project failure. Project managers must be on continuous guard to watch for signs that indicate problems with project scope. Figure 5.3 illustrates a simple but effective method of appraising the project scope.

The project scope appraisal process will ensure that the project manager will have an adequate definition of the works to be carried out. It will avoid a scenario where work being conducted may not necessarily be what should be done or does not lead to the owner's intended outcome.

Practical Suggestions to Project Managers

Literature research suggests that project managers should adhere to the following practices in defining project scope:

- Project scope tasks are a steering mechanism and are to be conducted before any other project management activities;
- Project scope is incomplete and cannot be conducted properly unless all relevant stakeholders have been identified and are actively involved at a suitable level;
- Document and define project scope in a simple, meaningful and easily understood manner so that it is unambiguous to those involved in the project;
- Formally acquire agreement and signature on the project scope document from all relevant and active stakeholders;
- Projects, particularly those involving organizational change, may be achieved by a number of interrelated projects rather than a big-bang approach;
- Carefully delineate what is included and excluded from the project;
- Proactive measures should be taken to minimize project scope creep;
- Identify all related projects, whether they are at the proposal, evaluation or implementation stage and define them on the project scope document;
- Project activities must support project scope. Note that there may be project managers who are operating to a different schedule that has not been formally specified in the scope;
- Continually monitor the project scope to ensure that project activities continue to align with it. Review the project scope and if necessary redefine it or bring the project back on track.

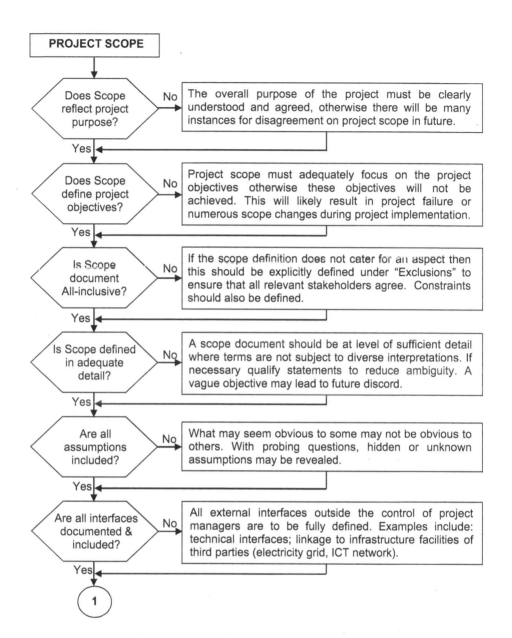

PROJECT SCOPE

Does Scope reflect project purpose? — No → The overall purpose of the project must be clearly understood and agreed, otherwise there will be many instances for disagreement on project scope in future.

Yes ↓

Does Scope define project objectives? — No → Project scope must adequately focus on the project objectives otherwise these objectives will not be achieved. This will likely result in project failure or numerous scope changes during project implementation.

Yes ↓

Is Scope document All-inclusive? — No → If the scope definition does not cater for an aspect then this should be explicitly defined under "Exclusions" to ensure that all relevant stakeholders agree. Constraints should also be defined.

Yes ↓

Is Scope defined in adequate detail? — No → A scope document should be at level of sufficient detail where terms are not subject to diverse interpretations. If necessary qualify statements to reduce ambiguity. A vague objective may lead to future discord.

Yes ↓

Are all assumptions included? — No → What may seem obvious to some may not be obvious to others. With probing questions, hidden or unknown assumptions may be revealed.

Yes ↓

Are all interfaces documented & included? — No → All external interfaces outside the control of project managers are to be fully defined. Examples include: technical interfaces; linkage to infrastructure facilities of third parties (electricity grid, ICT network).

Yes ↓

(1)

Figure 5.3 Appraising project scope

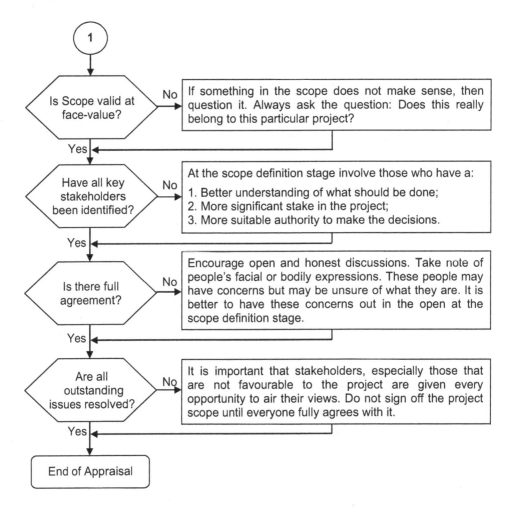

Figure 5.3   Appraising project scope (continued)

Conclusion

Projects may encounter difficulties because they are not well defined, resulting in unnecessary work effort that often does not lead to the intended outcome. This may eventually lead to discarding the project or conducting substantial rescheduled work during an advanced stage of project implementation. The main points made by this chapter are the following:

1. Project scope defines what needs to be done. It provides a common understanding as to what is included or excluded from a project;
2. Project scope ensures that the project identifies all the work that is required by breaking down project deliverables into smaller manageable components, which collectively produce the desired project outputs and outcomes;
3. Project scope is required at all times irrespective of the type and size of projects. However, larger and more complex projects require a more detailed project scope definition;

4. It is difficult for project scope to remain static. Hence, to minimize scope changes, prepare project scope guidelines and adhere to them;

5. Allow ample time for the definition of project scope since an inadequate definition will haunt a project throughout its life cycle. Ensure that project scope is defined in a way that is unambiguous and does not lead to conflicts.

Project scope has a three-way link. It has backward integration to corporate strategy and forward integration to project activity identification and the eventual project plan. Project scope seeks to provide information on three levels, how it supports corporate strategy, project objectives and the project domain. A standard template for defining project scope is to be incorporated as part of the project scope preparation guidelines. Once project scope has been prepared, conduct a review appraisal by examining whether project scope reflects the points addressed by Figure 5.3.

Project managers should carry out the project scope tasks before any other project management activities and ensure that all relevant stakeholders are identified and actively involved. Project scope must be defined in an unambiguous manner, defining precisely what is included and excluded in the project. Project managers should also ensure the all relevant and active stakeholders agree and sign the project scope document. In addition, the project manager must take proactive measures to minimize project scope creep by continually monitoring the scope so that project activities remain aligned with it. Finally, the project manager must safeguard the project by ensuring that all project activities support the project scope and that related projects are identified and documented in the project scope document.

References

Cleland, D.I. and King, W.R. 1988. *Project Management Handbook*. New York: Van Nostrand Reinhold.

The Project Management Institute Standards Committee. 2004. *A Guide to the Project Management Body of Knowledge*. Upper Darby, PA, USA: PMI.

Turbit, N. 2005. Defining the Scope of a Project. [Online] Available at: http://www.projectperfect.com.au [accessed: 8 June 2009].

Turner, J.R. 1993. *The Handbook of Project-Based Management*. Maidenhead: McGraw-Hill.

Yimin Zhu and Shu-Ching Chen. 2004. *SCOPE: A Conceptual Framework of Ontology-based Program/Project Scope Control*. Second LACCEI International Latin American and Caribbean Conference for Engineering and Technology (LACCET'2004) "Challenges and Opportunities for Engineering Education, Research and Development" Miami, Florida, USA, 2–4 June 2004, Available at: http://users.cs.fiu.edu/~chens/PDF/LACCEI04.pdf [accessed: 10 June 2009].

CHAPTER

6 *Project Organization Structure*

I believe the real difference between success and failure in a corporation can be very often traced to the question of how well the organization brings out the great energies and talents of its people.

Thomas J. Watson, Jr., former IBM Chief Executive

Having the appropriate organization structure for carrying out a project is an essential element for ensuring project management success. The project organization structure is the management framework that supervises the various activities and tasks that make up a project. However, the achievement of project management success in this context also depends on the appropriate project team. A suitable project team is required to bring about high performance and overcome two major obstacles:

1. The diversity and complex nature of different project undertakings;
2. The dynamic operational environment that normally exists in all types of industries.

Therefore, the goal is to have a suitable project organization structure that supports the project team to achieve high performance through gains in efficiency and effectiveness. The focus of this chapter is the project organization structure. The issue of project team organization will be addressed in the next chapter. It should be recognized that the corporate organization structure framework can weaken or strengthen the ability of an entity to deliver projects. For example, an entity that has a corporate organization structure that carries out support work as well as project implementation will normally give the support work priority over project implementation. Hence, when support issues occur they will take the focus away from the project. This will tend to weaken project deliverables.

In addition, the size of an entity may also be a determining factor in defining the corporate organization structure framework. In a small enterprise it may be normal practice for support services and project implementation to be performed collectively, sharing the same resources. In this situation, the human resources are shifting from one mode to another with a resultant loss in effectiveness. It is important to note that the corporate organization structure may facilitate or hinder an entity's ability to share resources. For example, if the project requires a resource with a particular specialist capability, it may be difficult to share this skilled resource with another functional area. The above issues illustrate that the project organization structure framework is essential to project management success and needs to be addressed in an appropriate manner.

Organization Structure Concepts

The abundant literature on organization structure recognizes that the task of organizing is a distinctive managerial function. Numerous studies of organization structures have been undertaken in diverse industries, such as manufacturing, finance, administration and multinational organizations, demonstrating that organization theories and practices are well established.

Organization structure theory is typically applicable to the study of complex organizations. Small to medium enterprises where the organization structure consists of one or a few supervisors and the number of employees is relatively modest do not usually need to spend a lot of effort on:

- Organizational structure design;
- Job design;
- Departmentalization;
- Building relationships between the job holders or between units.

The basic reason for this is that in these types of enterprises the corporate organizational framework is often informal and resource utilization is very flexible. However, there is a threshold where the size of the enterprise reaches a stage of development in which the informality of the organization structure and the flexibility of resource utilization become unmanageable and a more formal complex organizational framework is required. Research conducted by Harvard University (Lawrence and Lorsch, 1967) identified four major characteristics of an organization structure:

1. Span of control;
2. Number of levels to a shared superior;
3. Time span and specificity of review of departmental performance;
4. Importance of formal rules.

Although these characteristics may be valid for all types of organizations, they imply that organization size is an important factor in the magnitude of the applicability of each characteristic to a particular organization. Drazin and Van de Ven (1985) view organizational structure in terms of specification, standardization, discretion and personnel expertise. Note that specialization is the only attribute that is common with the Harvard University research findings. Likewise, research conducted by Mintzberg (1989) identified several types of organizations, namely, entrepreneurial, machine, professional, diversified, innovative, missionary and political. Mintzberg (1989) found that these organization types are based on the key functional components of the organization, the type of decentralization and their coordinating mechanism.

Contemporary and traditional researchers have identified organization structure as being characterized not only by the aspect of specialized divisions, but also by their horizontal and vertical interactions. The literature research highlights that there appears to be general agreement on two aspects:

- The structure of an organization is an essential aspect to the performance of the organization. This suggests that the project organization structure would without doubt affect the project delivery performance.
- The two basic components of the organization structure are its horizontal breadth as implied by the spans of control, and its vertical height as denoted by the hierarchal levels of decentralization.

There is evidence to suggest that the organization structure of an enterprise reflects the management style of corporate management and more importantly, supports the organizational corporate strategy.

Organization Structure Models

Researchers conceive that modifying the form of the organizational structure in terms of its horizontal and vertical span would affect organizational performance. Hence, two extremes for possible models of organization structures have been presented (Robbins, 1996). This spectrum of the organization structure models consists of the organic structure at one end and the mechanistic structure at the other. The organic structure model would represent a flat and cross-functional team, with low formalization, possessing comprehensive information and relying on participative decision making. The mechanistic structure model is the reverse of the organic structure and would be characterized by extensive departmentalization, high formalization, limited information and centralization.

As illustrated in Figure 6.1, the mechanistic structure model would consist of minimum horizontal width and maximum vertical height, while the organic structure model would have the maximum horizontal span but the minimum vertical hierarchical levels. While applied research on organizational structures is a continuous process, the main difficulty is attributed to the highly diverse features of projects and the high intrinsic uncertainties in the various processes of different type of industries. Hence, these factors have made it very complex to establish a credible model that will reflect all the diversities and uncertainties in the various operating organizational environments.

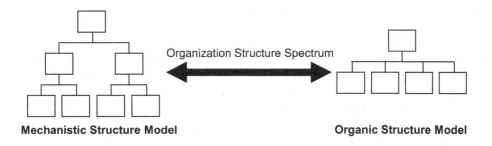

Figure 6.1   Spectrum of organization structure models

However, in the construction industry, Yinghui and Eng (2002) consider two elements as basic characteristics of a construction project. They are the *contract amount* and *project duration*. Yinghui and Eng (2002) suggest that these two elements provide the three-dimensional aspects of the project. The *contract amount* would indicate the two dimensions of size and complexity of the project, and *project duration* would express the third dimension of time, during which changes in the project take place. Hence, Yinghui and Eng (2002) propose that these dimensions may provide an indication of the organization structure model to be applicable, in terms of where it should lie in the organization structure spectrum.

Yinghui and Eng (2002) in a study of 40 random selected construction projects in Singapore found that the site project organization structure is inclined to be more organic as the project size increases in terms of contract amount, but not in terms of project duration. They also found that the site project organization would need to be enlarged in terms of number of supervisors as the production rate in terms of contract amount per day increases. However, their results suggest that a limit would be reached whereby any further increase in the production does not necessarily demand an enlargement of the site project organization. When this threshold is reached, changes in the levels of the organization structure would not have an impact on productivity. Generally, current structural and contingency theories on organizations indicate that there is no ideal rigid structure suitable for all situations.

Project Organization Structure

Conventional organization structures have restrictions when utilized for managing projects. Research literature suggests that these constraints are indicative when:

1. Organizational technical competencies are acceptable, but project outputs (deliverables) are not being achieved within the estimates;
2. Performance results are not consistent across the organization;
3. Tendency of growing employee discontent from perceived manipulation;
4. Difficulties result in not knowing who is accountable for the lack of project performance;
5. There is a lack of job satisfaction from project organization team members.

The structural design of the organization must address the social and technical needs of the works being undertaken. However, project management environments are dissimilar to normal management situations and therefore there is a need to customize the organization to support the intrinsic nature of the particular project environment. Organizations may be defined as groups of people who must coordinate their efforts to meet organizational objectives. However, The Project Management Institute Standards Committee (2004) specifically differentiates between an organization and project organization. They define project organization as any organization structure in which the project manager has full authority to assign priorities and to direct the work of individuals assigned to the project.

The setting up of a project organization is a delicate and essential issue at the initiation of any project. In the previous section, it was established that the diversity of projects and project magnitudes applicable to numerous assorted industries does not allow a standard project organization structure to be defined. However, the fact remains that establishing the project organization is one of the most important tasks that needs to be accomplished at the commencement of every project. This is especially so for large projects and particularly for those projects which have no precedent and therefore are considered to be of very high risk. At the same time,the research literature indicates that the suitability of a particular structure is influenced by a number of factors, including:

- Technology and technology trends;
- Complexity and resource availability;
- Type of product or service provided;
- Level of competitive rivalry;
- Organizational culture and decision-making process.

It is emphasized that a project organization structure is required to facilitate three important elements:

1. Internal and external communication;
2. Establishing interdependencies;
3. Assigning responsibility and authority.

Moreover, in selecting the most appropriate project organization structure, it must be recognized that all those participating in a project have to be conscious of the fact that a project is an undertaking that is likely to require the involvement and cooperation of different organizational function areas. Once this notion is fully understood and its implications comprehended, the project organization framework may be reduced to four possible options:

1. Coordination project organization;
2. Task force project organization;
3. Pure product (or service) project organization;
4. Matrix project organization.

COORDINATION PROJECT ORGANIZATION STRUCTURE

The coordination project organization structure formation evolved from the traditional organization structure approach to overcome a number of anomalies, when applied to a project management setting. The anomalies of the traditional organization structure when applied to a project management environment include:

- No formal direct accountability and responsibility for the project;
- Response to client concerns is often too slow;
- Bias towards a task or process achievement functionality rather than project orientation;
- Decision-making process is based on the individual's power and political strength;
- Difficult to attain interface management;
- Often difficult to inspire innovation and the motivation of employees.

The coordination project organization structure evolved to overcome the above inconsistencies by seeking to improve integration through the intensification of coordination as a result of:

1. Developing rules and procedures;
2. Reviewing and redesigning the planning processes;
3. Instituting hierarchical referral methods;
4. Fostering direct contact across functional boundaries.

Furthermore, the advantages of the traditional organizational structure approach were maintained, these included:

1. Ease of budgeting and control;
2. Facilitation of technical control;
3. Enhanced flexibility in manpower utilization;
4. Provision of continuity;
5. Permitting efficiencies in repetitive operations.

A coordination project organization structure permits most of the employees to remain in their current functions. However, this depends on the nature and complexity of the project. Figure 6.2 shows a coordination project organization structure for a very complex project that was utilized in the implementation of the Euro currency adoption at one European Union Member State (Malta). The various hierarchical levels are occupied by individuals on a part-time basis, except for the Chief Executive Officer (CEO) of the National Euro Changeover Committee and the support staff. Moreover, the entities that have the execution (implementation) role would each contain a full-time project leader with the necessary employees to carry out the identified modifications.

Figure 6.3 provides a representative example of a standard coordination project organization structure. This structure illustrates that the project managers are attached to the functional divisions. However, the project manager positions are frequently on the same hierarchical level as the functional managers, thus often resulting in role ambiguity and conflict for the employees that work in such structures. Experience has shown that role ambiguity and conflict may negatively affect employee commitment and motivation, resulting in higher project employee turnover rates and lower project performance. Coordination project organization structures have tended to provide inconsistent research results in terms of their effectives in implementing projects.

TASK FORCE PROJECT ORGANIZATION STRUCTURE

The Task Force Project Organization Structure is based on having the chairperson of the task force as the project director, who would have the overall leadership role for the project. An example of a task force project organization structure is illustrated in Figure 6.4. This example shows an actual project structure that was utilized in the implementation of the accrual accounting methodology at a national government level, across all government Ministries in one European Union Member State (Malta).

The members of the task force, including the chairperson, would dedicate their time to the project on a part-time basis. However, there may be instances where the chairperson

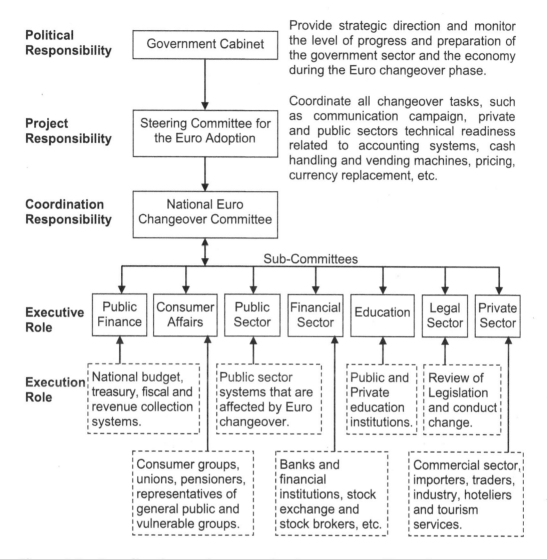

Figure 6.2   Coordination project organization structure (Euro changeover)

may be assigned to the task force on a permanent basis, until project completion. The task force policy sub-committees would work on defining and formulating policies, for example, accounting policies related to government pension liabilities or heritage assets. However, the employees within these committees would be provisionally detached from their daily business function for a short period of time, until a particular policy has been defined and approved. All employees in the technical project team would be on a full-time basis and are assigned to the project under the leadership of the project manager. The members of the project team would remain assigned to the project according to the exigencies of the project circumstances.

It should be noted that unless the task force chairperson has strong leadership qualities and formal procedures are applied, task force project structures may result in:

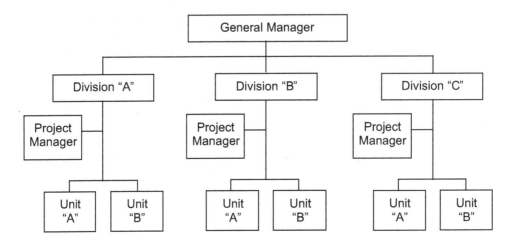

Figure 6.3   Classic coordination project organization structure

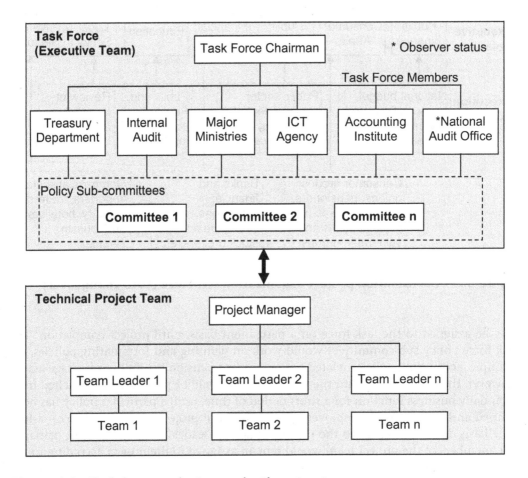

Figure 6.4   Task force project organization structure

- Inefficient meetings with discussions going off track, wasting precious time;
- Under-optimization of team members assigned to the tasks;
- Lack of information and authority for decision making at task force level;
- Concerns regarding project integration and coordination;
- Divided loyalties between the project and functional areas.

This style of project organization structure appears to be more successful when applied to corporate wide projects, involving different functional domains that cut cross-departmental organizational boundaries. It is for this reason that the task force project organization structure is popular with Government organizations, where projects may involve a number of ministries and their respective departments.

PRODUCT (OR SERVICE) PROJECT ORGANIZATION STRUCTURE

A product (or service) project organization structure is better suited to project driven organizations. This type of project organization structure has the objective of surmounting the concerns related to single point accountability and providing client focus. A product (or service) project organization structure is particularly applicable to environments where the outcomes involve new products or services, such as research and development, information systems, construction, marketing and engineering projects. Figure 6.5 provides a simple product (or service) project organization structure illustrating the concept of having a product manager being responsible for a particular product or service project.

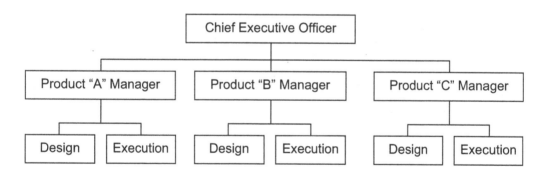

Figure 6.5   Product (or service) project organization structure

A product (or service) project organization structure provides a clear chain of command over a specific project, thus facilitating effective communication and rapid response time to resolve concerns. This type of project organization structure encourages product rather than functional loyalty, therefore facilitating interface management. A product (or service) project organization structure also provides the opportunity for management to assess a specific product or service with the objective of removing any that are unprofitable.

However, unless particular care is taken, this type of project organization structure tends to encourage higher costs due to the duplication of operational processes and resource utilization. Furthermore, being focused on a particular product or service may result in a lack of career opportunities and staff development, with consequential negative effects on innovation and staff retention.

MATRIX PROJECT ORGANIZATION STRUCTURE

A matrix project organization structure allows an enterprise to operate according to the number and type of projects that are being carried out in a specific time frame. Hence, in this type of project organization structure, individuals operate as a collective work group to achieve their projects goals. However, an individual assigned to a particular project would have two supervisors, the manager of the department they are normally assigned with on a permanent basis and the project leader of the particular project that they are assigned to at a particular moment.

With a matrix project organization structure, it is very important to describe precisely the roles of individuals in the project and their respective authority. Figure 6.6 illustrates that a project may obtain its resources from the organization's departmental functional areas according to it requirements. For example, Project "A" requires resources from every functional area, Project "B" does not have an "R & D" resource element, whilst Project "C" does not have a "Production" resource element.

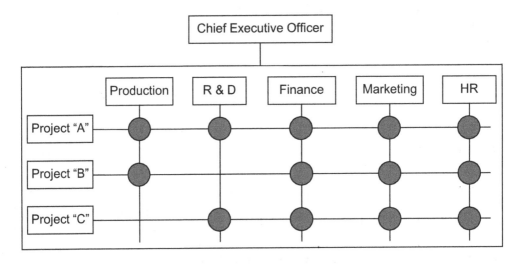

Figure 6.6   Matrix project organization structure

A practical example of a matrix project organization structure may be applicable to a government high technology agency that develops application systems and installs infrastructural components, such as data communication networks. A government department may request an accounting system to be developed and implemented, whilst another government department may request the installation of a wireless data communication network. The government high technology agency may possibly organize itself to complete both projects by establishing two project work groups, both of which would utilize resources from the different departments in the organization according to their specific requirements. When the projects are concluded, the two project work groups are disbanded and their respective members return to their permanent postings, to await other project assignments. The advantages of a matrix project organization structure include:

- Providing maximum control over resources to the project manager;
- Independent project components may be instituted on a project by project basis;
- Project managers have the capability to pledge resources of the entire organization within a set of prescribed parameters;
- Minimizing conflict and interface concerns on a particular project;
- Providing a means of having a single point of accountability, with work group responsibility;
- Ability to develop a strong technical base;
- Ability to balance cost with time performance schedules;
- Functional base (permanent posting) provides the employee with security and career path.

However, matrix project organization structures usually require dual and multiple reporting, with a resultant duplication of administrative effort. What is more, a change in project priority and the management of conflict between projects and functional responsibilities may cause significant operational difficulties.

Influencing Factors in Selecting a Project Organization Structure

As stated previously, current organization structural and contingency theories indicate that there is no ideal rigid project organization structure suitable for all situations. However, by identifying the project characteristics and the project implementation environment, the most suitable structure may be specified. The factors that determine the type of project organization structure that is most appropriate in a given situation are as follows:

1. *Coordination Project Organization Structure.* This type of project organization structure is more suitable for:
   a) Having high budgetary control and activity based accounting processes as an essential feature in the implementation of projects;
   b) Providing better vertical exchange and achieving least role conflict and ambiguity;
   c) Situations where the technology is dominated by one specific functional area.
2. *Task Force and Product (or service) Project Organization Structure.* This type of project organization structure is more suitable for:
   a) Providing better horizontal exchanges;
   b) Providing better accountability and responsibility by having one major authorization reference point, particularly for large and complex projects;
   c) Providing better synchronization and harmonization of activities between project work group members;
   d) Providing better client interface resulting in a closer client relationship;

e) Situations when both the number and importance of the projects increase, particularly when quality and project significance become a major issue;

f) Situations when the level of project uncertainty increases;

g) Developing of new products (or services);

h) High complex projects that require higher levels of harmonization.

3. *Matrix Project Organization Structure*. This type of project organization structure is more suitable for:

a) Short-term projects where resources are not tied down for a lengthy period of time;

b) Projects that have very high overhead costs and therefore cost sharing becomes a major consideration;

c) Sharing resources where resource utilization becomes a priority issue.

The above illustrates that the product (or service) and task force project organization structures appear to be the most suitable structures for organizations that primarily carry out projects on a continuous basis. However, it should be noted that many enterprises undertake projects on an individual project basis where a multiple project orientation approach may not be a feasible option. For these enterprises, coordination and a matrix project organization structure approaches are both feasible. Coordination or matrix project organization structures have a tendency to provide better financial control and minimize both role conflict and ambiguity among supervisors and work group members. A matrix approach is very effective for short duration projects and where resource and cost sharing becomes essential.

Conclusion

The project organization structure is an essential component of project governance, which seeks to ensure that the outputs from each project will deliver outcomes that are consistent with the policy and strategic objectives of the enterprise. It is therefore important to establish a project management organization structure that focuses on achieving results through managing opportunities and risks, and making the best use of resources.

It is an accepted axiom that project management environments are dissimilar to normal management situations. Therefore, there is a need to customize the organization structure, to support the intrinsic nature of a particular project environment. The Project Management Institute, in defining the term *project organization*, places emphasis on the need to provide the project manager with the full authority to assign priorities and to direct the work of individuals assigned to the project. Establishing the project organization structure is one of the most important tasks that must be addressed at the commencement of a project. An appropriate project organization structure is required to facilitate communication with internal and external stakeholders, determine the project interdependencies and the assignment of responsibility and authority. Executive management basically has four possible project organization framework options to choose from:

1. Coordination project organization;
2. Task force project organization;
3. Pure product/service project organization;
4. Matrix project organization.

COORDINATION PROJECT ORGANIZATION STRUCTURE

The coordination project organization structure seeks to improve integration through the intensification of coordination as a result of developing communication rules and procedures, redesigning the planning processes, instituting hierarchical referral methods and fostering direct contact across functional boundaries. A coordination project organization structure allows most of the employees to remain in their current functions. However, this will depend on the nature and complexity of the project.

A concern with this type of organization structure is role ambiguity and conflict. These role states may occur because typically, the project leader will have a similar hierarchical position as the functional managers. Hence, the project work group members may be confused about their supervisory relationship and resultant chain of command with the project leader and the functional manager. Role ambiguity and conflict may lead to lower employee commitment and motivation, resulting in high project employee turnover and lower project performance.

TASK FORCE PROJECT ORGANIZATION STRUCTURE

The task force project organization concept has a mixture of part-time and full-time project members. The task force chairperson and members are normally on a part-time basis. However, all employees in the technical project team would be on a full-time basis and are assigned to the project under the leadership of a full-time project manager.

This type of organization structure requires a chairperson with strong leadership attributes and the establishment and application of formal procedures. This style of project organization structure appears to be more successful when applied to corporate-wide projects involving different functional domains that cut cross-departmental organizational boundaries.

PRODUCT (OR SERVICE) PROJECT ORGANIZATION STRUCTURE

A product (or service) project organization structure is appropriate to project driven entities. This type of project organization structure has the objective of surmounting the concerns related to single point accountability and providing client focus. A product (or service) project organization structure provides a clear chain of command over a specific project, thus facilitating effective communication and rapid response time to resolve concerns. However, unless particular care is taken, this type of structure tends to increase costs due to duplication of operational processes and resources.

MATRIX PROJECT ORGANIZATION STRUCTURE

A matrix project organization structure is particularly suited to multiple project organizations that perform relatively short term projects and require human resources with specialist skills. A concern with matrix organization structures is that they usually require dual and multiple reporting, with a resultant duplication of administrative effort. Therefore, in a matrix project organization structure, it is very important to describe the chain of command and level of authority for particular project circumstances. Furthermore, a change in project priority and the management of conflict between projects and functional operations may cause significant difficulties for implementing a particular project.

GENERAL CONCLUSION

It may be generally concluded that functional project organization structures (Coordination Project Organization), provide better financial control. Functional project organization structures appear to minimize role conflict and ambiguity among supervisors and employees. Matrix structures seem to be more applicable to projects that have a very short duration horizon, and they strongly facilitate resource and cost sharing, particularly when high overhead costs are likely to be experienced.

Project oriented organization structures (Product Service or Task Force) have a single authorization reference point and therefore require strong leadership. They also provide the most efficient mechanism for synchronizing project activities and are very strong when the communication requirements have to cross organizational boundaries. These characteristics tend to achieve the clearest interface between the client and the organization. Projected oriented organization structures are more appropriate in environments that have high project complexity and uncertainty levels. Hence, they are particularly fitting when developing new products and services, specifically research and development projects. Moreover, project oriented organization structures are highly suitable for organizations that carry out numerous projects of high importance or significance.

References

Drazin, R. and Van de Ven, A.H. 1985. Alternative forms of fit in contingency theory. *Administrative Science Quarterly*, 30, 514–39.

Lawrence, P.R. and Lorsch, J.W. 1967. *Organization and Environment: Managing Differentiation and Integration*. Boston, USA: Division of Research, Graduate School of Business Administration, Harvard University.

Mintzberg, H. 1989. *Mintzberg on Management: Inside our Strange World of Organizations*. Ontario, Canada: Collier Macmillan.

Robbins, S.P. 1996. *Organizational Behavior: Concepts, Controversies, Applications* (7th Edition). New York: Prentice-Hall.

The Project Management Institute Standards Committee. 2004. *A Guide to the Project Management Body of Knowledge*. Upper Darby, PA, USA: PMI.

Yinghui, B. and Eng, G.C. 2002. *The Impact of Organizational Structure on Project Performance*. School of Building & Real Estate, National University, Singapore. [Online] Available at: http://www. buildnet.csir.co.za/cdcproc/docs/1st/yinghui_b.pdf [accessed: 12 June 2009].

7 *Project Teams Structure*

Teamwork is the ability to work together toward a common vision. The ability to direct individual accomplishments toward organizational objectives. It is the fuel that allows common people to attain uncommon results.
Andrew Carnegie (1835–1919), businessman and philanthropist

Project teams have become the indispensable work components of the modern business enterprise. The ability to complete projects successfully depends on the ability to work as a well-synchronized team. In addition, interpersonal relations, team spirit and collaboration become important ingredients in managing successful projects. For example, Akintoye, Macintosh and Fitzgerald (2000) argue that to engage in innovative procurement and business practices such as partnering, lean construction and supply chain management, requires the acceptance of a conciliatory approach, a collaborative spirit and trust. These elements in turn highlight the importance of social, human and cultural factors in the management of organizations and projects. Nicolini (2002) introduces the concept of *project chemistry*, where *project chemistry* is viewed as embracing an attitude of interaction between project participants, based on their kinship of purpose and temperament.

Thamhain (2004a) argues that while effective teamwork is crucial to project performance and is apparently obvious, few managers understand their organizations well enough to create a team setting that is optimally conductive to the professional needs of their team members. However, the way a team is structured can also play a primary role in how it functions. Current business culture expects project teams to engage in numerous responsibilities that cross organizational boundaries, involving a wide range of exchanges. These exchanges range from professional people, support groups, suppliers, contractors, government entities and clients. Therefore, different team structures will have different characteristics, with the composition and reporting relationships making a significant difference to the results achieved.

Group dynamics was initially highlighted as being important in the Hawthorne Studies of the late 1930s. These studies provided significant knowledge about group behaviour and illustrated the benefits that work group identity and cohesion may have on performance. Thamhain (2004b) argues that in today's more complex multinational and technologically sophisticated environment, the group has re-emerged in importance as the project team. Furthermore, this researcher contends that the roles and boundaries of teams are expanding towards self-direction, with a more open and organizationally transparent processes. He argues that this is happening because it is consistent both with the concepts of stakeholder management and learning organizations, and due to the support being provided by modern information and communications technologies.

There is no doubt that effective work teams contribute to the success of projects. However, the key element in having an effective work team is the interactions among the team members responsible for the specific undertaking. These interactions among team members include support groups, subcontractors, suppliers, strategic or collaborative partners, client entities and other project stakeholders. It is these numerous interactions that make the process of team building a complex issue that requires more advanced management competencies.

Research literature suggests that there are two critical factors that are strongly linked with project performance; these are team leadership and the team environment. Team leadership will be covered when discussing the project behavioural and managerial support factors. The main focus of this chapter is the project team environment.

The Concept of Teams

A project by its very nature requires a team approach. However, the team approach may be influenced by national cultures. For instance, a team mind-set tends to be contrary to Western culture, where individualism is a common trait. However, in Asian and African societies, collectivism is more of a natural phenomenon. Therefore, in a Westernized society, more effort is needed to make project work teams successful. However, on a more positive note, it must be recognized that individuals have moved away from merely wanting to satisfy only their material needs. Individuals want also to satisfy their social needs. These social needs include:

- A sense of belonging and recognition;
- Self-actualization by being innovative;
- Influencing and sharing responsibility by being involved in the decision-making process.

These social needs are obliging individuals to seek a collaborative environment. Hence, social forces are facilitating the trend towards the acceptance of the work team approach. Figure 7.1 illustrates that there are aspects that facilitate and hold back a team approach in both cultures.

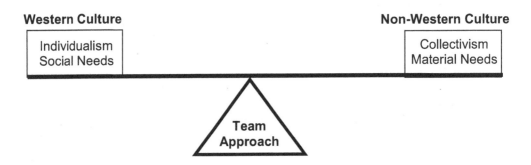

Figure 7.1   Cultural influences in implementing a team approach

The literature research suggests that teams generate synergy by amassing complementary talent, knowledge and experience that far surpass those of any team member. It is also argued that team membership may enhance an individual's qualities in terms of commitment, loyalty and general organizational citizenship behaviour. Therefore, when teams have unambiguous objectives and procedures, they are capable of undertaking new challenges, they enhance their problem-solving process and develop effective communication. It is precisely these qualities that enable work teams to be more responsive and clear-cut in the way they react to work concerns.

Work teams encourage a collectivist approach and satisfy the social needs of the individual members, thus enhancing work motivation in the process. Foster, Heling and Tideman (1996) make a distinction between friendship groups and task groups. They view task groups as being more applicable to an organizational setting and see them as being formally created by management to achieve specific goals. They lay emphasis on the notion of teams in relation to performance, in that teams are viewed as the collective performance of individuals who come together to work on projects as team members. Foster, Heling and Tideman (1996) argue that when employees are grouped together to perform a process, they do not necessarily form a team.

Taking the above into consideration, a project team may be defined as a group of individuals who possess the appropriate and complementary professional, technical or specialist competencies that are responsible for conducting the tasks specified in the project plan, working under the direction of the project manager. The size and composition of the team will also depend on the nature of the project being undertaken. However, it should be emphasized that a project may consist of many teams, with each team having a specific responsibility. It should be noted that as the number and/or membership size of teams increase, the bigger and more complex the communications network is likely to become. Research suggests that the ideal team size is between five to nine individuals. This team composition will allow the optimum personal interaction between the team members and create an atmosphere of belonging.

A concept that is often mentioned in the literature is that of self-managing teams. According to Foster, Heling and Tideman (1996), these are teams that operate automatically, with leadership and management roles being divided among the team members. They argue that self-managing teams have the ability of evolving into "high performance teams". They stress that in a normal team the individual feels as being part of the team. However, in high performance teams, the individual views the team as being part of the individual. Hence, high performance teams develop very strong "affective" commitment towards achieving the team performance objectives. This is a very important concept, especially in a project environment, where autonomous teams have the potential to increase productivity and quality workmanship on specific undertakings.

Autonomy is also an important issue for self-managing teams. It defines the magnitude of flexibility, which team members have in making decisions regarding a range of aspects related to their tasks, independently from their immediate supervisor. Foster, Heling and Tideman (1996) argue that members of self-managing teams share management tasks that were previously viewed as being the sole prerogative of the manager. They cite examples, such as scheduling of work and vacation leave, rotation of different job tasks and assignments, ordering of materials and setting of goals. However, the extent that the self-managing team concept will be applied in a project management context is highly dependent on the leadership style of the project director and the technical complexity of the project being undertaken.

Another important issue with self-managing teams is the notion of ambition. There is a need to differentiate between individual and team ambition. Individual ambition is related to enhancing one's personal position, whereas team ambition refers to the attainment of specific performance objectives of the project being undertaken. Hence, there is a need to align individual ambition with team ambition.

Goal congruence is also viewed as an essential concept in work teams. All team members must pull the same rope in the same direction to achieve both the project and organizational mission. The goals of the team should be clearly defined and understood by all the team members. Team members should also be informed how the objectives impact the holistic project deliverable, so that they may see the full picture and not just an isolated snapshot of the segment they are working on. It is emphasized that when individuals are assigned specific responsibilities and they perceive that they have achieved their tasks, both their self-esteem and work motivation increase accordingly.

Conflict resolution in work teams is very important. It is an axiom that whenever individuals work together, interpersonal rivalry and discord are likely to take place. It is important that the project manager knows when and how to resolve such issues. A divergence of opinion can develop into a difference of attitude that can intensify into a deviation in behaviour. Role conflict and ambiguity are often a source of discord in work teams. Hence, it is important that each team member knows their individual role and responsibility in the project being undertaken.

It is important that teams work in an atmosphere of openness and mutual trust, since much of the team's intelligence is based on shared experiences. It is through this process that work teams are able to cope with and resolve demanding problematic circumstances. McGregor's (1967) research itemized the following characteristics of an effective managerial team, which are considered as critical factors for effective teamwork:

- Mutual understanding and agreement of the tasks being undertaken;
- Identification with the assigned tasks;
- Open communications between team members;
- Mutual trust and support between team members;
- Management of human conflicts;
- Selective application of the team;
- Appropriate skills and competencies of team members;
- Leadership.

Leadership has a unique meaning in a team environment. It is viewed as being a shared responsibility of all team members and not just the responsibility of the formal appointed leader. According to Bragg (1992) individuals that are members of a work team must adhere to a number of prerequisites:

- Communicate the same vision;
- Dedicated to ensuring that the team functions effectively;
- Contribute to leadership responsibilities;
- Collaborate with other team members;
- Share ideas freely;

- Pay careful attention to what other team members have to say;
- Assist other team members to resolve their concerns;
- Find innovative solutions when team members have different opinions;
- Forfeit personal recognition for the sake of the team;
- Recognize and support the contributions of the other team members.

The above prerequisites will enable the team to flourish but they necessitate very high team commitment. These prerequisites do not normally occur naturally, so they must be instilled in the team members through guidance and coaching.

Drexler, Sibbet and Forrester (1988) have defined a comprehensive team performance model that shows the predictable stages involved in both creating and sustaining teams. They view team development as having seven stages, four to create the team and three to describe the levels of performance. The Drexler–Sibbet team performance model consists of the following phases:

1. *Creative Phase*. This phase has three stages:
   a) Orientation (the basis for the individual to be part of the team). When teams are forming, members wonder why they are there, how they are likely to fit within the team and whether they will be accepted by the others. These individuals need some kind of answer as a basis to continue being part of the team. The facilitators for this stage include team purpose, identity and membership; whilst the inhibitors are disorientation, uncertainty and fear.
   b) Trust building (team members get to know each other). Members want to know who they will work with, their expectations, competencies and personal agendas. Sharing is likely to build trust and fosters free exchange among team members. The facilitators for this stage include mutual regard, forthrightness and reliability; whilst the inhibitors are caution, mistrust and façade.
   c) Goal clarification (objectives of the team). Team members need to know their priorities. The facilitators for this stage include explicit assumption, clear and integrated goals, and a shared vision; whilst the inhibitors are apathy, irrelevant competition and scepticism.
2. *Constraints Phase*. This phase comprises one stage:
   a) Commitment (team direction to achieve goals). Decisions must be made about the allocation and management of resources, time and people. The role of each team member must be defined and agreed. The facilitators for this stage include assigned roles, allocation of resources and decisions made; whilst the inhibitors are dependence and resistance.
3. *Sustaining Phases*. This is comprised of three stages:
   a) Implementation (how to achieve goals). Teams must establish who does what, when and where. The facilitators for this stage include clear processes, alignment of individual and team goals and disciplined execution; whilst the inhibitors are conflict, confusion and non-alignment of goals and missed deadlines.
   b) High performance (accomplishing goals). This refers to surpassing expectations. The facilitators for this stage include spontaneous interaction, synergy and surpassing results; whilst the inhibitors are role overload and disharmony.
   c) Renewal (reason to continue with the team). Teams reach a stage when they complete projects, experience large organizational changes or new members join

the team. All these changes will require a reaction. It is at this stage that questions are asked: Why continue? Is the work of the team over? Is it time to form a new team? The facilitators for this stage include recognition and celebration, staying power and change mastery; whilst the inhibitors are boredom and burnout.

Each stage within a phase evolves, as a particular stage is resolved. However, if the concern is unresolved the team may revert to a previous stage. Furthermore, stage succession may not occur sequentially. For instance, decision making may be continuous and trust building may occur at any time particularly if new members join the team. The quality of the effectiveness of the team depends not only on the value of each member's contribution but also on the level of the interaction between team members and the capacity of team learning.

The objective of the Drexler–Sibbet team performance model is to make it possible for individuals to have positive and productive exchange of ideas with each other, regarding how they view their organization. This process ensures that the team members possess common knowledge, which may be utilized as a basis for making important decisions. The basis of the Drexler–Sibbet team performance model is the empowerment of the team; by allowing all employees to share in the responsibility for taking decisions and resolving concerns.

Project Chemistry

The term *project chemistry* (Nicolini, 2002) implies a mixture of the right ingredients to provide the formula for the successful management of projects. These ingredients are moulded together by the level of interaction between the people involved in the project. The concept is similar to chemical bonding. In general, strong chemical bonding is associated with the sharing or transfer of electrons between the participating atoms. In other words, if the level of *people interaction* is high, the project molecular bonding is strong. The level and quality of the interaction of those involved in the project basically depends on two elements, namely their proximity of outlook or attitude towards the project and the strength of their goal congruence.

However, the moulding elements that determine the level and quality of people interaction within projects do not happen automatically. Organizations need to determine ways to develop a culture that promotes a common project outlook and goal congruence of those participating in the projects undertaken by the organization. Nicolini (2002) and other researchers advocate that common project outlook and project goal congruence can be nurtured by having a proper organizational and team environment, the use of cross-functional project teams and promoting the right balance of societal characteristics.

DEVELOPING A PROPER ORGANIZATIONAL AND TEAM ENVIRONMENT

The first step to developing a suitable organizational and team environment is for executive management to define a formal business strategy that explicitly describes the organizational mission and vision, including the short- and long-term objectives. However, the formulation of the mission and vision cannot be defined in an ivory tower; employees must be given the opportunity to provide their input to the strategy formulation process.

This process would provide a shared vision, leading to an organizational common outlook and goals.

Participation should not be restricted merely to providing an input to the strategic formulation process but also in decision making, particularly in the continuous improvement in task procedures and practices involving the project activities. Participation should be organized as a team effort to allow the growth of open communication and team interaction. This must take place in a non-threatening atmosphere that encourages those involved in the project to freely express their opinions, while respecting the opinions of others. Moreover, executive management must be committed to the team participative process and have an appropriate scheme for rewarding creativity. Finally, participation in a project environment should also include (if practical) contractors and other external stakeholders. Developing a proper organizational and team environment is an important step towards developing the notion of *project chemistry*.

USE OF CROSS-FUNCTIONAL PROJECT TEAMS

The use of cross-functional project teams is an important tool for developing *project chemistry*. In a project environment, it is essential to recognize that projects often require a wide variety of competencies to complete the numerous activities. Hence, project managers will be overseeing teams of individuals with different skills and experience backgrounds who may come from different organizational divisions and at times from external sources for example, contractors). It is this diversity of skills, experience and background that give rise to "cross-functional" teams.

However, unless correctly managed, a cross-functional team could be a barrier to the notion of project chemistry, because it is more difficult to achieve trust and cohesiveness, which are both essential factors for successful project teams. On the other hand, a mixture of personalities, skills and experience backgrounds often generates innovative ways of conducting the various project tasks. At the same time, trust and cohesiveness within teams develop when functional strategies have the goal of supporting the holistic corporate strategy; the organization adopts a participative project teamwork approach, supported by an appropriate communication mechanism; management is genuinely committed to the needs of the team and the project by having a supportive leadership style; and the reward scheme reflects the team effort and specifically the attainment of the agreed goals.

PROMOTING THE RIGHT BALANCE OF SOCIETAL CHARACTERISTICS

An important role of project managers is to influence the project internal and external stakeholders. Internal stakeholders do not only include the project team members but also other employees from other divisions within the organization, particularly those related to financial, human, logistical and infrastructural resources. These internal stakeholders often are responsible for allocating the resources that are essential for sustaining project focus and impetus. On the other hand, external stakeholders include the client, subcontractors, and other social groups that have an interest in the project. Hence, project managers need to build relationships within and outside the project team to inspire a sense of collective project ownership and resolve conflicts that threaten to form a barrier to adequate project progress.

Promoting the right balance of societal characteristics is influenced by the involvement of the holistic project community (internal and external stakeholders) and ensuring that their specific interests are addressed. This requires continuous communication that is specifically designed to address the concerns of the different stakeholders. Moreover, the selected project manager must have the appropriate leadership qualities that match the specific project challenges and must be given a clear mandate to implement the project. For example, projects that have environmental connotations should be lead by a project manager who is sensitive to community concerns and knowledgeable of environmental issues. Finally, two further requirements are needed to develop the right balance of societal characteristics. These are project team composition and an appropriate team development process. Project team composition consists of selecting the right team structure and having team members with the proper mixture of skills and expertise. A team development process is based on having regular team building workshops specifically design around the project being implemented. This ensures team cohesiveness and that team members are aware of the challenges and issues that confront the project.

BENEFITS FROM A PROJECT CHEMISTRY MIND-SET

A project that is able to achieve the right project chemistry will generate a number of important benefits that directly impact project performance. Project teams that have a common shared vision ensure the development of a cooperative project outlook and collective project goals. In other words, everyone involved in the project has the same achievement focus, and project team members that take the opportunity to participate in formulating the project vision and associated goals will identify themselves with and become owners of the defined vision and goals.

The direct benefit of cross-functional project teams is the optimization of the application of human resources. Having the correct balance of skills, knowledge and expertise will improve the timeliness for problem detection and expand the problem-solving capability of project teams through innovative approaches. This improved responsiveness will often result in reduced rework and defects; reduced waste, bureaucracy and related costs; and absence of litigation and legal costs. What is more, promoting the right balance of societal characteristics in the implementation of projects generates community sensitivity, a lack of which often leads to controversy and public protests. Having the right societal characteristics will minimize the social gap and generate mutual understanding between the project team and the stakeholders who may be opposed to the project. This will often lead to lowering the conflict level and promote constructive disagreements that encourage the relevant parties to discuss and resolve conflicts that may arise. The three project bonding elements described above allow the interaction between the people involved in the project, thus achieving project chemistry.

Team Structure

As stated previously, a project team structure has a major role in how a team functions. A specific team structure approach will have its own unique characteristics. Project teams may be visualized as a matrix as illustrated in Figure 7.2.

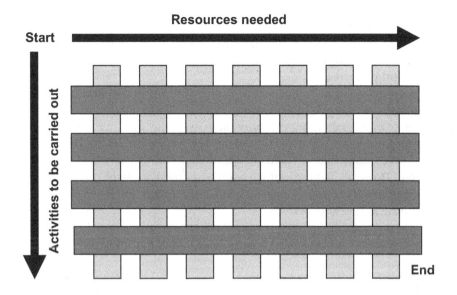

Figure 7.2   Project team organization matrix

Matrix teams may include work groups, cross-functional teams, task forces, problem-solving teams, committees and special project teams. They are usually composed of a small number of people from different departments, functional areas or organizations, who are brought together to solve a common problem or achieve a goal through collaboration. What distinguishes a team from just a mere group is the ability to achieve higher outcomes, through the collective use of knowledge and skill sharing. Many organizations have working groups that call themselves teams. However, their work is produced by a combination of individual contributions. Teams produce work that is based on a collective effort through collaboration.

Team members with their own particular skills will need to work closely together and share their knowledge, in order to ensure a consistent and proper solution. The team members will also need to work together on the various processes or functional areas. Projects may consist of a single team or multiple teams. Each of these teams, whether they work vertically or horizontally, will require a leader and will need to comprehend their individual roles and responsibilities. Hence, care must be taken in how to structure the team in terms of reporting, monitoring and controlling the activities undertaken and the resources consumed. There are some basic conventions that need to be taken into consideration in how teams are structured. These conventions include:

1. Individuals working collectively in a team usually perceive the team members as being supportive. Hence, they will normally work in partnership and help each other to achieve their combined goals;
2. Teams normally generate an atmosphere of collaboration, knowledge sharing and skills transfer. It is this environment that determines the level of synergy the team generates;
3. Team structure will affect team behaviour. Hence, the objective is to form a collaborative team, where team members share their knowledge, support and assist each other and are motivated to attain the team objectives;

4. Interaction between team members through an effective communication mechanism allows the project leader to obtain a balanced view of all the viewpoints, be they client related, business requirements, realistic and practical practices, technical viability, efficiency and performance;
5. Endeavour to take full advantage of the understanding, knowledge and capabilities of team members working in other teams;
6. Encourage team members to see individuals working in other teams as a source of learning and not as an irritation that get in the way of the team's development;
7. The size and composition of the team will depend on the nature of the project being undertaken. However, having a single team composed of a large number of individuals creates more interaction than progress, since the bigger the team the more complex the communications network;
8. Having five to nine persons in a team allows optimum personal interaction between the team members and creates an atmosphere of belonging.

The basic principle in team formation is to ensure knowledge sharing among the team members. It should be emphasized that the main factor that inhibits a team from obtaining its goal optimally is knowledge hoarding, rather than knowledge sharing.

Project Roles and Responsibilities

It is essential that project roles and responsibilities are defined as early as possible in the project life cycle to avoid role conflict and ambiguity. Role conflict and ambiguity can only serve to confuse the project team members, with a resultant decline in project execution progress. Note that the project team is collectively responsible for:

*   Assisting the project manager to deliver the project objectives;
*   Conducting the tasks assigned to them within their technical knowledge;
*   Providing administrative support to the project manager;
*   Advising the project manager of any risks that arise and which are likely to influence the delivery of the project objectives;
*   Participating in the risk reduction and avoidance process;
*   Providing data for documenting the specific project life cycle progress.

The project team should also be able to understand the project aim and how their expertise contributes to this aim; provide their technical expertise in support of the project objectives; be knowledgeable and use the applicable project management standards; and maintain the project documentation in line with the project quality plan. The above are the general collective roles and responsibilities of the project team. However, the roles of the team members and their relationship to the organizational management structure have to be established for every project, taking into consideration the two important factors:

1. Project magnitude in terms of expenditure, amount of work and complexity;
2. Nature of the project in terms of whether it is a construction, engineering, information system, change process, new product or service development or other type of project.

The research literature regarding projects identified various categories of individuals or groups that may make up the full project responsibility boundary. The project type is an important factor in determining project roles and responsibility categories. For instance, a software development project will have many roles and responsibilities that are not found in engineering or construction projects and vice versa. A general examination of the literature regarding software development projects revealed 36 different project roles and responsibilities, while those related to construction had well over this number, depending on the project magnitude. However, there are many roles and responsibilities that are common to all projects. These include:

- Client (or Customer);
- Project Sponsor;
- Programme Manager;
- Project Manager;
- Project Team Leader;
- Project Team;
- Contractors/Suppliers/Vendors;
- Executive Committee/Steering Committee/Project Board;
- Legal Adviser;
- Change Control Board;
- Internal Auditor;
- User;
- Stakeholders;
- External Auditor;
- External Regulator.

Some projects will combine some of the above categories into a single class, because the respective roles and responsibilities of a category are conducted by the same person. However, the roles and responsibilities of each category will remain with each category having its distinct role and responsibilities within the project boundary.

CLIENT OR CUSTOMER

The client is a person or group often representing an entity that is the direct beneficiary of a project or service. They are the people for whom the project is being undertaken. It should be noted that an entity may have both internal and external clients. However, external clients are usually referred to as "customers". The client has the role of ensuring that projects support the strategic objectives of the entity. In addition, the client must ensure adequate and timely funding so that the project is implemented according to an agreed schedule. The client also has the role of ensuring that the business benefits identified in the project justification document are accomplished. Finally, the client is responsible for allocating the necessary resources to participate on the project organization and approving any changes to the project scope.

PROJECT SPONSOR

The project sponsor is the project initiator, in other words, the person who saw the need for the project and has the authority to make it happen. The project sponsor is the person who commissions others to deliver the project and champions the cause throughout the project. This is the person who often chairs the project board sessions and has the ultimate authority over the project. The sponsor secures project funding, resolves issues and scope changes, approves major deliverables and provides high-level direction. Hence, the sponsor is often a senior executive with a relevant area of responsibility that will be affected by the outcome of the project.

The project sponsor provides clarity of the project vision and the executive authority necessary to overcome organizational obstacles and barriers. The project sponsor has several important responsibilities, such as being accountable for the delivery of planned benefits associated with the project; ensuring the resolution of issues escalated by the project manager; assuring the availability of the project resources; approving the project budget; and making major organizational decisions for the project.

PROGRAMME MANAGER

The programme manager is the person responsible for a portfolio of related projects. This person has a coordination management function with the specific goal of ensuring that the portfolio of projects under his/her responsibility achieves the identified strategic objectives and benefits.

PROJECT MANAGER

The project manager is the person with day-to-day responsibility for the successful implementation of the project. The project manager typically has control over all project resources and has the authority to manage a project. This includes planning and achieving all project deliverables. The project manager is also responsible for managing the budget, adhering to the project schedule and all project management procedures related to scope management, conflict resolution and risk management.

The project manager is responsible for developing, in conjunction with the project sponsor, the project domain. The project manager is responsible for coordinating and integrating activities across multiple functional lines and managing stakeholder communications. This is achieved by ensuring that the project is delivered on time, to budget and to the agreed specifications. The project manager is also responsible for managing the work of contractors, specifically ensuring that the contractors integrate with the project team's efforts. The project manager has a wide range of responsibilities that include:

- Managing and leading the project team;
- Recruiting project team members and contractors;
- Implementing appropriate project planning and control mechanisms;
- Developing and maintaining project plans;
- Managing project deliverables according to the approved project plan;
- Escalating issues that are beyond their control;

- Resolving cross-functional issues, particularly resource allocation;
- Managing project scope and change control issues;
- Monitoring project progress and taking appropriate action to achieve the desired level of performance;
- Compiling regular project status reports for the project sponsor, client and other relevant stakeholders.

PROJECT TEAM LEADER

Usually a project will consist of several teams, with each team having a team leader. The number of teams will depend on the nature and magnitude of the project. Team leaders are responsible for the day-to-day management of the team and providing support to team members. The team leader is normally responsible for a phase of a project segment, ensuring that the tasks are delivered on schedule, within the cost estimate and specifications.

The team leader has the responsibility of assigning tasks to the team members and recording the time and resources utilized on each task, thus updating the consolidated project plan with actual data. A team leader is required to be aware of any issues that are of concern to the team members and that may threaten the delivery schedule of the tasks under the team's responsibility. This may involve taking appropriate action to resolve a particular issue or seeking consultation with the project manager and providing recommended action.

PROJECT TEAM MEMBERS

A team member is an individual who is part of a project team. Some team members have a specific role while others are more flexible in the way they are utilized. Team members who have a specific role often have specialist skills and are assigned their tasks accordingly. Furthermore, some team members are full-time while others are part-time. A cross-functional team has members from various organizational divisions. A cross-functional team is usually an indication that the organization is utilizing a matrix project structure.

Team members are responsible for understanding the tasks to be completed; breaking down the assigned tasks into more detail; completing the assigned tasks within schedule, cost and agreed specifications; keeping the team leader informed about issues that threaten the completion of the tasks to the defined time, cost and quality parameters; and providing the daily status of the tasks and associated utilization of resources to the team leader.

CONTRACTORS/SUPPLIERS/VENDORS

Projects often involve the utilization of third-party companies or individuals that provide a specific skill that the organization does not possess. These subcontractors may work directly under the direction of the project manager or they may be supplying material, equipment and supplies to the project. Subcontractors working directly under the direction of the project manager should be considered as part of the project team and monitored as such. However, subcontractors that are not working directly under the direction of the project manager must be monitored closely to ensure that they provide their assigned deliverable on time, to the agreed quality and contracted cost.

EXECUTIVE COMMITTEE/STEERING COMMITTEE/PROJECT BOARD

These types of committees often consist of senior management who are responsible for providing guidance on the overall strategic direction of the project. They are also responsible for overseeing the progress of the project and reacting to any strategic problems. Moreover, they address issues that threaten project delivery which are not under the control of the project manager. Project committees are a formal team of executives from across the organization that ensure projects meet the corporate goals.

LEGAL ADVISER

A legal specialist has the responsibility to address various contractual issues, such as detailed contracts regarding the entire project scope and contracts regarding the provision of services, equipment and project financing.

CHANGE CONTROL BOARD

Very often project scope will change during the project implementation stage. It is imperative that these changes are kept to an absolute minimum because they often result in escalating project cost and delaying the project delivery schedule. Projects may also fall behind schedule and require a number of activities to be expedited to recover lost time. Expediting project activities ultimately results in cost escalation. The Change Control Board has the responsibility to evaluate the proposed project scope changes or changes to the project cost structure with the aim of either rejecting or accepting the changes of the projects requirements.

INTERNAL AUDITOR

An internal auditor is an individual within the organization who has the responsibility for maintaining project standards and procedures and ensuring their compliance.

USER

These are the people who will actually use the deliverables of the project. Project users should be constantly involved throughout the project, particularly at the design and project acceptance stages.

PROJECT STAKEHOLDERS

Project stakeholders are individuals, groups or organizations that are actively involved in the project or whose interests may be positively or negatively impacted by execution or implementation of the project. Stakeholders may be internal or external to the organization. Internal stakeholders include clients, management and employees. External stakeholders include community groups, trade unions, investors, government and suppliers.

EXTERNAL AUDITOR

An external auditor is an accountant who is responsible for the audit of the organization. External auditors may review project plans, designs and the completed solution, including any aspect that is linked to financial transactions. An external auditor ensures that the project meets an adequate standard from an audit perspective.

EXTERNAL REGULATOR

Many projects involving construction, engineering and pharmaceuticals are subject to various forms of regulation by external regulators. There may be legal and ethical requirements to cooperate with these regulators or to maintain specific records or information to meet their requirements.

Rewarding the Project Team

An organization needs to pay competitive salaries to employ those who posses suitable qualifications and experience. However, money seldom motivates individuals to hit the peak of their performance. The literature on work motivation indicates that monetary rewards are important but they are a short-term motivator. Research suggests that first and foremost, most employees desire verbal or written praise from their immediate supervisor. These two simple appreciation gestures have been shown to be very effective motivators.

Moreover, informal acclamations, particularly peer praise, have been found to be essential for building and sustaining high performance teams. However, appreciation and praise are not enough. Management needs to implement formal incentive schemes that are suitable for a project team environment. Yet, formal incentive schemes must be fine-tuned to the particular environment one operates in, since what may work in one environment may not work in another. Having said this however, there are a number of basic principles that are required for formal incentive schemes to provide the proper benefits to both the organization and the employee. These principles include:

* The incentive scheme must support organizational objectives. Management must identify the appropriate behaviour that facilitates the organization to achieve its strategic objectives and then choose the best method to reward this behaviour.
* The incentive scheme must be equitable. Research shows that there is a positive link between performance and equity. However, equity is subjective, with individuals perceiving that rewards are unfair if only a few qualify for them. Experience shows that the minority of employees will achieve the majority of the results. Hence, organizations must reward its top performers. However, the remaining employees must somehow be motivated as well. To motivate these employees, one must devise a reward scheme that sets goals within their reach, given that they put in the appropriate effort.
* The incentive scheme must strike a balance between rewarding team effort and individual effort. Whilst the incentive system must cater for team achievements, it must ensure that top performers are adequately rewarded.

- The incentive scheme should not encourage individual competition but foster collaboration. Individual competition can be a destructive mechanism for team work and will most likely generate the perception of winners and losers. Collaboration enables everyone in the team to be a winner. The reward should be given to all the team members for their contribution to the achievement of the set goals. Let peer pressure stimulate the productivity of the team members that are slack in their performance.
- The incentive scheme must have a positive effect on performance. Ensure that performance measures are established and are measurable in a practical sense. Use a trial and error method for devising and fine-tuning the appropriate incentive scheme against the selected performance measures.
- Incentive schemes must be effective in all economic conditions. Establish a method of rewarding top performers even during difficult economic times.
- The client should be a major focus of incentive schemes. It is clients that determine the success of the organization. Unhappy clients lead to a decline in clients and ultimately lead to business failure. Align the incentive scheme to focusing on serving the client.

These key principles will enable management to introduce incentive schemes that motivate and unite project team members to perform at levels that satisfy the organization's strategic objectives, the client and the individual team member.

Assessing the Project Team Environment

Below is a simple but effective method for assessing whether the project team environment in an organization is conducive to high performance achievement. The project team environment assessment is based on five key measures:

1. Level of role conflict and ambiguity within the project team;
2. Adequate definitions of roles and responsibilities for project team members;
3. Appropriate level of processes and procedures within the project team;
4. Level of collaboration between the project team members;
5. Level of cooperation between the project team and external stakeholders.

LEVEL OF ROLE CONFLICT AND AMBIGUITY WITHIN THE PROJECT TEAM

It is very difficult to entirely eliminate role conflict and ambiguity in a team environment. At one time or another, conflicts and ambiguous situations between team members will occur. However, it is important that a way is found to minimize conflicts and ambiguous circumstances. This assessment (see Figure 7.3) basically measures whether the level of role conflict and ambiguity is at an acceptable level.

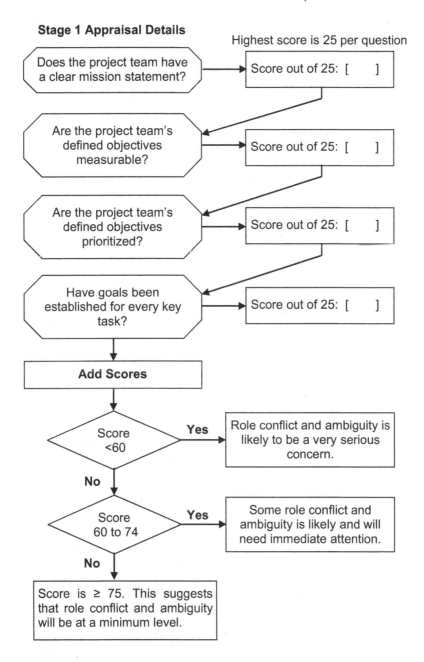

Stage 1 Appraisal Details

Highest score is 25 per question

Does the project team have a clear mission statement? → Score out of 25: [ ]

Are the project team's defined objectives measurable? → Score out of 25: [ ]

Are the project team's defined objectives prioritized? → Score out of 25: [ ]

Have goals been established for every key task? → Score out of 25: [ ]

Add Scores

Score <60 — Yes → Role conflict and ambiguity is likely to be a very serious concern.

No

Score 60 to 74 — Yes → Some role conflict and ambiguity is likely and will need immediate attention.

No

Score is ≥ 75. This suggests that role conflict and ambiguity will be at a minimum level.

Figure 7.3   Assessing project team environment – role conflict and ambiguity

A score of greater than 75 suggests that role conflict and ambiguity within the project team will be at a minimum level. A score of 60 to 74 suggests that some role conflict and ambiguity is likely and will need immediate attention. A score of less than 60 suggests that role conflict and ambiguity is likely to be a very serious concern.

ADEQUATE DEFINITIONS OF ROLES AND RESPONSIBILITIES FOR PROJECT TEAM MEMBERS

For the project team to function properly, each team member must know their role and responsibilities. These must be adequately defined and understood by all the project team members. This assessment (see Figure 7.4) measures whether the roles and responsibilities of the project team members are adequately defined.

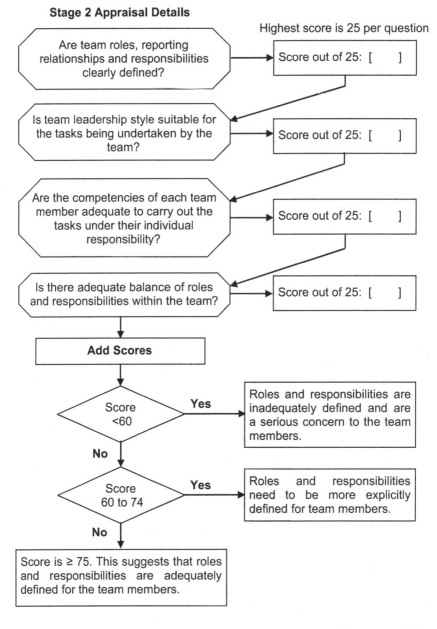

Figure 7.4   Assessing project team environment – roles and responsibilities

A score greater than 75 suggests that roles and responsibilities are adequately defined for the project team members. A score of 60 to 74 suggests that the roles and responsibilities need to be more explicitly defined. A score of less than 60 suggests that the roles and responsibilities are inadequately defined and will be a serious concern.

APPROPRIATE LEVEL OF PROCESSES AND PROCEDURES WITHIN THE PROJECT TEAM

Appropriate processes and procedures are required for the project team members to be kept adequately informed of project developments and to actively participate in the decision-making process. This assessment (see Figure 7.5) measures whether suitable processes and procedures are in place to enable the project team to be actively involved in the decision-making process.

A score greater than 80 suggests that appropriate processes and procedures are in place to enable the project team to work effectively. A score of 65 to 79 suggests that processes and procedures need to be explicitly defined if the team is to work as an effective team. A score of less than 65 suggests that processes and procedures are a hindrance to the effective contribution of the project team members.

LEVEL OF COLLABORATION BETWEEN PROJECT TEAM MEMBERS

The basis for a successful project team is collaboration. However, collaboration is built on many factors, such as equitable incentive schemes, mutual trust, adequate feedback and healthy work relationships. This assessment (see Figure 7.6) measures the extent that a collaborative environment is in place to enable the project team to work in harmony.

A score of greater than 80 suggests that the internal relationships between the project team members are based on the principle of collaboration. A score of 65 to 79 suggests that collaboration between project team members needs to be improved. A score of less than 65 suggests that collaboration between project team members is a serious concern and needs immediate action for improvement.

LEVEL OF COOPERATION BETWEEN PROJECT TEAM AND EXTERNAL STAKEHOLDERS

Project team members need to maintain a good relationship with external stakeholders, particularly the client. This relationship is facilitated by having the appropriate communications channels that allow a two-way consultative process to take place. This assessment (see Figure 7.7) measures whether suitable processes are in place to allow an appropriate level of external relationships between the project team and the external stakeholders.

A score greater than 80 suggests that relationships with key external stakeholders facilitate cooperation; while a score of 65 to 79 suggests that cooperation with key external stakeholders needs to be improved. A score of less than 65 suggests that cooperation with key external stakeholders is a serious concern and needs immediate action for improvement.

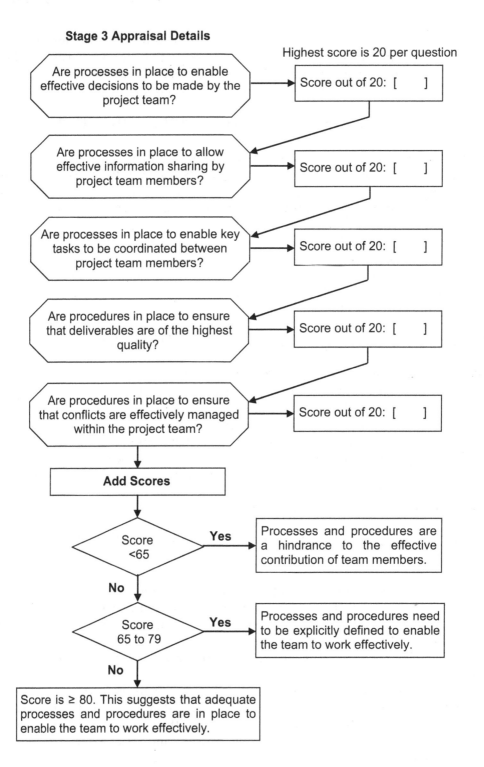

Figure 7.5   Assessing project team environment – processes and procedures

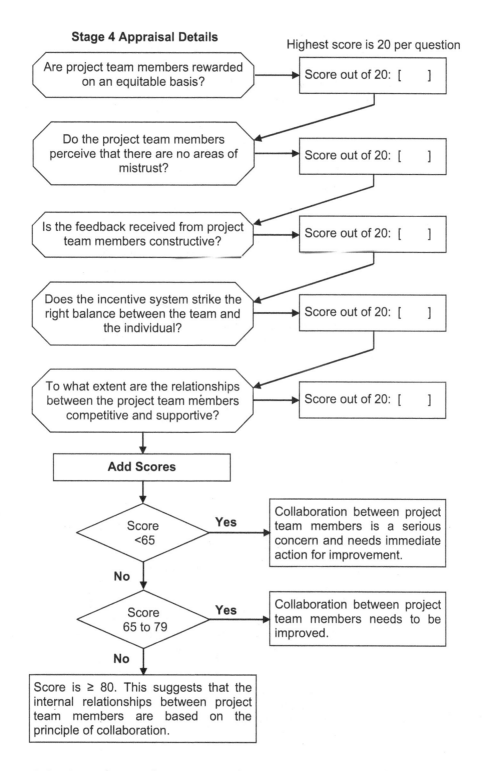

Figure 7.6   Assessing project team environment – internal collaboration level

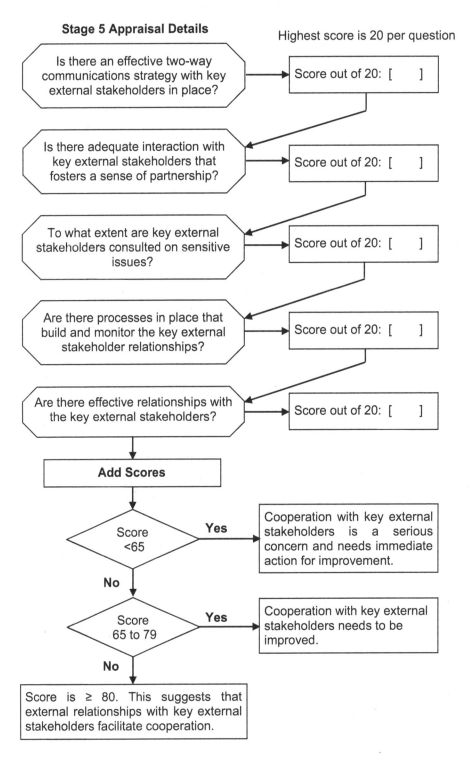

Stage 5 Appraisal Details

Highest score is 20 per question

Is there an effective two-way communications strategy with key external stakeholders in place?

Score out of 20: [   ]

Is there adequate interaction with key external stakeholders that fosters a sense of partnership?

Score out of 20: [   ]

To what extent are key external stakeholders consulted on sensitive issues?

Score out of 20: [   ]

Are there processes in place that build and monitor the key external stakeholder relationships?

Score out of 20: [   ]

Are there effective relationships with the key external stakeholders?

Score out of 20: [   ]

Add Scores

Score <65

Yes

Cooperation with key external stakeholders is a serious concern and needs immediate action for improvement.

No

Score 65 to 79

Yes

Cooperation with key external stakeholders needs to be improved.

No

Score is ≥ 80. This suggests that external relationships with key external stakeholders facilitate cooperation.

Figure 7.7   Assessing project team environment – external cooperation level

Conclusion

A project by its very nature requires a team approach. The key element in having an effective work team is the level and quality of the interactions among the team members. Teams generate synergy by amassing complementary talent, knowledge, and experience that far surpass those of any team member. Work teams encourage a collectivist approach and satisfy the social needs of individual members, thus enhancing their work motivation in the process.

A project team may be defined as a group of individuals who possess the appropriate and complementary professional, technical or specialist competencies that are responsible for conducting the tasks specified in the project plan working under the direction of the project manager. The ideal team size is between five to nine individuals. This team composition will allow the optimum personal interaction between the team members and create an atmosphere of belonging. Project teams should evolve into self-managing teams. The concept of self-managing teams develops when teams are able to operate automatically, with leadership and management roles being divided among the team members. In addition, self-managing teams have the ability of evolving into "high performance teams" when the individual members view the team as being part of themselves. The key elements that make project work teams effective include:

- *Autonomy.* This determines the magnitude of flexibility that team members have in making decisions independently from their immediate supervisor;
- *Team ambition.* This refers to the attainment of specific performance objectives of the project by aligning individual ambition with team ambition;
- *Goal congruence.* The objectives of the team are to be clearly defined and understood by all team members, hence establishing common team goals;
- *Feedback.* Team members should be informed how the objectives impact the holistic project deliverable, so that they see the full picture;
- *Self-esteem and work motivation.* These increase when team members are assigned specific responsibilities that are realistic and attainable;
- *Conflict resolution.* Whenever people work together, interpersonal rivalry and discord are likely, therefore the project manager must know when and how to resolve such issues;
- *Role conflict and ambiguity.* It is important that each team member knows their individual responsibility and role in the process being undertaken;
- *Trust.* Teams must work in an atmosphere of openness and mutual trust, since much of the team's intelligence is based on shared experiences.

Furthermore, a number of basic principles for rewarding the team must be adhered to. Hence, an incentive scheme must:

- Support the organizational strategic objectives;
- Be seen to be fair;
- Strike a balance between rewarding team effort and individual effort;
- Not encourage individual competition but fosters collaboration;
- Have a positive effect on performance;
- Be effective in all economic environments even during difficult times;
- Focus on the client, since clients determine the success of the organization.

These main principles will enable management to introduce incentive schemes that motivate and unite the project team members to perform at levels that satisfy the organization's strategic objectives, the client and the individual team member.

References

Akintoye, A., Macintosh, G. and Fitzgerald, E. 2000. A survey of supply chain collaboration and management in the UK construction industry. *European Journal of Purchasing and Supply Management*, 6, 159–68.

Anderson, N. and West, M. 1998. Measuring climate for work group innovation: development and validation of the team climate inventory. *Journal of Organizational Behavior*, 19, 235–58.

Bragg, D.D. 1992. Team basics: how to develop teamwork in training organizations. *Performance & Instruction*, 31(9), 10–14.

Drexler, A.B., Sibbet, D. and Forrester, R.H. 1988. The team performance model. In: *Team Building: Blueprints for Productivity and Satisfaction*, W. Breden Reddy and K. Jamison (eds). NTL Institute for Applied Behavioral Science. San Diego, CA: Alexandria, VA and University Associates.

Foster, S.F., Heling, G.W.J. and Tideman, B. 1996. *Teams in Intelligent Process Based Organisations*. Leiderdorp, The Netherlands: Lansa Publishing BV.

McGregor, D. 1967. *The Professional Manager*. New York: McGraw-Hill.

Nicolini, D. 2002. In search of 'project chemistry'. *Construction Management and Economics*, 20, 167–77.

Thamhain, H.J. 2004a. Team leadership effectiveness in technology-based project environments. *Project Management Journal*, 35(4), 35–46.

—— 2004b. Leading technology-based project teams. *Engineering Management Journal*, 16(2), 35–42.

8 *Project Planning and Control*

Execution is the ability to mesh strategy with reality, align people with goals, and achieve the promised results.
Larry Bossidy, Chairman and CEO, Allied Signal

Project planning and control is a predominant and critical issue in project management. When we refer to project management, we inevitably think about project planning and control. Therefore, care, skill and an appropriate amount of time and effort should be applied immediately at the project outset towards the establishment of a planning and control mechanism. Often project managers argue that when considering the project planning and control issue, one should differentiate between small and large projects. For example, small projects have tight budgets and short schedules that translate into project managers having very little room for error in planning, tracking and control. However, whatever the project, a suitable planning and control mechanism is required that is sufficiently flexible to accommodate a diverse range of projects in terms of size and complexity. The outcome without such a mechanism is an outwardly disorganized muddle that exhibits excessive duplication of effort, enormous cost overruns in proportion to the original cost estimate and critical shortages of resources.

An important aspect of the planning and control process is to understand what the project is to deliver, in other words the outputs. If you do not know the project deliverables, you cannot plan for project completion. In a previous chapter (see Chapter 5, pp. 63–73) the importance of project scope was specifically emphasized. When defining the project scope, the project manager is developing a common understanding as to what is included in or excluded from a project. No matter the magnitude of the project, a clear definition and statement of the impacted areas and project domain must be determined and provided. The project scope embraces the clients, work packages, human and financial resources, outputs and outcomes. The detail of the project scope depends on the project magnitude, therefore, the larger and more complex the project is, the more detail the definition. Project scope should also take into account the time frame and resource constraints. In simple terms, the project scope definition deals with the "what" and "why" the project is being undertaken.

The project planning and control aspect deals with the "how", "by whom" and "when" the project activities are to be undertaken. Project planning and control embraces a number of functions, such as generating a network of actions that depicts the relationship between these actions and their order of occurrence. It also includes project scheduling, which links a plan into a time frame, as well as smoothing out resource level variations and measuring job progress, reviewing the plan and rescheduling when conditions change. When one considers the amount of effort needed with planning a project, the novice may sometimes be astonished that projects are accomplished at all.

However, projects do get done, but not always in the manner initially planned and often need continuous prodding. This is where project control comes into play. Planning a project is a good start, but to put the plan into action needs continuous monitoring, control and action. Besides, plans are not static, circumstances, especially with large and complex projects, are continuously changing and need reviewing. The point is that executing a project requires detailed planning and tight control, but the method is not optimal and will require regular and frequent reviews. One should note that a lack of a proper planning and control mechanism has serious consequences. These consequences include:

- Clients are dissatisfied by late delivery;
- Employees experience low moral and low motivation due to insistent demands to achieve unattainable targets;
- Project managers are constrained to take short cuts that apart from being dangerous in certain circumstances, such as in engineering projects, may harm the organization's reputation;
- Each project will encounter and need to overcome the same concerns as the previous projects.

However, having an appropriate planning and control mechanism in place will facilitate a project being executed on time and be able to interact effectively with the client, suppliers and the tasks assigned to the organization's employees. A proper planning and control mechanism allows those involved in the project to fully understand what is required. In addition, any arising concerns are anticipated and dealt with before they may cause harm to the project.

The Planning and Control Process in the Information Age

A planning and control mechanism takes into consideration a wide range of functions and incorporates a number of key activities, such as:

- Generating a network of actions that depicts the relationship between these actions and their order of occurrence;
- Project scheduling that links a plan into a time frame as well as smoothing out resource level variations;
- Measuring job progress, reviewing the plan and rescheduling when conditions change.

It should be noted that planning and scheduling are not synonymous. Planning specifically considers the "what", "how" and "by whom" aspects of the project, whereas scheduling considers the "when" aspect. Planning is therefore the process of choosing the method and order of work from among various methods and possible sequences, while scheduling is the calculation of the timing for the selected sequences and provides the completion of project time. Planning provides detailed information and is the basis for estimating time and concurrently providing a baseline for project control. However, scheduling reflects the plan in terms of time scales. Unfortunately, when project managers refer to the planning process they often include both the planning and scheduling aspects of the project.

The distinction between planning and scheduling is important. When planning a project, the project manager will normally discuss the project scope and the specific deliverables to determine the tasks, order of work, possible sequences and time estimation for each task. The discussions may take the form of dynamic interaction, brainstorming and assessments exercises among the project participants. A lack of integration between the project stakeholders, including the contractual parties, clients, suppliers, line supervisors and others may lead to plans being ignored or misunderstood. Therefore, project scope together with the integration of those involved in the project, provides a solid basis for accurately deciding the material and work requirements and determining the works quantity, labour and other resource requirements. It is important to note that this planning aspect is the result of human knowledge, informational intelligence and human interaction.

The information age plays a significant role in this planning aspect. The information age, particularly through the internet allows for two-way information dissemination. Physical distance is no longer a hindrance to having close integration and interaction between those involved in a project. The quality of information is dependent upon two critical factors, having a comprehensive data collection process and the timely dissemination of information. In addition, gathering information and making the appropriate decisions on the information obtained is central to planning. The project manager becomes the "control" centre as a repository for and disseminating relevant, timely and meaningful information.

The information-gathering process requires considerable resources and may be based on a business intelligence platform that is capable of integrating data from different sources, including information search from previous but similar projects; analysis of ad hoc queries; and processing of data for the appraisal of alternatives. The information-gathering process must also cater for a range of transmission modes ranging from face-to-face meetings to video conferencing. Hence, planning is to a large extent a data intelligence exercise that integrates the interactions of different data sources be they human or electronic. The information age not only facilitates such a process, but it is the focus of the process. Without the Information and Communications Technology (ICT) such a process is not possible.

The scheduling aspect is normally the result of a computer-based tool, such as Critical Path Method analysis (CPM) or Project Evaluation Review Technique (PERT). However, CPM and PERT are not tools for gathering and assessing intelligence; they both make use of the information gathered in the planning stage and calculate a schedule. It is emphasized that as with all computer systems, the golden rule applies: garbage-in garbage-out. Hence, the accuracy of the results from the CPM and PERT systems are dependent on the accuracy and relevance of the information provided. The CPM and PERT tools do not question the validity of the data; these systems assume that the planner has addressed the input issues and they take the data at face value.

The full planning process needs to be viewed in the light of the evolution of the internet and intranet facilities that are available to organizations. It is now possible for every relevant stakeholder to access a common work breakdown structure and project schedule showing the milestones and activities. It is now also possible to link the supply value chains of material suppliers, contractors, subcontractors, financial institutions and the client with the entity undertaking the project, so that payments, orders and other relevant business transactions are instantly conducted in a highly secure manner. The information revolution facilitates the implementation of the Information Resource Management (IRM) concept. The IRM concept is based on the premise that information is an asset that should be fully utilized like any other capital asset. IRM allows the gathered information to be integrated into the business processes of different organizations through a fully interactive data sharing mechanism.

Planning a Project

Project planning consists of a number of steps that should be conducted with great care. It is emphasized that time invested in planning a project is time and resources saved in the execution of the project. Furthermore, the project plan establishes the base line against which a project is monitored and controlled. Hence, the project planning phase is fundamental to project management success. The ten steps required to define a suitable project plan are as follows:

1. Review project scope;
2. Identify the project components;
3. Prepare a Work Breakdown Structure (WBS);
4. Break down each project component into activities;
5. Determine physical, technological, resource and management constraints;
6. Determine the relationships between the activities;
7. Prepare the project network diagram;
8. Prepare duration and cost estimating data for activities;
9. Prepare the Cost Breakdown Structure (CBS);
10. Schedule activities for time, cost and resources.

It should be noted that planning a project requires a considerable amount of manual and mental effort and rigorous human interaction. Numerous computer software packages are available to aid the project team with project scheduling (Step 10) but the preceding steps require information and manual decision making at a micro human level.

In preparing a project plan it is wise to keep in mind that planning is a process of selecting the one method and sequence of work to be adopted for a project from among many alternative ways and sequences that a particular project can be carried out. Therefore, there may be various methods of carrying out a project but the proper plan is regarded as the optimum plan and is the method adopted to execute the project. The optimum plan is viewed as the most advantageous in terms of both time and cost. It is precisely for this reason that planning requires extensive human interaction and intervention to allow the project manager to determine and select the optimum plan from the many alternative methods, with their resultant numerous permutations of executing various tasks. On the other hand, scheduling utilizes the optimum plan and determines the timing of the various activities to give the overall project completion time. Thus, scheduling is easily facilitated through the application of computer application software using CPM or PERT.

REVIEW PROJECT SCOPE

The project scope is the definition of the project, a statement of the problem, not the solution. It is essential that the project scope is understood by all those involved in the project. It is normal to assume that the project scope will have inaccuracies, ambiguities, misunderstandings and other misconceptions that unless clarified will cause serious problems at the project implementation stage. It is therefore important that the project scope is thoroughly reviewed. One may question the need for reviewing the project scope. However, in many projects, the project scope is defined by persons who are not part of the project team and in many cases by non-technical persons. Hence, the need for a project scope review is a necessity not a luxury.

The major objective of the project scope review is to ensure that everyone concerned with the project from the instigator, the designer, the project team, right up to the client who will take delivery of the end product have the same understanding. The result from this review should be a formally written document defining what is required (end deliverables) and by when. This document must be agreed and signed by all involved and is regarded as the fundamental definition of the project. View the time spent on this task as an investment. Having a formal written project scope review document has the following benefits:

- Clarity will disclose misunderstandings and misinterpretations;
- Comprehensiveness will eliminate inconsistent assumptions;
- Thoroughness will draw attention to the technical and practical aspects;
- A formal signed agreement will motivate all concerned to fully contemplate all the details.

The project scope review integrates quality management into the planning process. Whilst project scope changes are always possible during project execution, it is essential that these changes do not become the order of the day. A thorough project scope review has the objective of minimizing project scope changes. One should note that once the project is being implemented, scope changes consume time, resulting in higher costs. When reviewing the project scope assess the following five aspects:

1. Ensure that project scope takes an holistic approach, with project elements being consistent and fitting together as a whole. Look for duplication, mismatching and missing elements.
2. Examine the project interfaces. The value chain between the client, suppliers and project organization are important. Ensure that interfaces are defined and agreed to. Contact persons from all concerned will help to maintain friendly relations throughout the project.
3. Appraise the holistic time scales. Optimistic time scales usually lead to project time and cost overruns. Ensure that the project scope review document does have realistic time scales.
4. Assess external dependencies. Ensure that any deliverable that depends on others is clearly highlighted. All project links should be defined and every entity or individual outside the immediate project team are aware of their responsibilities and the difficulties that they will cause, should they fail to deliver on the specified deadline.

Ensure that appropriate communication channels are established with the external dependencies.

5. Assess resources. The project scope should identify the holistic resources needed. The agreed and signed final project scope document should include a commitment by management to allocate the necessary funds for the project. Ensure that the holistic resource estimates are realistic.

The project scope review document should state in simple, clear, concise and unambiguous terms the definition of the project. The project scope may change, but those involved in the project will be able to have an understanding of the project at a particular point in time.

IDENTIFY PROJECT COMPONENTS

The project scope review document will provide an adequate initial input for identifying the project components. The identification of the project components consists of a breakdown of the general project deliverables. This breakdown is normally referred to as the decomposition process and has the objective of subdividing the project deliverables into smaller and more manageable parts or components. The level of the project deliverable breakdown will normally depend on the size and complexity of the project and how far into the future the project extends.

Caution should be exercised in deciding the level of decomposition. The excessive breakdown of a project may lead to:

*   An increase in management effort;
*   Ineffective utilization of resources;
*   Decrease in performance efficiency.

On the other hand, a lower lever of detail provides a higher capability to plan, manage and control the work being carried out. Therefore, there is a need to maintain equilibrium between insufficient and excessive planning detail.

Example for indentifying project components – steel warehouse frame

Let us consider an example. Assume that a project manager has been assigned a project to erect a steel warehouse frame. The project team have discussed and reviewed the project scope and understand exactly what is required. The project manager must now bring the project team together to discuss the erection of the steel warehouse frame. This meeting could take the form of brainstorming session or a focused group discussion under the guidance of a facilitator. The objective of the meeting is to consider the various components that would comprise the project.

After a detailed discussion there was consensus among the project team members that the project would consist of the following components:

1. *Preliminary phase.* The project team decided that this phase would consist of three sub-work components. Furthermore, the project team decided that this level of detail is sufficient for the proper management of this project segment. The three sub-work components are:

a) Prepare site;
b) Fence site;
c) Erect site workshop.

2. *Steel fabrication phase*. It was decided that the fabrication phase is fairly straightforward and therefore it would consist of two sub-work components, as follows, with no further breakdown being necessary:
a) Fabricate steel work;
b) Paint fabricated steel work.

3. *Foundation phase*. The foundation phase is critical to the project and requires more detailed thinking. It was decided that this phase would consist of three major segments, but each segment required further detail, particularly, the concrete stage. The project team consider that the concrete stage is rather tricky, so they want a further breakdown of this stage. The sub-work components for this phase areas follows:
a) Excavation works. This consists of two further sub-work components:
   • Mark out excavation site;
   • Excavate site.
b) Concrete Reinforcement (steel). This consists of two further sub-work components:
   • Bend reinforcement steel;
   • Place reinforcement steel in excavated foundation.
c) Concrete works. This consists of two further sub-work components:
   • Procure concrete for excavated foundation;
   • Pour concrete in excavated foundation. Pouring of the concrete is considered critical so a further breakdown was considered necessary:
     – Construct temporary formwork;
     – Pour concrete in foundation;
     – Cure and let concrete to set (harden);
     – Dismantle formwork.

4. *Assembly Phase*. The assembly phase was considered an easy process and required only one component:
a) Assemble Steel Frame.

The above example illustrates the process that a project team must go through to identify the project components. The identification of the project components will be used as input information to prepare the work breakdown structure (next step).

PREPARE WORK BREAKDOWN STRUCTURE

The work breakdown structure (WBS) is a schematic diagram of the project components identified in Step 2. If any of the project components are still too complex for them to be easily organized, the WBS provides an opportunity to break them down into another level of simpler descriptions, and so on until in the opinion of the project team they can be fully and effectively managed. This method allows a complex project to be organized as a set of simple tasks which together achieve the desired outputs.

Example for preparing work breakdown structure (WBS) – steel warehouse frame

The WBS will enable the project team to acquire a real grasp of the project. It is easier to visualize a project in manageable slots, rather than trying to process the complexity of the project in its entirety, simultaneously. Therefore, each level of the project can be understood as a combination of a number of simply described smaller units. Figure 8.1 provides the WBS for the construction of a steel warehouse frame.

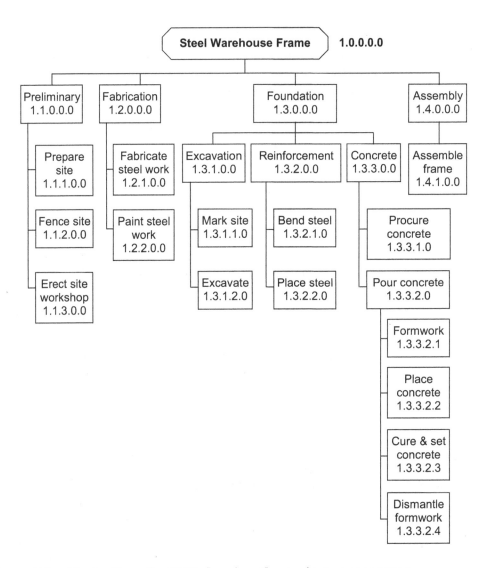

Figure 8.1 Illustration of a WBS showing the project components

The example at Figure 8.1 illustrates that not all project components are decomposed to the same level. The breakdown of a project component should stop when sufficient description of the component is provided to give a clear indication of the work that needs to be done and to have a reasonable estimate for the total time and effort involved. Therefore, some components to be completely understood will need less information and others more. Therefore, the WBS and its components, including the work packages are allocated a code that acts as a control account. These control account codes are unique identifiers and will be used for monitoring and controlling the progress of the project in terms of work components.

DETERMINE THE ACTIVITIES FOR EACH PROJECT COMPONENT

The WBS makes it easier for the project team to define the project components into manageable work units, but it does not inform them of the activities that are required to carry out each work unit. This step requires the project team to further examine each project work component and respective work units, and decide what activities are required to achieve them. Hence, this will result in a further breakdown of the project work components into specific tasks. The degree of this further breakdown will depend on the level of control desired. Some factors influencing the level of control include:

1. *The type of work being undertaken.* If the project has a short time span, tight control is essential. Therefore, the breakdown needs to be at a detailed level to attain the required degree of control. But if the work is of a highly technical and complex nature, more detail may also be required.
2. *The features of the resources needed.* If a special class of labour, equipment or material is required that is considered to be in very short supply then the use of such resources may need to be closely monitored and controlled. Hence, more detail is required in an attempt to segregate the tasks that utilize these scarce resources.
3. *Project geographical location and dispersion.* If certain project components are conducted away from the organization's place of work then more detail may be needed to exercise better control. For instance, road building, construction sites and international projects represent more risk and logistic concerns than if the work was being conducted at the organization's place of work. Hence, the level of detail may need to be increased so that any concerns encountered are exposed in a very short time frame.
4. *The cost information system.* Management may require a detailed degree of costing information at the project implementation phase. The plan must therefore reflect the level of detail required by the cost management system.
5. *Broad general sequence of project.* The way the project is to be conducted in terms of the sequence in which the components are executed may require a more detailed breakdown, particularly if some components are (partially or fully) conducted concurrently.

The lowest level of the project components breakdown is normally referred to as an activity or task. An activity consumes time and very often resources.

Example for determining the activities for each project component

Let us continue with the example of the erection of the steel warehouse frame. The project manager would continue the meeting with the project team to ascertain the activities that would be needed to accomplish each of the identified project components and their respective work units. After a detailed discussion the project team members ascertain the activities for each project component and work units as shown in Figure 8.2.

WBS Code	Component	Activities
1.0.0.0.0	Steel Warehouse Frame	
1.1.0.0.0	Preliminary	
1.1.1.0.0	Prepare Site	• Secure bulldozer and trucks • Move onto site • Level site area • Clear grass and other rubble from site • Move bulldozer and trucks from site
1.1.2.0.0	Fence Site	• Calculate fencing material needed • Secure and deliver fencing material • Erect fence
1.1.3.0.0	Erect Site Workshop	• Secure prefabricated workshop • Deliver prefabricated workshop • Erect prefabricated workshop
1.2.0.0.0	Fabrication of Frame	
1.2.1.0.0	Fabricate Steel Work	• Examine warehouse design plans • Calculate frame steel requirements • Calculate frame steel joining brackets • Secure steel needed • Delivery of steel • Fabricate frame steel joining brackets • Fabricate steel frame structure • Group frame structure according to design
1.2.2.0.0	Paint Fabricated Steel	• Calculate volume of paint needed • Secure paint • Secure spray painting equipment • Paint fabricated steel joining brackets • Secure steel lifting equipment • Spray paint fabricated steel frame structure • Release and return equipment • Return unused paint to stores
1.3.0.0.0	Foundation	
1.3.1.0.0	Excavation	
1.3.1.1.0	Mark Site	• Secure services of surveyor • Mark foundation location with pegs
1.3.1.2.0	Excavate	• Secure excavating equipment and trucks • Excavate foundation & remove excess rubble • Internal inspection of foundation • Move excavator and trucks from site
1.3.2.0.0	Reinforcement	
1.3.2.1.0	Bend Steel	• Secure reinforcement steel • Cut and bend steel • Deliver steel on-site
1.3.2.2.0	Place Steel	• Organize inspection of steel • Placement of steel • Inspection of steel and foundation

Figure 8.2 Activities for WBS project component and work units

WBS Code	Component	Activities
1.3.3.0.0	Concrete	
1.3.3.1.0	Procure Concrete	• Determine concrete mix • Test concrete mix • Calculate concrete quantity • Order concrete
1.3.3.2.0	Pour Concrete	
1.3.3.2.1	Formwork	• Arrange inspection of foundation works • Secure and delivery of formwork • Assemble formwork • Internal inspection of formwork
1.3.3.2.2	Place Concrete	• Inspection of foundation works • Delivery of concrete • Test concrete mix • Place concrete in foundations
1.3.3.2.3	Cure & Set Concrete	• Arrange for final foundation inspection • Cure and set concrete
1.3.3.2.4	Dismantle Formwork	• Dismantle formwork • Remove formwork from site • Backfill • Final foundation inspection
1.4.0.0.0	Frame Assembly	
1.4.1.0.0	Assemble Frame	• Arrange for frame inspection • Delivery of steel frame and accessories • Assemble pillars • Assemble supporting beams • Assemble rest of frame • Touch up paint • Clean up site • Frame inspection • Leave site

Figure 8.2   Activities for WBS project component and work units (continued)

DETERMINE THE ACTIVITY CONSTRAINTS

Each activity normally consumes time and often resources. What is more, there may be constraints in the way an activity may be conducted that affects the sequence in which the other related activities are carried out. There is thus a need to examine each activity to determine the management, resource, technological and physical constraints.

It is important to note that the allocation and levelling of resources will be conducted at a later stage during the scheduling phase. It is emphasized that at this stage, the constraints are examined only from the point of view of how the activities may be carried out in relation to the other activities.

Management constraint

An example of a management constraint is a union agreement which may stipulate that certain activities are to be conducted by two persons as a safety precaution, even though the work content itself may be sufficient for one person. Another example is that there could be strict budgetary limitations which prohibit the use of overtime.

Resource constraints

Resource constraints result due to various reasons. For example, an activity may require five technicians to complete within one working week, but the organization has only two technicians at its disposal. Another example of a resource constraint is that an activity may require a particular piece of equipment that may not be available, therefore an alternative apparatus is utilized that may not be as efficient.

Technological constraints

There may be technological constraints that do not allow an activity to be conducted until the right conditions are attained. For example, when pouring concrete into a foundation, the concrete must set hard. The setting period varies depending on cement type, mixture and temperature but construction may not be able to commence until the concrete attains its full strength. Another example is paint work. Paint must be allowed to dry before other related activities may be carried out.

Physical constraints

There may be a physical condition that does not permit two or more activities to be carried out concurrently at the same location. For example, in shipbuilding, there may be confined spaces where a pipe-laying activity in a particular area cannot take place while electrical cabling is being laid because there is not enough space for two categories of labour to work concurrently in the same location.

DETERMINE THE RELATIONSHIP BETWEEN ACTIVITIES

Planning is the process of choosing the method and order of work from among various methods and possible sequences. Hence, this step takes into consideration the identified management, resource, technological, and physical constraints to decide the relationship between activities, so that these activities may be conducted in the optimal order.

A number of activities may proceed concurrently with other activities because they are independent of each other. However, other activities must be constrained to a given sequence. For instance, in the example regarding the construction of a steel warehouse frame, one cannot pour the concrete into the foundations unless the excavation works have been completed and the reinforced steel is in place. Moreover, the steel warehouse frame cannot be erected unless the concrete in the foundation has attained the required hardness. This is the reason why the constraints were identified, to help the project team determine the optimum and proper sequence of the activities.

Example for determining the relationship between activities – steel warehouse frame

Let us continue with the example regarding the construction of the steel warehouse frame. To determine the relationship between activities, the project team must ask the following questions for each activity:

1. What activities must be achieved immediately before this activity?
2. What activities may be carried out concurrently with this activity?
3. What activities must immediately follow this activity?

This procedure allows each activity to be closely examined and the appropriate order of conducting the activities is determined. Figure 8.3 provides an illustration of this process for the "Preliminary" project component of the construction of a steel warehouse frame.

WBS Code	Component/Activities	Activities		
		Before	Concurrent	After
1.0.0.0.0	01 Steel Warehouse Frame	nil	nil	2 (*)
1.1.0.0.0	02 Preliminary	1	nil (*)	3,9,13
1.1.1.0.0	03 Prepare Site	2	9, 13	4
	04 Secure bulldozer and trucks	3	nil	5
	05 Move onto site	4	nil	6
	06 Level site area	5	nil	7
	07 Clear grass and other rubble from site	6	nil	8, 12
	08 Move bulldozer and trucks from site	7	nil	17
1.1.2.0.0	09 Fence Site	2	3, 13	10
	10 Calculate fencing material needed	9	nil	11
	11 Secure and deliver fencing material	10	nil	12
	12 Erect fence	7, 11	nil	15
1.1.3.0.0	13 Erect Site Workshop	2	3, 9	14
	14 Secure prefabricated workshop	13	nil	15
	15 Deliver prefabricated workshop	12, 14	nil	16
	16 Erect prefabricated workshop	15	nil	17
	17 Finish Preliminary (end)	8, 16	nil	nil

* Other activities are not shown since example is on "Preliminary" project component.

Figure 8.3   Relationships between project activities

The following observations may be made from Figure 8.3:

- The activities for a particular project component inherit the WBS code for that component. For example, all the activities belonging to the "Prepare Site" sub-component will all have the same WBS code (that is, 1.1.1.0.0).
- The project components and their respective activities have been allocated a unique sequence number. This is being done to make it easier for referencing purposes when entering information in the "before", "concurrent" and "after" columns.
- The numbers in "before", "concurrent" and "after" columns refer to the component/ activity sequence number. At this stage it is purely a reference number.
- The last activity, "Finish Preliminary (end)" has been added in this example to signify the end of this particular segment of the project.

PREPARE PROJECT NETWORK DIAGRAM

The project network diagram may be prepared concurrently with Step 6 (determine the relationship between activities). It is emphasized that the input of all key persons concerned with the project is essential when deciding the method and order of conducting the project activities. The objective of the project team at this stage should be to establish an optimal method of conducting the project. There are basically two types of project network diagrams:

1. Arrow network;
2. Precedence network.

Arrow network

Figure 8.4 is an example of an arrow network depicting a simple project, namely "Painting a Room". In an arrow network, each line represents an activity. The relationship between the activities is represented by the relationship of one arrow to the other arrows. Arrows must always point in a forward direction to give the perception of forward motion. Each circle represents an event and is uniquely numbered. However, the number at the head of the arrow is always greater than the number at the tail. Likewise, an activity is referenced by its start and end event number. For example, the activity "Prepare walls" in Figure 8.4, would be referenced as activity 1–3.

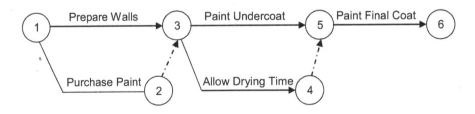

Figure 8.4   Example of arrow network – painting a room project

Events are separated by activities, with an activity having an event to mark its beginning. This event may be the commencement of the project or the completion of a preceding activity. For example, event "1" signifies the beginning of the project and also of the beginning of the activity "Prepare walls". The relationship between activities is based on the various constraints identified in Step 5. For example, activity 3–4, "Allow drying time" is a technological constraint, and activity 5–6 "Paint final coat" cannot commence until the undercoat has dried. Then again, some activities occur concurrently with other activities. For example, activity 1–2 is carried out concurrently with activity 1–3. Also, activity 3–4 occurs concurrently with activity 3–5.

The completion of an activity is also regarded as an event that signals the successful achievement of work. Hence, activities normally consume time, but events do not. The length of the arrow has no significance; it merely represents the passage of time in the direction of the arrow. The start of all activities leaving the event depends on the completion of all the activities entering that event. Therefore, an event is not achieved until all the activities entering that event have been completed. For example, event "5" is deemed complete only when both activities 3–4 and 3–5 are accomplished. Thus, activity 5–6 cannot start unless both activities 3–4 and 3–5 are completed.

Arrow networks may have dummy activities that are signified by a dotted arrow. These dummy activities do not normally consume time. They are used because each activity must be uniquely referenced. For example, activity 1–3 may be carried out concurrently with activity 1–2. Since these activities must be uniquely referenced, a dummy activity 2–3 is created because "Prepare walls" and "Purchase paint" cannot be allocated the same activity identifier. It should be noted that the dummy activity 2–3 would not consume time.

Precedence network

Figure 8.5 is an example of a precedence network depicting the "Painting a Room" project. In precedence networks the nodes (rectangles) represent activities and the arrows represent logical time relationships between activities. The length of the arrows has no significance. Again, precedence networks do not need dummy activities to maintain their unique identity.

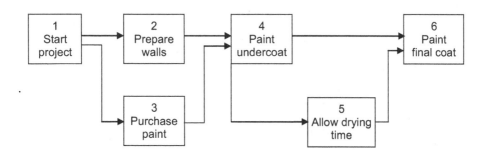

Figure 8.5 Example of precedence network – painting a room project

In Figure 8.5 activities "2" and "3" are conducted concurrently, and activity "4" cannot start until both these activities are completed. Moreover, activity "6" cannot start until activities "4" and "5" are both finished. A precedence network has a major advantage over an arrow network in the way relationships are represented. Figure 8.6 illustrates the four types of relationships that are permitted in a precedence network.

Type 1: Finish-to-start

In the example, Activity 4 may not start until both Activities 2 and 3 have been completed. Hence, in the *finish-to-start* link, one or more activities must finish before the succeeding activity can start.

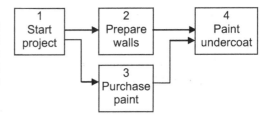

Type 2: Start-to-start

In the example, Activity 5 starts with the start of Activity 4. When one activity lags behind the start of another activity it is often referred to as a "lag-start" relationship.

In reality, drying time commences as soon as painting starts.

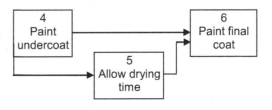

Type 3: Finish-to-finish

Activity 5 must be completed before Activity 6 can be completed. This link is possible if you have for example two persons painting, one the undercoat and the other the finish coat. Activity 5 would signify the start of drying time at the start of Activity 4, but Activity 6 cannot be completed until the entire painted surface is dry. This is also known as "lag-finish" relationship.

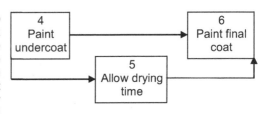

Type 4: Start-to-finish

Activity 4 must begin before Activity 6 can be completed. This situation is possible if you have two persons painting, one the undercoat and the other the finish coat. The person doing activity 4 would need a head start before the second person starts the finishing coat (assume that paint drying is taking place without having an activity specifically for it).

Figure 8.6   Relationships permitted in precedence network

It is emphasized that the correct use of the four permitted relationships requires a high level of training and experience in planning and scheduling projects. Abuse of the precedence network method has resulted through the excessive use of the *start-to-start* and *finish-to-finish* dependencies by those who do not fully understand their application and the resulting implications to the scheduling process. The main issue at the planning stage is to develop a plan that is clear and easily understood. Therefore, be careful in the use of the *start-to-start* and *finish-to-finish* relationships and ensure there is a valid reason for using them. If the purpose for using these relationships is to provide a preferred sequence of execution of the work, a constraint date is a better way to handle this. It should be noted that dates are easy to change whereas logic changes to the precedence network may have a drastic impact on the entire network analysis at the scheduling stage.

The precedence network method can be applied at two levels, namely basic and complex. In the basic application, only the *finish-to-start* relationship is used. The use of the complex precedence network method should only be utilized when:

- There is a valid need for other relationships besides *finish-to-start*;
- Application of the relationships is fully understood by the planning team;
- Limited to situations where the full consequences of applying these advanced dependencies are fully comprehended.

Example for preparing network diagram – steel warehouse frame

Figure 8.7 illustrates the precedence network of the "Preliminary" WBS project component and its respective activities as shown in Figure 8.3. Note that the illustration uses only the *Finish-to-Start* relationship and normally the activity descriptions (and other activity scheduling details) would appear in the rectangle.

The advantages of a precedence network over an arrow network include:

- The use of dummy activities is eliminated;
- The concept is easier to grasp;
- Relationships if used properly are more representative of the practical world;
- Modification and correction of a precedence network is easier;
- Each activity is assigned a single unique number that may be adapted to include the WBS number and other code designations, such as a cost code and location code.

PREPARE DURATION AND COST ESTIMATING DATA FOR ACTIVITIES

This step is concerned with the duration and cost that each activity will take to be completed and is often termed as "utility data". In other words, the utility data is concerned with the detailed time and cost information regarding each project activity. It should be noted that:

- A plan deals with the "what" and "how"?
- Utility data deals with the estimation of how long and how much?
- Scheduling deals with "when" and "by whom"?

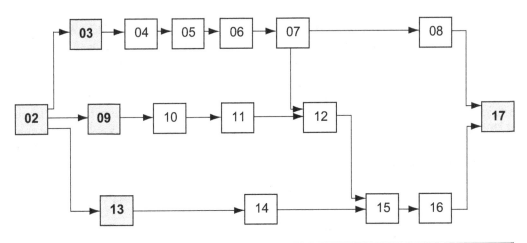

Figure 8.7   Precedence network of "Preliminary" WBS project component

Hence, before the scheduling of activities may take place, both the plan (what and how?) and basic utility data (how long and how much?) are required. It is also important to note that an activity may be performed by different:

- *Combination of methods.* For example, if one was digging a trench the method could be manual or mechanical or a combination of both.
- *Equipment.* The trench may be dug using various apparatus. For instance, pick and shovel; front-end loader or trench-digging machine.
- *Crew sizes.* The crew size for digging the trench could be two, five or more labourers.
- *Working hours.* The working hours for conducting the trench-digging activity may vary. For instance, working an eight-hour shift, working a three-shift system (24 hours per day) or working overtime.

The major factors dominating the selection of the optimum combination to perform an activity may be cost, time or both. However, no matter what the combination of methods, equipment, crew size and working hours selected, the work content and effort remains the same. For example, an activity that requires the removal of 2,000 cubic meters of rubble remains the same no matter what method is used. However, it is the time and cost to complete the activity that will change with the combination of methods, equipment, crew size and the working hours selected.

Likewise, both time and cost are equally important. However, cost may be viewed as being made up of two distinct categories, direct and indirect cost. Direct cost predominates and is normally variable, whereas indirect cost is usually proportional to time and is usually at a fixed rate (linear). The information that is normally required for the overall project and individual activities are the following:

1. On a whole project basis.
    a) Prepare a list of all resources that may be required for the project and their respective estimated resource usage rates. For example, labour cost per hour, fuel cost per litre, equipment cost per day, and so on;
    b) Prepare a list of all indirect costs involved as separate items. For example, supervisory costs, administrative charges, water and electricity, site expenses and permits are normally classified as indirect costs. However, you may need to consult the accountant to establish the indirect costs within your organization;
    c) Prepare information regarding work shifts, public holidays, length of the working week (five or seven days) and other important calendar details (for example, annual shut down).
2. On an activity basis.
    a) Provide for each activity the estimated duration. For example, person effort in hours or days or weeks, and so on;
    b) Provide for each activity the estimated direct resource usage required in units. For example, two labourers; one overhead crane; 200 litres of paint, and so on;
    c) Provide for each activity the estimated indirect costs if applicable.

It should be noted that the time–cost issue has an infinite number of solutions and may be viewed as occurring within two extremes:

1. *At one extreme is time.* If time is not a concern, then an activity may be performed by a method that attains the lowest direct cost;
2. *At the other extreme is cost.* If cost is not a concern, each activity may be hurried to be accomplished in the minimum time.

There are an unlimited number of solutions within these two limits. These solutions are normally depicted by a direct time–cost graph as illustrated by Figure 8.8. These graphs are calculated from the basic data itemized previously and as the name suggests, only the direct costs are considered because they are usually variable; whereas the indirect costs are normally proportional to time and are often charged at a fixed rate.

The direct time–cost graphs are obtained by plotting the calculated direct cost of achieving an activity for each method against the duration required to conduct the activity through a particular method. A judicious review of an activity will disclose many possible ways of shortening its duration.

The normal time–cost point is the optimum application of resources to complete an activity. However, if the project manager wishes to shorten the activity duration time then the activity must be expedited. The expedite time (also referred as crash time) on the graph represents the shortest duration an activity may be executed.

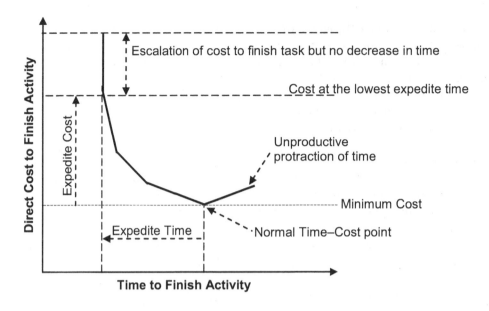

Figure 8.8   Example of an activity direct time–cost graph

Normally an increase in resources will shorten the activity duration time at an increase in cost. However, there is a limit to the amount of resources one may engage to perform an activity. Thus, increasing resources may increase cost but may not shorten the duration time. For instance, if one was to paint a small room, having four persons may shorten the duration time because each person would paint a wall without interfering with each other. However, increasing the number of persons to ten will result in an increase in cost but not a decrease in time, since the ten persons will not be able to work in a small room, resulting in resource wastage.

The preparation of the direct time–cost graphs for the various activities is an important process. However, these graphs in practice will only be prepared for a small proportion of the project activities depending on the resources being utilized. The cost elements for carrying out an activity may include:

- *Direct costs.* These consist of different categories of labour, material and equipment;
- *Indirect costs.* These consist of cost elements, such as administrative and supervision charges, security costs, interest on financial loans, penalty payments and other ad hoc expenses.

The direct costs are normally linked with activities, whereas indirect costs are often assessed and allocated for the project as a whole and behave in a linear manner over the entire project time. Hence, direct time–cost graphs are prepared for activities using only the direct cost elements.

Example of time–cost graph – earth excavation activity

The example below is regarding the preparation of the direct time–cost graph for an activity such as earth excavation for a drainage channel. This activity may be performed using manual labour, a number of mechanical methods and subcontractor. However, in the example only manual labour is considered to be practical. The following assumptions are made:

1. Work effort. It is assumed that after taking into consideration the earth quantities, timbering requirements and other relevant factors, the workload for the activity is 450 person days of labour. Again, assume that the efficient work crew size is nine persons.
2. Other assumptions include:
   a) Number of work days per week is five;
   b) Number of hours per working day is eight;
   c) Day shift pay rate is five units per eight-hour working day;
   d) Second shift pay rate is six units per eight-hour working day;
   e) Third shift pay rate is seven units per eight-hour working day.

Applying the above assumptions the following calculations are made:

1. Day shift.
   a) Duration for working the day shift = 450 ÷ 9 = 50 working days.
   b) Day shift cost = 50 work days × 9 persons × 5 units = 2250 units.
2. Second shift system.
   a) Duration for working two shifts = 450 ÷ (9 × 2) = 25 working days.
   b) Day shift cost = 25 work days × 9 persons × 5 units = 1125 units.
   c) Second shift cost = 25 work days × 9 persons × 6 units = 1,350 units.
   d) Total cost for working two shifts = (1,125 + 1,350) = 2,475 units.
3. Third shift system.
   a) Duration for working three shifts = 450 ÷ (9 × 3) = 17 working days.
   b) Day shift cost = 17 work days × 9 persons × 5 units = 765 units.
   c) Second shift cost = 17work days × 9 persons × 6 units = 918 units.
   d) Third shift cost = 17 work days × 9 persons × 7 units = 1,071 units.
   e) Total cost for working three shifts = (765 + 918 + 1071) = 2,754 units.

Note that there may be other work methods apart from work shifts. These include extending the working day and/or working week and paying overtime rates; having incentive bonus payments for more efficient work output; and many other innovative methods.

Let us now assume that the management requires the duration of the activity to be a lot less than the 17 days minimum period under a three-shift system. Usually, there is a tendency to increase the work crew. However, the nine-person work crew was the optimum size, therefore labour utilization inefficiency will result and hence the original estimate of 450 person days of work effort will increase. There will also be a minimum limit that the activity may be achieved. For instance, it is impractical to have 450 persons working for one day.

In situations when it is vital that the duration of an activity is at an absolute minimum, resource availability becomes critical and costs are of secondary importance. In this example, the project manager may assess that 60 persons are available in three work crews of 20 persons each. Due to resource inefficiency, the activity is now estimated to require 540 person days of labour. This means expediting the activity, known as the least time solution.

The calculations for expediting the activity are as follows:

a) Least Duration = 540 ÷ (3 × 20) = 9 working days.
b) Day shift cost = 9 work days × 20 persons × 5 units = 900 units.
c) Second shift cost = 9 work days × 20 persons × 6 units = 1,080 units.
d) Third shift cost = 9 work days × 20 persons × 7 units = 1,260 units.
e) Total cost for working three shifts = (900 + 1,080 + 1,260) = 3,240 units.

The resultant time–cost graph for the earth excavation activity using manual labour and applying all the calculations above is shown in Figure 8.9.

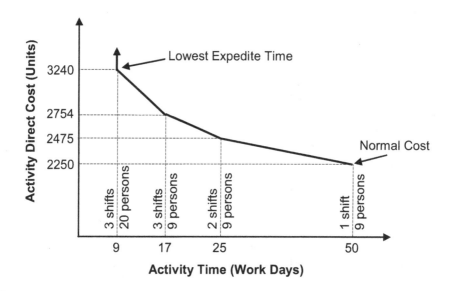

Figure 8.9   Time–cost graph for earth excavation activity (manual labour)

If the earth excavation activity as shown in Figure 8.9 is conducted using a trenching machine instead of manual labour, the resultant calculations would be as shown below. The following assumptions are made:

•   Number of work days per week is five;
•   Number of hours per working day is eight;
•   Work crew is three persons;
•   Normal working days is 18;
•   Trenching machine cost is 125 units per shift of 8 hours;

- Day shift pay rate is five units per eight-hour working day;
- Second shift pay rate is six units per eight-hour working day;
- Third shift pay rate is seven units per eight-hour working day.

Applying the above assumptions the following calculations are made:

1. Day shift.
   a) Duration for working the day shift = 18 working days.
   b) Equipment cost for day shift = 18 work days × 125 units = 2,250 units.
   c) Labour day shift cost = 18 work days × 3 persons × 5 units = 270 units.
   d) Total cost for working day shift = (2,250 + 270) = 2,520 units.
2. Second shift system.
   a) Duration for working two shifts = 18 ÷ 2 = 9 working days.
   b) Equipment cost (two shifts) = 9 days × 2 shifts × 125 units = 2,250 units.
   c) Day shift cost = 9 work days × 3 persons × 5 units = 135 units.
   d) Second shift cost = 9 work days × 3 persons × 6 units = 162 units.
   e) Total cost for working two shifts = (2,250 + 135 + 162) = 2,547 units.
3. Third shift system.
   a) Duration for working three shifts = 18 ÷ 3 = 6 working days.
   b) Equipment cost (three shifts) = 6 days × 3 shifts × 125 units = 2,250 units
   c) Day shift cost = 6 days × 3 persons × 5 units = 90 units.
   d) Second shift cost = 6 days × 3 persons × 6 units = 108 units.
   e) Third shift cost = 6 days × 3 persons × 7 units = 126 units.
   f) Total cost working three shifts = (2,250 + 90 + 108 + 126) = 2,574 units.

In the mechanical situation the three-shift system would be the expedite solution because the machine has to work continuously (24 hours per day) to accomplish the activity in the six days. The examples show that utility data are the detailed time–cost information obtained from the initial estimate for each individual activity. It should be noted that not all activities will have a direct time–cost graph. Some activities will have complex graphs similar to the example shown, others will have a straight line relationship with the cost being proportional to time and yet others will have one single cost. The direct time–cost graphs are required to:

- Determine whether a project is economically feasible;
- Find the optimum project plan;
- Satisfy a management decision about the overall project completion time;
- Determine whether the normal project solution is acceptable;
- Determine a project execution approach if the normal project outcome is not acceptable;
- Provide the necessary data for the recovery of lost time during project execution.

Generally, this basic information will be applied at the project scheduling stage to determine the optimum project duration and cost for the entire project.

PREPARE COST BREAKDOWN STRUCTURE (CBS)

The cost breakdown structure is utilized for keeping track of the activity costs, particularly the cost elements. Costs are categorized under two major classes:

1. *Direct costs.* These are typically costs related to the utilization of different categories of labour, material and equipment;
2. *Indirect costs.* These may include:
   a) Administration and supervision charges;
   b) General project costs, such as permits, electricity and water charges;
   c) Interest on loans for financing the project;
   d) Penalty payments.

The cost classification system will depend on the cost management accounting methodology adopted by a particular organization as illustrated by Figure 8.10. Furthermore, the accounting division within the organization would normally provide the cost categories for both the direct and indirect cost classes.

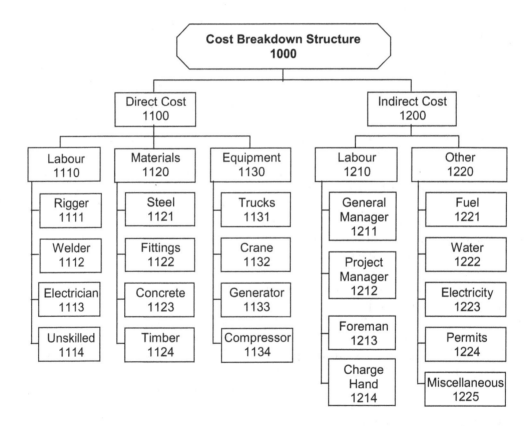

Figure 8.10 Illustration of a Cost Breakdown Structure (CBS)

Two important points need to be emphasized at this stage:

1. The preparation of duration and cost estimating data for activities and the cost breakdown structure (Steps 8 and 9) would normally be applicable to organizations that are geared for the continuous execution of projects. Hence, these types of organizations would operate in a multiple project environment and would require the concurrent monitoring of many projects.
2. The cost breakdown structure would be prepared for the organization as a whole and applicable to all projects undertaken by the organization. Hence, the CBS is not prepared specifically for a particular project. It is prepared only once and updated by the accounting department and is applicable to all projects undertaken by the organization.

Hence, Steps 1 to 7 and 10 are mandatory for all types of projects, while Steps 8 and 9 are essential for organizations that operate in a multiple project environment or where a specific project is of a complex nature and requires rigorous monitoring.

SCHEDULE ACTIVITIES: TIME, COST AND RESOURCES

The objective of the project manager at this stage is to ascertain the optimum solution for the execution of a project as a whole. However, to find the optimum project solution requires a detailed assessment of concurrent, interrelated and overlapping activities, and the individual activity duration and cost data. In other words, the scheduling of activities stage requires two major information inputs:

1. Information from Step 7 (Prepare Project Network Diagram). The project network diagram specifies what and how the project activities will be executed.
2. Information from Step 8 (Prepare Duration and Cost Estimating Data for Activities). The preparation of duration and cost estimating data for activities specifies the duration and cost that each activity will take to be completed, commencing with normal time and cost.

However, in determining the optimum solution for the project on a holistic basis, the project manager must also be aware that expediting one activity will increase its cost and shorten its time, but may not decrease the overall time of the project. It is therefore essential for the project manager to find the proper combination of activities that should be expedited in order to determine the most economical project schedule, taking into consideration both the direct and indirect costs. This is not a simple matter since all costs vary with time. Direct costs tend to decrease if more time is available for an activity, but indirect (overhead) costs will tend to increase with time. Hence, it is the proper balance between time and cost that will provide the optimum solution. The scheduling activities stage has three fundamental objectives:

1. Determines when these activities are to be conducted (the time plan);
2. Determines all the resources that will be required to conduct the project on an individual activity basis taking into account the time plan;
3. Determines the optimum project duration and cost for the entire project by conducting resource scheduling and resource levelling.

Two popular techniques to help the project manager achieve these objectives are the Critical Path Method (CPM) and Project Evaluation Review Technique (PERT). For the purpose of this text, CPM will be mainly considered. The project manager has a wide selection of computer application software that utilizes one or both of these techniques. CPM and PERT provide a systematic method for correlating the effects of time and cost to provide an optimum solution for the project as a whole.

Determining the project schedule requires numerous calculations for every activity that holistically establish project completion time and cost. While these calculations are normally provided by the chosen computer application software, it is important that the project team understand the terminology associated with the various calculations.

Example of time scheduling calculations and terminology used – painting a room

This is a simple example regarding the painting of a room. The network at Figure 8.11 shows five activities. The "Start Project" activity has zero duration time. Assume that a working day is from 08:00 to 17:00 hours with a one-hour break at 12:00 hours (an eight-hour working day).

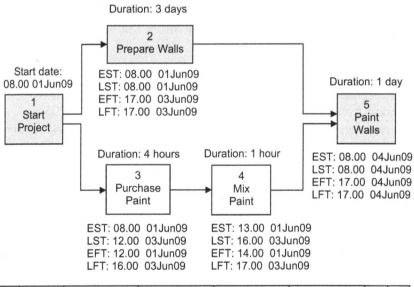

Act.	Duration	EST	LST	EFT	LFT	TF	FF
1*	0 days	08.00 01Jun09	08.00 01Jun09	08.00 01Jun09	08.00 01Jun09	0	0
2*	3 days	08.00 01Jun09	08.00 01Jun09	17.00 03Jun09	17.00 03Jun09	0	0
3	4 hrs	08.00 01Jun09	12.00 03Jun09	12.00 01Jun09	16.00 03Jun09	20h	0
4	1 hrs	13.00 01Jun09	16.00 03Jun09	14.00 01Jun09	17.00 03Jun09	19h	19h
5*	1 day	08.00 04Jun09	08.00 04Jun09	17.00 04Jun09	17.00 04Jun09	0	0

* Critical Activities.

Figure 8.11 Time scheduling calculations for painting a room

All the computations are usually calculated by the project management computer software. Four calculations are initially computed:

1. *Earliest Start Time (EST)*. The EST is the earliest time and date that an activity can start, taking into consideration that there may be other preceding activities that need to be completed;
2. *Earliest Finish Time (EFT)*. The EFT is the earliest time and date that an activity can finish;
3. *Latest Start Time (LST)*. The LST is the latest time and date that an activity can start, taking into account concurrent and other preceding activities;
4. *Latest Finish Time (LFT)*. The LFT is the latest time and date that an activity can finish.

Note that for Activity 2 (Prepare Walls) the EST and LST, and the EFT and LFT are the same because there are no restrictions for this activity to start except for the fact that the project is to commence at 8.00am 1 June. However, an examination of Activity 3 (Purchase Paint) and Activity 4 (Mix Paint) reveal that EST and LST, and the EFT and LFT for these activities are different. The reason is that even though Activity 3 and Activity 4 have durations of four hours and one hour respectively, these hours may be carried out at any time within the three-day period allocated to Activity 2. The reason is that as the network diagram illustrates, Activities 3 and 4 are conducted concurrently with Activity 2, and Activity 5 cannot start until Activities 2, 3 and 4 are all finished. Two other important terms are important in time activity scheduling:

1. *Total float (TF)*. TF is the amount of time by which the start of an activity may be delayed without extending the project duration. Such a delay may cause delays in succeeding activities but will not hold up the project as a whole. TF is calculated by subtracting the EFT from LFT (LFT minus EFT). Activities that have a TF of zero are referred to as critical activities. Hence, TF for Activities 2, 3, 4 and 5 are 0, 20, 19 and 0 hours respectively.
2. *Free float (FF)*. FF is the amount of time by which the start of an activity may be delayed without delaying the start of succeeding activities. FF is calculated by subtracting the activity's own EFT from the EST of the succeeding activity (EST of succeeding activity minus its own EFT). FF can never be greater than TF. FF for Activities 2, 3, 4 and 5 are 0, 0, 19 and 0 hours respectively.

Note that all Activities with zero TF (total float) are critical and are said to be on the critical path. Hence, any delay of the critical activities results in a delay of the project. Therefore, Activities 1, 2 and 5 are considered to be critical activities and cannot be delayed without delaying the project.

Let us assume that the cost for unskilled labour is 5 units per hour for a normal shift of 8 hours per day and the overtime rate is 1.5 times normal rate (that is, 7.5 units per hour). The cost for a painter is 10 units per hour. Furthermore, all activities utilize unskilled labour, except for Activity 5 which utilizes a skilled painter.

Figure 8.12 shows the normal cost calculations and the resultant Gantt chart. The duration and cost calculations are for the normal time to complete an activity. For illustration purposes only the direct labour costs are being shown in the example.

Activity	Normal Cost at Normal Duration
1*	0 units
2*	3 days × 8 hours × 5 units = 120 units
3	4 hours × 5 units = 20 units
4	1 hour × 5 units = 5 units
5*	1 day × 8 hours × 10 units = 80 units

The normal duration and cost schedule is represented by the following Gantt Chart:

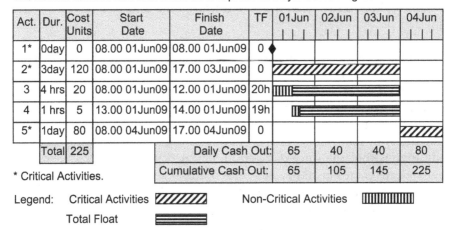

Figure 8.12 Normal cost calculations and resultant Gantt chart

The project manager has received instructions from the client to shorten the project completion time by one day. The only activities that are suitable for expediting are those activities that have a total float of zero, in other words, the critical activities. The reason being that expediting non-critical activities will result in shortening the duration of these activities, but will not shorten the overall project duration. In this example, only Activity 2 and Activity 5 are candidates for expediting. However, before determining the optimum project solution, the cost of these two activities at various time durations must be calculated as shown below:

1. Assume that Activity 2 (Prepare Walls) may be carried out by one of the following methods:
   a) Completing Activity 2 by working at normal duration of 3 days at 8 hours per day.
      Total cost = 3 days × 5 units per hr × 8 hrs × 1 person = 120 units.
      Average Cost per Hour = 5 units.
   b) Completing Activity 2 in 2 days by working 4 hours overtime per day.
      Total cost = (2 days × 5 units per hr × 8 hrs × 1 person) +
      (2 days x 7.5 units per hr × 4 hrs × 1 person) = 140 units.
      Average Cost per Hour = 5.83 units.

c) Completing Activity 2 in 1.5 days by having 2 persons working on the task and paying them a bonus of 15 units each.
Total cost = (2 persons × 1.5 days × 8 hours × 5 units per hr) +
(2 persons × 15 units bonus) = 150 units.
Average Cost per Hour = 6.25 units.

d) Completing Activity 2 in 1 day by having 2 persons working at 8 hours per day and working 6 hours overtime per day per person due to the labour inefficiency in having 2 persons in the same room simultaneously.
Total cost = (2 persons × 5 units per hr × 8 hrs x 1 day) +
(2 persons × 7.5 units per hr × 6 hrs × 1 day) = 170 units.
Average Cost per Hour = 6.07 units.

2. Assume that Activity 5 (Paint Walls) may be carried out by one of two methods:

a) Completing Activity 5 by working the normal duration of 1 day at 8 hours per day.
Total cost = 1 day × 10 units per hr × 8 hrs × 1 person = 80 units.
Average Cost per Hour = 10 units.

b) Completing Activity 5 in 4 hours by having two persons. However, pay a bonus of 5 units each person for having them working in the same room simultaneously.
Total cost = (4 hrs × 10 units per hr × 2 person) +
(5 units bonus × 2 persons) = 90 units.
Average Cost per Hour = 11.25 units.

When deciding which activity is to be expedited first, always chose the least costly. Hence, Activity 2 is selected to be expedited by one day at an average hourly rate of 5.83 units. The revised duration and cost schedule, and resultant Gantt chart to expedite Activity 2 by one day is shown in Figure 8.13.

Act.	Dur.	Cost Units	Start Date	Finish Date	TF	01Jun	01Jun	03Jun
1*	0day	0	08.00 01Jun09	08.00 01Jun09	0	◆		
2*	2day	140	08.00 01Jun09	17.00 02Jun09	0	/////////	/////////	
3	4 hrs	20	08.00 01Jun09	12.00 01Jun09	12h	‖‖‖≣		
4	1 hrs	5	13.00 01Jun09	14.00 01Jun09	11h	‖≣		
5*	1day	80	08.00 03Jun09	17.00 03Jun09	0			///////
	Total	245		Daily Cash Out:		95	70	80
				Cumulative Cash Out:		65	105	245

* Critical Activities.

Critical Activities ///// Non-Critical Activities ‖‖‖‖‖‖ Total Float ≣≣≣

Note: The project completion time has been expedited by 1 day, but the cost has increased from 225 units to 245 units. Furthermore, the total float time available for Activities 3 and 4 has been reduced by 8 hours.

Figure 8.13 Revised Gantt chart for time schedule

The project may be fully expedited within the allowable limits. For instance, Activity 2 may be completed in one day at a cost of 170 units and Activity 5 may be expedited by half a day at a cost of 90 units. The full project expedited schedule shown in Figure 8.14 also illustrates the direct time–cost graph for the full project.

Act.	Dur.	Cost Units	Start Date	Finish Date	TF	01Jun	02Jun	03Jun
1*	0day	0	08.00 01Jun09	08.00 01Jun09	0	◆		
2*	8 hrs	170	08.00 01Jun09	17.00 01Jun09	0	▨		
3	4 hrs	20	08.00 01Jun09	12.00 01Jun09	4h	▥		
4	1 hrs	5	13.00 01Jun09	14.00 01Jun09	3h	▥		
5*	4 hrs	90	08.00 03Jun09	12.00 02Jun09	0		▨	
	Total	285				Direct Cost	195	90
						Cumulative Direct Cost	195	285

* Critical Activities.

Critical Activities ▨ Non-Critical Activities ▥ Total Float ▤

Note: The full project expedited schedule is reduced by 2.5 days at an increase in direct cost from 225 to 285 units.

Direct Time–Cost Graph Data

Project Effort	Project Duration	Cost Units
37 Hrs	32 Hrs	225
29 Hrs	24 Hrs	245
25 Hrs	20 Hrs	255
21 Hrs	16 Hrs	275
17 Hrs	12 Hrs	285

Direct Time–Cost Graph

Figure 8.14 Full project expedited Gantt chart for time schedule

The above simple example provides the basic principles in scheduling activities in a project. Note that if any activity is delayed by an amount that is greater than its free float (if any) this delay will interfere with the start of subsequent activities in the project network but may not delay the total project. However, if the delay of the activities is greater than the total float available, the project will be delayed. Therefore, total float may be viewed as a safety margin that may be utilized to offset unforeseen delays or deliberate delays in activities along the non-critical paths in the project network.

Moreover, as critical activities are expedited, the total float will decrease and the non-critical activities will approach being critical. Moreover, if critical activities are further expedited, a situation may occur where all available total float is utilized and therefore all the project activities will become critical. Remember that when expediting activities, always start with the least costly ones, and if further expediting is warranted then select the next costly activity and so on, until the expedited least time solution is finally achieved.

Each expedited stage provides the coordinates for the optimal solution and permits the project manager the possibility to plot the cost–time graph of the optimal project direct costs against the project duration. In addition, by plotting the indirect cost along with the direct cost and adding these costs together will produce the optimum overall economic project solution. Figure 8.15 assumes that the indirect costs are linear at 2.75 units per hour, and shows the optimum solution as being of 20 hours project duration (with a project time effort of 25 hours) at a total cost of 310 units.

Total Project time-cost graph data (direct & indirect costs are considered).

Project Time Effort	Direct Cost (Units)	Indirect Cost (Units)	Total Cost (Units)
4 days 5 hrs (37 Hrs)	225	32hrs x 2.75=88	313
3 days 5 hrs (29 Hrs)	245	24hrs x 2.75=66	311
3 days 1 hrs (25 Hrs)	**255**	**20hrs x 2.75=55**	**310**
2 days 5 hrs (21 Hrs)	275	16hrs x 2.75=44	319
2 days 1 hr (17 Hrs)	285	12hrs x 2.75=33	318

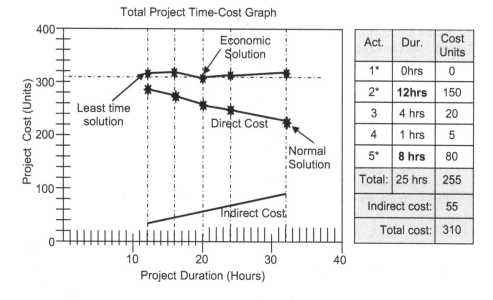

Total Project Time-Cost Graph

Act.	Dur.	Cost Units
1*	0hrs	0
2*	**12hrs**	150
3	4 hrs	20
4	1 hrs	5
5*	**8 hrs**	80
Total:	25 hrs	255
Indirect cost:		55
Total cost:		310

Figure 8.15 Optimum overall economic project solution

The Gantt chart in the scheduling process enables the project manager to see at a glance the critical activities that must be given special attention and not be delayed, if the project is to finish on time. It also shows how much delay may be tolerated in other activities. Knowledge of the available float enables the project manager to shift activities within the available float to help smooth out the application of resources (labour, equipment, and so on). This process is referred to as resource scheduling and levelling. The above example considered time and cost. In the example, resources, such as unskilled persons and skilled painter were considered only in terms of cost. The solution would be acceptable to the project manager only if there are no restrictions on resource availability. However, when resource constraints are applicable, resource scheduling and levelling becomes essential. Now we shall consider the application of resources for resource scheduling and levelling purposes.

In resource scheduling and levelling, three primary factors must be taken into consideration; the priority for the resources to be utilized, activity type and total float available to the activities. Projects may use many resources, such as human resources, equipment, and so on. However, human resources and equipment may also vary. For instance, skilled persons may be scarcer than unskilled ones; one class of skilled workers may be scarcer than another. A specialized type of equipment may be scarcer than a common type. Therefore, it is important for the project manager to prioritize the resources in terms of scarcity or specialization and schedule them in order of priority.

A further consideration in the resource scheduling and levelling process is the activity type. Some activities may be continuous, therefore once started they cannot be interrupted. For example, pouring concrete in a foundation may be a continuous activity. Once the concrete ready mix is delivered it must be poured and cannot be interrupted. However, other activities may be intermittent, that is, they may proceed progressively in a piecemeal fashion, for example, laying ceramic tiles. Such an activity may be commenced and interrupted until the resources (skilled worker and/or material) are available. Furthermore, total float provides the project manager with a certain amount of flexibility in delaying non-critical activities. Therefore, resources may be allocated to the critical activities, thus delaying the non-critical ones within the total float tolerance limits.

Example of resource scheduling and levelling – painting a room

Consider the previous example regarding the painting project. However, the project has been expanded to include two similar painting jobs as shown in Figure 8.16. For illustration purposes Project "A" and Project "B" are kept as separate projects however the resources assigned to the project manager may be shared. Hence, this simple example is illustrating a multi-project environment where a pool of resources must be optimally shared.

Assume that the human resources allocated to the project manager are restricted to two unskilled workers and one skilled painter. Therefore, the human resources are critical to the project since the material, namely the paint, may be simply purchased and is available on demand. The project manager must find the most feasible solution for scheduling and levelling the resources, giving the skilled painter priority in the resource levelling process. Furthermore, the estimated durations and costs for the activities are as defined previously. A summary of the estimated durations and costs are as shown below:

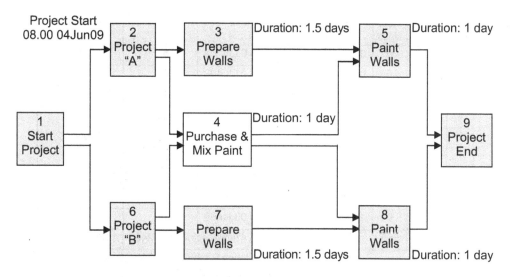

Note: (1) Allow one activity for purchasing and mixing paint at a duration of 1 day.
(2) Activities 1, 2, 6, and 9 have zero duration.

Figure 8.16 Painting project

1. Activity 3 and Activity 7 (Prepare Walls) may be carried out by one of the following methods:
   a) Working the normal duration of 3 days at 8 hours per day.
      Direct cost = 120 units.
   b) Completing the activities in 2 days by working 4 hours overtime per day.
      Direct cost = 140 units.
   c) Completing the activities in 1.5 days by having 2 persons working on the task and paying them a bonus of 15 units each.
      Direct cost = 150 units.
   d) Complete the activities in 1 day by having 2 persons at 8 hours per day and working 6 hours overtime per day per person due to labour inefficiency for having 2 persons in the same room simultaneously.
      Direct cost = 170 units.
2. Activity 5 and 8 (Paint Walls) may be carried out by one of the following methods:
   a) Working the normal duration of 1 day at 8 hours per day with one person.
      Direct cost = 80 units.
   b) Complete activity in 4 hours by having two persons. However, pay a bonus of 5 units each person for having them working in the same room simultaneously.
      Direct cost = 90 units.

The objective in resource levelling is to ensure that the available resources are utilized in a continuous manner, thus eliminating as much as possible peaks and troughs in resources usage. Figure 8.17 provides the time, cost and resource schedule as depicted by the project network at Figure 8.16 without resource levelling.

Act.	Dur.	Cost Units	Start Date	Finish Date	TF	01Jun	02Jun	03Jun
1*	0	0	08.00 01Jun09	08.00 01Jun09	0	◆		
2*	0	0	08.00 01Jun09	08.00 01Jun09	0	◆		
3	12 hrs	150	08.00 01Jun09	12.00 02Jun09	0	▨▨▨		
4	8 hrs	40	08.00 01Jun09	17.00 01Jun09	4hrs	▥▥▤		
5*	8 hrs	80	12.00 02Jun09	12.00 03Jun09	0		▨▨	
6*	0	0	08.00 01Jun09	08.00 01Jun09	0	◆		
7*	12 hrs	150	08.00 01Jun09	12.00 02Jun09	0	▨▨▨		
8*	8 hrs	80	12.00 02Jun09	12.00 03Jun09	0		▨▨	
9*	0	0	12.00 03Jun09	12.00 03Jun09	0			◆

	Total	**500**			

	01Jun	02Jun	03Jun
Daily Cash Out:	240	180	80
Cumulative Cash Out:	240	420	500
No. Unskilled Persons:	5	4	0
No. Skilled Persons:	0	2	2

* Critical Activities.

Only direct labour costs are shown.

Critical Activities ▨▨▨ Non-Critical Activities ▥▥▥ Total Float ▤▤▤

Resource Utilization without Resource Levelling

Unskilled Persons Utilization				
Resource Units	01 June	02 June	03 June	04 June
Usage:	5	4	0	0
Constraint:	2	2	2	2
Variance:	3	2	-2	-2

Skilled Persons Utilization				
01 June	02 June	03 June	04 June
0	2	2	0
1	1	1	1
-1	1	1	-1

Resource Usage ■   Resource Constraint ▨▨

Figure 8.17 Human resource utilization schedule with no resource levelling

When examining the project costs, it will be noted that the direct labour is 500 units. However, without resource levelling the usage of both skilled and unskilled persons is over the constraint established by management. Therefore, the project manager must reschedule the project within the imposed human resource constraints giving the skilled persons priority in the smoothing process. The project manager must also examine the total float available to see whether this will enable the smooth levelling of the resources

Act.	Activity Description	Cost Units	Dur.	TF	01Jun	02Jun	03Jun	04Jun
1*	Start Project	0	0	0				
2*	Project "A"	0	0	0				
3*	Prepare walls (Proj. "A")	150	12 hrs	0				
4	Purchase and mix paint	40	8 hrs	4hrs				
5*	Paint walls (Proj. "A")	80	8 hrs	0				
6*	Project "B"	0	0	0				
7*	Prepare walls (Proj. "B")	150	12 hrs	0				
8*	Paint walls (Proj. "B")	80	8 hrs	0				
9*	Project End	0	0	0				

Total Cost Units:	500	Direct Cost	140	190	130	40
		Indirect Cost	22	22	22	11
		Total Cost	162	212	152	51
		Cumulative Cash Out	162	374	526	577
		Unskilled Persons	2	2 & 1	1	0
		Skilled Persons	0	1	1	1

* Critical Activities.

Both direct labour and indirect costs are shown.

Critical Activities   ▨

Non Critical Activities   ⬚

Total Float   ▤

Resource Utilization with Resource Levelling

	Unskilled Persons Utilization			
Resource Units	01 June	02 June	03 June	04 June
2				Resource Limit
1.5				
1				
.5				

Usage:	2	2	2	1	1	0	0	0
Constraint:	2	2	2	2	2	2	2	2
Variance:	0	0	0	-1	-1	-2	-2	-2

	Skilled Persons Utilization			
	01 June	02 June	03 June	04 June
		Resource Limit		

0	0	0	1	1	1	1	0
1	1	1	1	1	1	1	1
-1	-1	-1	0	0	0	0	-1

Resource Usage ▮   Resource Constraint ▨

Figure 8.18 Human resource utilization schedule with resource levelling

without increasing costs by prolonging the project. Note that the lengthening of the project time will not affect the direct labour component (or material usage) but the indirect costs will increase linearly at 2.75 units per hour, thus increasing the total project cost.

Moreover, the solution at Figure 8.17 is based on the optimum overall economic project solution at Figure 8.15. Therefore, most of the total float available has already been consumed by expediting the activities related to "Prepare Walls". The solution at Figure 8.17 shows that only Activity 4, "Purchase and Mix Paint" is not on the critical path with a total float of four hours. Hence, the project manager has no other option but possibly to utilize this total float and prolong the project duration at an extra cost.

Figure 8.18 illustrates that by extending the project with one additional day, the resources are levelled within the established management resource constraints, giving the skilled persons (painters) priority.

The total project cost due to the indirect cost element has increased from 555 (500 direct cost plus 20 indirect hours at 2.75 units per hour) to 577 units, an increase of 22 units (8 hours times 2.75 units per hour). However, this extra cost is mitigated because one unskilled person day may be utilized on another project. Also note that the float time available for Activity 4 cannot be utilized for decreasing the indirect cost element. A possible way to utilize the float time would be to commence Activities 5 and 8 (paint walls) half a day earlier without waiting for Activities 3 and 7 (prepare walls) to be fully completed. However, this utilization would depend on the physical and technological constraints. In other words, the physical space available where these activities are being conducted and whether the dust and rubble from preparing the walls would impede the paint finish quality.

In summary, time, cost and resource scheduling and levelling consist of the following process:

1. Prepare the project network diagram (steps 1 to 7);
2. Prepare the duration and cost estimating data for those activities that utilize resources, particularly those that have a variable cost characteristic, such as human resources and equipment (step 8);
3. Using project management computer software to:
   a) Compute the time and cost schedule utilizing the project network diagram and the estimates of duration and cost using the normal duration as the initial base input;
   b) Identify the activities on the critical path;
   c) Note the non-critical activities and their respective float time availability;
   d) Find the optimum overall economic project solution in terms of time and cost. This is an iterative process and is calculated by expediting an activity at a time, starting from the least costly ones and using the relevant activity duration and cost estimates.
4. Identify the resource utilization constraints and resource levelling priorities.
5. Identify the continuous and intermittent activities, that is, those activities that cannot be interrupted and those that can be conducted in a piecemeal manner.
6. Using project management computer software:
   a) Compute the resource schedule for the optimum overall economic project solution;
   b) If the resources utilized are within the management constraints then the solution would be acceptable. However, try to smooth (level) the application of the resources within the computed time and cost schedule;

c) If the resources are not within the management constraints then smooth (level) the application of the resources first within the calculated time and cost schedule, followed by the possible minimum extension of the project duration until an acceptable solution is obtained. Note that the resource levelling process is an iterative process and requires patience and perseverance on the part of the project manager.

Once a project solution that conforms within the various constraints is found then this solution is ready for implementation. At the implementation stage the project must be tightly controlled so that it remains within the confines of the accepted project solution.

Controlling a Project

Once a project enters the implementation stage it moves in a path and at a rate of impetus that may be completely independent of the way it was predicted. The project manager must recognize that there is an important distinction between the planning and implementation phases. The planning phase is theoretical, whereas the implementation phase is reality. However, to minimize the gap between theory and reality, the project manager must establish within the plan a means of monitoring and influencing the project's progress. There are two fundamental factors that aid the project manager to control a project, namely:

1. Defining milestones that are clear and have unambiguous deliverables within the defined target dates;
2. Establishing exceptional and robust channels of communication.

For the project manager, milestones are an essential means to monitor progress. In addition, milestones provide the entire project team with short-term goals and deliverables that are tangible in the immediate time span rather than the vague holistic completion of the whole project. Hence, milestones sustain project thrust and stimulate effort by allowing the project team to ascertain the progress being made and to register incremental successes throughout the duration of the project, rather than merely at project completion. The best means of defining milestones is by examining the work breakdown structure and the project network to identify short-term deliverables that are specific and attainable within the time, cost and resources allocated to them. However, milestones must be effectively communicated so that the project team see how these milestones fit holistically into the project structure.

Communication is a critical feature in project control because it allows the project manager to monitor progress, obtain timely warning of delay, promote collaboration and facilitate motivation through the participation of project team members. The project manger should utilize an information system that provides continuous and frequent reports giving supporting evidence of (or lack of) progress. The project manager must insist that the project team monitors its own progress with specific, real and measurable achievements and failures that are formally reported.

ESSENTIALS OF PROJECT CONTROL

The literature indicates that many projects in different types of industries have the following characteristics:

- A wide variety of tasks and processes that require different techniques, equipment, human resource skills and competencies;
- Often the project team is physically working away from their organization's premises at work sites that are temporary and in some cases remote;
- The project management team rarely has full control of finance, HR and other policies, and can never be self-sufficient;
- Human resources on projects are normally of two classes, the relatively permanent members and transitory members. This may be a source of concern related to project commitment.

Therefore, organizations are to have the necessary procedures in place to ensure the proper control of their projects in this varied and sometimes complex environment. Project planning aids management to:

- Select the most economical method of conducting the project;
- Establish the various resource levels required;
- Secure human resources and financial needs;
- Procure materials, including their delivery;
- Determine the necessary management staff levels;
- Employ qualified subcontractors at the appropriate time;
- Carry out the project within the estimated cost constraints.

However, rarely do paper plans work continually in practice. The primary purpose of project control is to review the current methods and processes, and forecast the future requirements of the project so that it may be successfully completed within the constraints established by management. Expediting all tasks within a project that fall behind schedule is not the solution. Critical path methods provide the project manager with the necessary tools to achieve the appropriate project control. These tools allow project managers to predict concerns in adequate time to decide on rational project modifications for the concerns encountered.

Basically, project control with CPM (Critical Path Method) is achieved by the regular periodic appraisal of the tasks completed to date, together with the evaluation of the project network. As time on the project moves forward, the estimated activity durations and resources of the project network are updated, with actual time and resource utilization for the activities completed and being carried out at the time of the project review. Whenever the activity durations are revised, the project network is evaluated to determine whether the critical path and the project duration and cost have been affected. Hence, a report related to the WBS (Work Breakdown Structure) will reveal those project deliverables that have been completed or the extent of their completion. Furthermore, a report regarding the CBS (Cost Breakdown Structure) will disclose the various costs and variance by cost category for the deliverables and those deliverables being executed.

The project evaluation will reveal whether the project is on or behind the planned time and cost. If the project is delayed, the project network may:

1. Be amended and the relevant future activities expedited to restore the position at an increase in costs; or
2. Accept the delayed completion time rather than increasing costs to recover the position.

However, this decision will depend on the cost of expediting the activities behind schedule versus the loss of reputation and/or cost of penalties for late deliverables. However, delayed non-critical activities may be permitted to utilize the available float without any effect on project duration (but the cost of conducting these activities may be affected). Should the delay of non-critical activities exceed the float time available, a new critical path will result. Hence, the uncompleted project network segment must be reviewed so that the appropriate decisions and actions are undertaken.

Whatever the project evaluation result and consequences, CPM allows the project manager to analyse time, cost and resource usage, and respond in a timely manner. The investment made at the planning phase will prove very beneficial at critical stages of the project. For instance, the duration and cost estimating data for activities calculated at the planning stage enables the project manager to make a prompt assessment of the original estimates and will provide information for the project manager to employ a different execution method (if necessary) to recover lost time.

The project evaluation and the resultant decisions made by management will enable a new revised network to be computed, including the associated time, cost and resource schedules and Gantt charts. Hence, a new plan is available to the project manager for the uncompleted segment of the project. This process is a continuous one and is adhered to until the project is completed.

OTHER PREREQUISITES OF PROJECT CONTROL

The literature indicates that the common reasons for project delays are the following:

- Faulty duration and cost estimating data for activities and resource usage;
- Unavailability of the identified resources, particularly specialized human resources, equipment and materials;
- Unanticipated project conditions, such as technical and other complexities, site hazards, weather conditions, discovery of historical artefacts and a host of other issues;
- Insolvency of contractors and suppliers;
- Unexpected delays in the delivery of materials, equipment and other items;
- Industrial and other HR disputes (particularly with trade unions);
- Unanticipated project site conditions;
- Additional or deductions in works quantities and specifications.

The decisive factor in undertaking a project network revision is the magnitude of the project delay. For minor delays, such as a few days or delays that can be tolerated, the computation of the time schedule may be recalculated and an appropriate notation is made to the network. However, extensive delays that force the project manager to amend the sequence of tasks or the introduction of new tasks to adjust for the delay will require a full project network revision so that a new project plan may be computed. The frequency of the project review depends on a number of factors, such as:

- The overall duration and cost of the project or project phase and/or its rate of momentum;
- The degree of project risk and uncertainty;
- The project size and complexity;
- The assortment of difficulties being encountered.

Obviously, a project that has an overall duration of only a few weeks will require close scrutiny and may require a daily review; with more lengthy projects, a weekly or fortnightly review may be adequate. Again, the project review may not be based on a specific regular frequency, but on the occurrence of specific control issues, such as milestones. A full project evaluation need not be conducted every time that a review is undertaken, but restricted to assessing the critical or near critical activities. However, a full review is necessary at times to ensure that the non-critical activities do not fall behind time to such an extent that they become critical.

Note that a full project review will necessitate a substantial amount of costly effort. Deciding when to undertake a full review depends on the experience of the project manager and above all the circumstances. An easy and practical method to decide when to undertake a full review is to compare the progress expenditure with the scheduled rate of expenditure:

- If the critical activities are on time or ahead of schedule, but the expenditure rate is behind schedule, then it is likely that the non-critical activities are falling behind schedule;
- If the critical activities are on or ahead of schedule on both the time and cost elements, then it is likely that no significant slippage has occurred, unless the critical path activities have been maintained by the utilization of resources from the non-critical tasks;
- If the critical activities are only just on or behind schedule but the actual expenditure rate is higher than scheduled, then this could mean that either the non-critical activities are being given priority over critical activities or the cost of conducting critical activities was underestimated. In this case, a detailed cost analysis of each activity will be necessary to reveal the cause.

On large projects, therefore, it is best to appraise the critical and near-critical activities at frequent short-term periods (say weekly) as well as examining the actual expenditure rate. If this evaluation indicates a concern (falling behind schedule) then a complete activity review is conducted. The project control procedures described have provided the reader with some of the basic principles for controlling a project. However, these procedures must be supported by an information flow and reporting process, the subject of which will be covered in Part III: "Project Informational Support Factors".

CREATING A LEARNING ORGANIZATION

In a project management environment the creation of a learning organization is facilitated by conducting regular project reviews, particularly the post-project review, and documenting the findings. A post-project review is an evaluation of the project at the completion phase, where the project manager determines the time, cost and resource usage variances, and more importantly what went right and wrong with the project. The experience gained from implementing a project should not be lost.

The organization should have the proper mechanisms for capturing lessons learnt by documenting the good and bad things that occurred in the management of the project and recording all comments and recommendations for improvements. This will improve the management process in future projects. Project reviews must take into account any key performance indicators that were defined at the project definition stage.

This project learning experience must be fostered among the contractors by motivating them to improve the deliverables assigned to them. Such a process facilitates a commitment to long-term relationships amongst the project teams, with the primary objective of having continuous improvement through learning from project experience. The project manager in conjunction with the project team members should explain the lessons learnt and what would be done differently the next time round. These lessons are presented at the post-project review meeting in clear and precise terms.

Conclusion

The project planning and control aspect deals with the "what", "how", "by whom" and "when" the project activities are to be undertaken. A proper planning and control mechanism allows those involved in the project to fully understand what is required. Note that planning and scheduling are not synonymous. Planning specifically considers the "what", "how" and "by whom" aspects of the project, whereas scheduling considers the "when" aspect. Planning is therefore the process of choosing the method and order of work from among various methods and possible sequences, while scheduling is the calculation of the timing for the selected sequences and provides the completion of time.

INFORMATION COMMUNICATIONS TECHNOLOGY (ICT)

The information age, particularly through the internet, allows for two-way information dissemination and ensures that physical distance no longer hinders close integration and interaction between those involved in a project. In addition, information quality is improved because ICT facilitates a comprehensive data collection process and the timely dissemination of information.

Planning, to a large extent, is a data intelligence exercise that integrates the interactions of different data sources be they human or electronic. At the same time, ICT application tools using CPM or PERT allow the scheduling function to be achieved quickly and accurately. However, CPM and PERT are not tools for gathering and assessing intelligence, they both make use of the information gathered in the planning stage and calculate a schedule. CPM and PERT tools do not question the validity of the data; these systems assume that the planner has addressed the input validity issues.

Furthermore, ICT allows every relevant stakeholder to access a common work breakdown structure and project schedule, and permits the linkage of the supply value chains of material suppliers, contractors, subcontractors, financial institutions and the client with the entity undertaking the project, so that payments, orders and other relevant business transactions are conducted in a highly secure manner instantly.

PROJECT PLANNING AND SCHEDULING

Project planning and scheduling consists of a number of steps that should be conducted with great care. These steps consist of the following:

- Step 1: Review Project Scope. This is to ensure that everyone concerned with the project has the same understanding of the project. The result from this review should be a written formal document defining what is required (end deliverables) and by when;
- Step 2: Identify Project Components. This consists of a breakdown of the general project deliverables, normally referred to as the decomposition process. This step has the aim of subdividing the project deliverables into smaller, more manageable parts;
- Step 3: Prepare Work Breakdown Structure (WBS). The WBS is a schematic diagram of the project components identified in Step 2;
- Step 4: Determine the Activities for Each Project Component. This step requires the project team to decide how each individual project work component is to be achieved. This will lead to a further breakdown of the work components into specific tasks;
- Step 5: Determine the Activity Constraints. This step consists of reviewing the activities to determine the management, resource, technological and physical constraints;
- Step 6: Determine the Relationship between Activities. This step consists of closely examining all the activities to decide the proper sequence of conducting the activities;
- Step 7: Prepare the Project Network Diagram. The aim of the project team at this stage is to establish an optimal method of conducting the project. This optimal method is denoted by a network diagram taking into consideration the information from the previous steps, particularly, Steps 4, 5 and 6;
- Step 8: Prepare duration and cost estimating data for each activity;
- Step 9: Prepare the Cost Breakdown Structure (CBS). The CBS is utilized for monitoring activity costs by the cost elements. Costs are categorized under two major classes, direct costs, such as material, labour and equipment; and indirect costs, such as administration charges and general project costs like electricity and water charges. However, the accounting department will normally signify the direct and indirect cost elements;
- Step 10: Schedule Activities for Time, Cost and Resources. This step is concerned with determining the optimum solution for the execution of a project as a whole. The optimum project solution requires a detailed assessment of concurrent, interrelated and overlapping activities, and the individual activity duration and cost data.

The meticulous undertaking of the above ten steps will ensure that the project is well thought out and that all project stakeholders, particularly the project team, have a common and comprehensive understanding of the entire project.

PROJECT CONTROL

There is an important distinction between the planning and implementation phases of a project. The planning phase is theoretical, whereas the implementation phase is reality. To minimize the gap between theory and reality, the project manager must establish a means of monitoring and influencing the project's progress. This may be facilitated by identifying milestones that are clear and having unambiguous deliverables with defined target dates, and establishing exceptional and robust channels of communication.

The CPM provides the basic tools to achieve the appropriate level of control by allowing project managers to predict concerns in ample time and thus decide on rational project modifications for the concerns encountered. Basically, project control with CPM is achieved by regular periodic appraisal of tasks completed to date, together with the evaluation of the project network. Project evaluation will reveal whether the project is on or behind time. This prompts the project manager to take proper action to maintain or improve project execution performance.

The resultant decisions will enable a new revised network to be computed, hence, a new plan is available to the project manager for the uncompleted project segment. This evaluation process is a continuous one and is sustained until the project is completed. On large projects it is best to appraise the critical and near-critical activities at a frequent short-term periods as well as examining the expenditure rate. If this evaluation indicates a concern (falling behind schedule) then a complete activity review is conducted.

THE LEARNING ORGANIZATION

The experience gained from a project should not be lost. The organization should have the proper mechanisms for capturing lessons learnt through the documentation of the good and bad things in the management of the project and recording all comments and recommendations for improvements, in order to improve the management process in future projects.

References

Antill, J.M. and Woodhead, R.W. 1982. *Critical Path Methods in Construction Practice*. New York: John Wiley & Sons Inc.

Kliem, R.L. and Doughty, R. 1987. How to develop the project management manual. *Journal of Systems Management*, 38(3), 17–22.

Kuklan, H. 1993. Effective project management: An expanded network approach. *Journal of Systems Management*, 44(3), 12–16.

Herroelen, W. 2005. Project scheduling: Theory and practice. *Production and Operations Management*, 14(4), 413–32.

Schei, K.G. 1990. Small project management. *Civil Engineering*, 60(1), 42–4.

Project Informational Support Factors

The chapters in Part III will examine in detail the project informational support factors that consist of the following project success–failure dimensions:

- Information flow and knowledge management;
- Project risk management;
- Project competency development.

The project informational support factors are mainly applicable for project oriented organizations, in other words, a multi-project environment. Together with a standard project management methodology, these factors aim for repeatable project management success. Furthermore, these factors may be viewed as an extension of the project hygiene support factors. As one may recall, the project hygiene support factors have the objective of ensuring project management success of a specific project by introducing best project management practice.

The project informational support factors have the objective of ensuring that an organization is consistently achieving project management success on all its projects. The emphasis of these factors is reliability, in other words, the achievement of project management success time after time, without fail. This is achieved by having the proper information flow processes in place and maintaining an accurate data warehouse of current and previously undertaken projects. This accumulated project information and knowledge will aid the organization to resolve project concerns promptly, assess project risk and appraise the project related competencies possessed by the organization.

9 *Information Flow and Knowledge Management*

Not having the information you need when you need it leaves you wanting. Not knowing where to look for that information leaves you powerless. In a society where information is king, none of us can afford that.

Lois Horowitz, author

In Chapter 8, "Project Planning and Control", it was shown that there are two fundamental elements that aid the project manager to control a project, namely defining clear and unambiguous milestones, and having exceptional and robust channels of communication. However, these by themselves are not enough. Management must explicitly identify the critical information that is to be communicated for monitoring the project and have the right processes in place to facilitate the communication and dissemination of information to the relevant people.

Deciding what information is required and the processes needed to communicate this information depends on the organizational setting. For instance, in organizations where projects are carried out by individuals in isolation, the processes and data sets will most likely be a simple matter and restricted to a few people. However, in project oriented organizations, such as in building and construction, jobbing works and software development industries, the processes that determine the information flow can be quite intricate. In addition, the data that is received, processed and disseminated may have complex database structures and be voluminous.

Project managers have six types of resources at their disposal to carry out the projects under their responsibility. These are money, people, materials, equipment, energy and information. The focus of this chapter is information and the processes needed to support the information flow. Information is utilized for three major purposes:

1. Discussion, for example, project team dialogue about whether a particular task is to precede, succeed or be conducted concurrently with another task;
2. Decisions, for example, deciding whether to work overtime to expedite a particular activity;
3. Calculating or measuring, for instance, determining the amount of time and material an activity has consumed over a specified period.

An organization's value chain becomes an important notion when examining information and information flow, in a project-oriented environment. One should note that when referring to an organization's value chain, we are in reality referring to two separate and concurrent but complementary value chains. One portrays the physical value chain and the other depicts the informational value chain. Hence, the physical value chain is the transformation of tangible resources, such as materials and labour, to a finished product or service; while the informational value chain consists of the information and knowledge necessary to transform tangible resources to a finished product or service. Both value chains are necessary, each supporting the other and ultimately they shape the basis of the organization's business survival.

The informational value chain in this context is viewed to be similar to the knowledge hierarchy as defined by Nissen (2000). This researcher views the knowledge hierarchy as the traditional concept of knowledge transformations, where data is transformed into information and information is transformed into knowledge.

Processes that Control Project Information Flow

For information to be of value in the execution of a project it must meet three basic criteria. It must be:

1. Accurate and complete;
2. Timely. Having the right information delivered too late can be as useless as having no information at all;
3. Meaningful. Information must be adequate and relevant to the particular person that requires it.

Having the proper processes in place will help the organization to have accurate, timely and meaningful information. However, the processes must be simple with the information flow being comprehensive to ensure that every relevant individual receives the information needed for making specific decisions related to their particular job function. Figure 9.1 illustrates the typical processes that control project information flow in a project oriented organizational environment.

Figure 9.1 shows some basic principles that may be applicable to many project organizational settings. The information may be classified into three types: input information, generated information and output information.

Input information

Input information is the raw elementary data that is provided by individuals. For instance, employees working in the Planning Division would provide the input details regarding the various activities and their respective time and resource utilization estimates. The employees working on project execution would provide the input details regarding the actual time they consume on the specific activities, while the project manager or project leader would provide the input details regarding the equipment utilized to carry out the activities and the materials consumed.

Generated information

Generated information refers to information that is provided automatically by the application system. For example, the duration and cost estimating input data for activities provided by the Planning Division employees would be utilized by the critical path

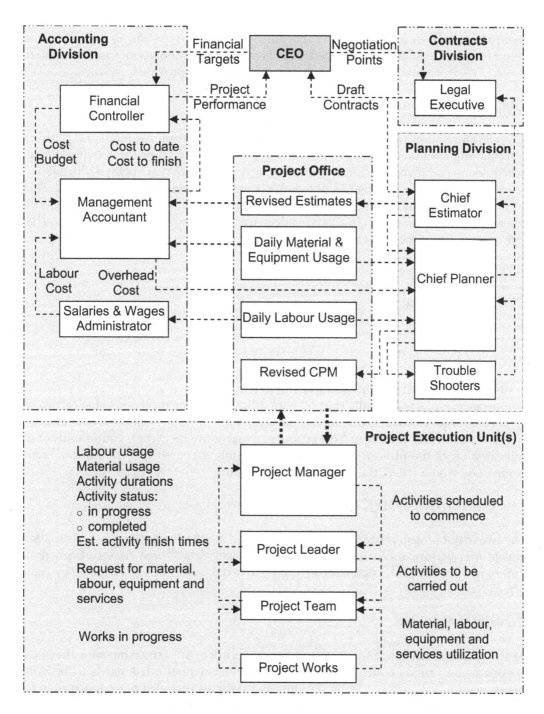

Figure 9.1   Processes controlling project information flow

method application to calculate the scheduled activity start and finish dates, and their respective total float duration that would indicate whether the activities are critical to the project. This information is computed from the input data provided.

Output information

Output information refers to the reports that are produced from the input and generated information. For example, the project manager may want to know the activities that are scheduled to commence within five working days or those that are behind schedule.

Figure 9.1 depicts an organization with six major information flow divisions. These organizational information flow divisions are linked, with each division requiring information from the others in a varying degree of detail and for various purposes. These information flow divisions consist of:

1. Chief Executive's Office;
2. Contracts Division;
3. Accounting Division;
4. Planning Division;
5. Project Office;
6. Project Execution Unit(s).

It should be noted that information flow in projects tends to move in a cyclical pattern. For instance, projects normally start off with estimates, as the project is being carried out actual data is collected, and this actual data is inputted into the project network and used to revise the various estimates. This estimate–actual–estimate cycle is continuous for the full duration of the project, until the project is fully executed and the information at completion would reflect the actual project position.

CHIEF EXECUTIVE'S OFFICE (CEO)

The two major project related links at the CEO level are the project contract negotiations and project performance monitoring. These linkages entail three classes of functional duties, namely the CEO, Legal Executive and Financial Controller as illustrated by Figure 9.2.

Contract definition

At the project award stage the CEO and Legal Executive, in partnership with the client, negotiate the various contract clauses. The contract defines what needs to be done, hence providing a common understanding as to what is included or excluded from the project. It also specifies the responsibilities of the project executor and the client. The contract ensures that all the works are identified and defined by itemizing all the project deliverables. The contract will normally have the project scope as an attached annex.

A poorly-defined contract will burden a project throughout its life cycle. Hence, it is in the interest of both the contractor and client to have a contract that is unambiguous and does not lead to future conflicts. The primary objective is to have a successfully completed project where all parties concerned are satisfied with the project outcome.

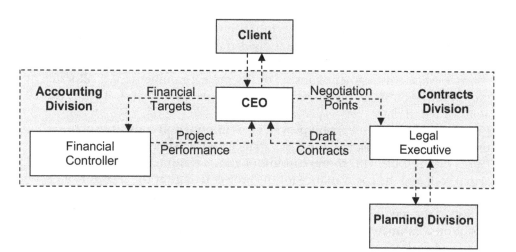

Figure 9.2   Legal–CEO–Accounting information flow link

Litigation during project implementation is a recipe for project failure. Moreover, the contract has a direct link to the project scope definition, which in turn is integrated to the project activity identification and the eventual project plan, thus linking this process to the Planning Division.

Project performance

Project performance monitoring is a continuous process and concludes when the project is fully completed. However, it is important to note that the contract has a direct relationship with project execution and completion. The contract normally defines the works to be delivered and the payment terms. Hence, the project performance monitoring stage has the objective of aiding management to determine and ensuring that the project realizes the profit margins calculated at the contract stage. As the project advances to completion, there is a convergence of anticipated and actual income that is generated by the project and the eventual profit made.

Project performance monitoring helps management to ensure that at worst, the estimated and actual profit variance is minimized and at best, attains a better profit margin by achieving lower actual costs than were originally estimated. The CEO initially provides the Financial Controller with the holistic financial targets for the organization so that these may be incorporated into the budgetary process. The Financial Controller on the other hand makes available the project performance details for every project being conducted to the CEO so that the overall organizational profitability may be determined and to ascertain whether the holistic financial targets are being achieved.

Figure 9.3 shows an example of a project performance report that the Financial Controller would prepare for the CEO's consideration for a specific accounting period. The accounting period may be weekly, monthly or quarterly, depending on the specific needs of management and the circumstances of the organization. Due to the page size restriction, the sample report shown at Figure 9.3 should be viewed as a template, as the actual column size, particularly for project title, in reality would be much wider than that shown. The project performance report is divided into seven major segments:

1. *Project Details.* This segment consists of the project number that is allocated at the project initiation stage, the project title and the percentage project effort carried out as at the report date.
2. *Project Period Cost.* This segment provides cost information consisting of the estimated project cost, actual cost and the cost variance for the report period.
3. *Project Cost To-Date.* This shows cost information regarding the project estimated and actual cost, and the cost variance for the project to-date at the report date.
4. *Project Cost To-Finish.* This segment provides the estimated cost to complete the project at the report date and the estimated forecast cost of the full project to finish. The project estimated forecast to-finish is equal to the actual cost to-date plus the estimated project cost to-finish at the report date.
5. *Project Status.* The project status segment provides two items of information, namely the project original cost estimate and the current project loss or gain. The project loss or gain figure is the difference between the original project estimate and the estimated project cost forecast to-finish.
6. *Project Contract Details.* The contract details segment has three items of information, namely the total value of the contract, payments received to-date and resultant project profit or loss to-date.
7. *Project Income on Completion.* This segment has also three items of information, forecast project income or loss, planned profit and the expected variance between the planned profit and the forecast project income or loss.

The project performance report provides the holistic financial position of the organization in general, and the respective projects being undertaken in particular. It should be noted that the degree of detailed provided to the CEO is at a project level and not on an activity basis.

CONTRACTS DIVISION

The Contracts Division has two major links, one with the CEO which has already been examined and the linkage with the Planning Division, particularly, the Chief Estimator. The focus of this section is with the latter process linkage as depicted by Figure 9.4.

The process linkage between the Contracts and Planning Divisions is mainly at the project contract phase. However, when the project requirements are modified during the execution phase, the project contract would also need to be amended. Hence, when the project contract is being defined or modified there is a continuous iterative process between the Contracts (Legal Executive) and Planning Divisions (Chief Estimator) to identify and define the project deliverables, including their respective delivery schedule, cost and profit margins. The project deliverables data would normally be included as an annex to the project contract that is signed between the CEO and the client.

Project Details			Period Cost			Cost To-Date			Cost To-Finish		Project Status		Contract	Contract To-Date		Income on Completion		
No.	Title	% Now Finished	Est.	Act.	Diff.	Est.	Act.	Diff.	Est.	Est. Forecast	Original Cost Est.	Loss Gain	Total Value	Payments Received	Profit Loss	Forecast	Planned Profit	Expected Difference
1	2	3	4	5	6	7	8	9	10	11	12	13	14	15	16	17	18	19
Total:																		

Project Details
Col. 01: Project number allocated at the project initiation stage.
Col. 02: Project title (short description to identify project).
Col. 03: Percentage project work carried out up to the report date.
Project Period Cost
Col. 04: Estimated project cost for report period.
Col. 05: Actual project cost for report period.
Col. 06: Project cost variance for report period.
Project Cost To-Date
Col. 07: Estimated project cost to-date for report period.
Col. 08: Actual project cost to-date for report period.
Col. 09: Project cost to-date variance for report period.

Project Cost To-Finish
Col. 10: Estimated project cost to-finish at report period.
Col. 11: Estimated project cost to-finish forecast = Col. 8 + Col. 10
Project Status
Col. 12: Original Estimated project cost.
Col. 13: Estimated Project Loss/Gain = Col. 12 - Col. 11
Project Contract Details
Col. 14: Contract value for total project.
Col. 15: Contract income to-date from project (payments received).
Col. 16: Contract profit/loss to-date = (Col. 3 X Col. 14) - Col. 15
Project Income on Completion
Col. 17: Final income forecast = Col. 14 - Col. 11
Col. 18: Planned Profit = Col. 14 - Col. 12
Col. 19: Expected Profit = Col. 18 - Col. 17

Figure 9.3 Project performance report

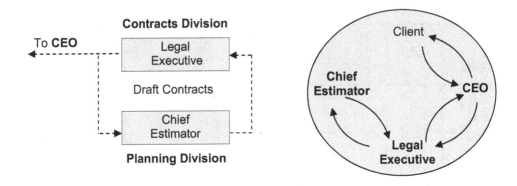

Figure 9.4   Contracts–Planning information flow link

PLANNING DIVISION

Apart from the link with the Contracts Division, the Planning Division has its own internal processes and is also linked in a significant way with the Projects Office as illustrated by Figure 9.5. As stated previously, the contract is drawn up in consultation with the Planning Division and is the basis for the project scope that is developed into a detailed project plan. The Planning Division has a number of functions, it provides:

- Overall project estimated costs and time durations;
- Determines the project network that identifies the activities and defines the sequence and relationships between the activities;
- Detailed activity time, cost and resource usage estimates;
- Calculates the original and subsequent revisions of the critical path, including the time and resource scheduling data;
- The overall revised project estimates.

The information flow within the Planning Division is mainly of two types. The planning employees (reporting to the Chief Planner) have the function of determining the project network and the estimating employees (reporting to the Chief Estimator) have the function of providing the detailed activity time, cost and resource usage estimates. All other processes within the Planning Division are derived from these two primary tasks. A sample of the project activity estimate details is shown in Figure 9.6.

The project activity estimate details are prepared for every activity in the project network. Collectively this information provides the full project estimate. Figure 9.6 illustrates that the activity estimate is based on four fundamental cost elements, namely overhead, labour, material and equipment costs; risk is addressed by having three scenarios, best, expected and worst. If a project activity has never been previously conducted and therefore there is high uncertainty, then the Project Evaluation Review Technique (PERT) formulae for the expected mean may be applied. Note that these estimates are used as the input data for the critical path method calculations normally carried out by the planning employees.

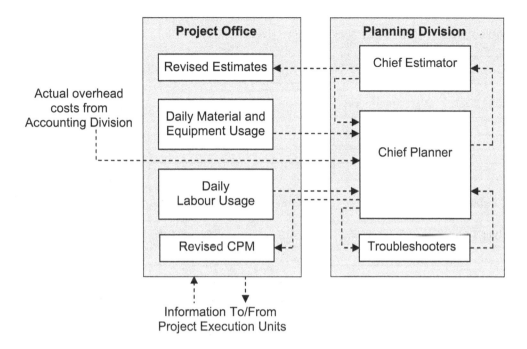

Figure 9.5 Planning Division – project office information flow link

Figure 9.7 provides the full project information broken down to the individual activity level. This report would be provided to the Project Office as the work schedule for the employees who are responsible for project execution. It should be noted that the information flow is mainly a two-way reoccurring process between the Planning Division and the Project Office (and vice .versa), except for the actual overhead costs that are conveyed directly to the Chief Planner by the Management Accountant. Also note that the information flowing out of the Planning Division is mainly estimates, while the information flowing into the Planning Division is actual data. However, as the project is being conducted the estimate data is being continually refined due to the recording of actual information until there is a convergence at the project completion stage. Obviously, the objective for management is to ensure that actual cost and time duration for the activities and the project as a whole do not exceed the estimate.

The focus of this section is the internal information flow within the Planning Division and the information flowing out of the Planning Division to the Project Office. Information flowing into the Planning Division will be addressed when discussing the Project office. The function of troubleshooting is an extension of the planning function in that the troubleshooters receive information from the Chief Planner about the critical activities that are in danger of delaying the project if they are not carried out in the allocated time duration. Their function is to expedite the activities by closely monitoring progress on a focused short-term basis and ensuring that all the necessary resources are made available when required for these activities. It should be noted that expediting activities should be the exception and not the norm. The troubleshooters would have an exception report with a similar format as depicted in Figure 9.7, but showing only the activities that are to be the focus (exceptions).

Project No.:	Activity No:	Description:		

Overhead Cost	Scenario:	Best	Expected	Worst

O/H Type	O/H Description	Best Cost	Expected Cost	Worst Cost	Remarks

Labour Cost		Best	Expected	Worst

Skill Type	Qty	Description	Best Hours	Best Cost	Expected Hours	Expected Cost	Worst Hours	Worst Cost	Remarks

Material Cost		Best	Expected	Worst

Type	Description	Unit	Best Qty	Best Cost	Expected Qty	Expected Cost	Worst Qty	Worst Cost	Remarks

Equipment Cost		Best	Expected	Worst

Type	Qty	Description	Best Hours	Best Cost	Expected Hours	Expected Cost	Worst Hours	Worst Cost	Remarks

Authorized Person:	Estimate Date: / /

Scenarios Regarding Estimates:

Best: Optimistic.   Expected: Most likely.   Worst: Pessimistic.

Note: In high risk situations an additional estimate computation may be calculated. This would be referred to as the *Expected Mean*. The *Expected Mean* is calculated by the simple formula: (Optimistic + 4 times Most Likely + Pessimistic) ÷ 6

Figure 9.6   Project activity estimate details

| Proj. No: | Title: | | % Complete: | Contract Value: | Payments To-date: | Cost To-date: |

Act. No.	Activity Details						Scheduled Dates		Earliest Dates		Latest Dates		Float	
	Title	Primary Responsibility	Est. Duration	Est. Cost	% Complete	Status	Start	Finished	Start	Finished	Start	Finished	Total	Free
1	2	3	4	5	6	7	8	9	10	11	12	13	14	15

Project Information:

Project No: Project number allocated to the project.

% Complete: Project work carried out at report date.

Payments To-date: Payments received project.

Activity Details:

Col. 01: Activity number.

Col. 02: Activity description.

Col. 03: Person/division responsible for activity.

Col. 04: Estimated activity duration.

Col. 05: Estimated activity cost.

Col. 06: Actual % activity completion.

Col. 07: Status (Critical or Non-Critical)

Activity Scheduled Dates:

Col. 08: Time an activity is scheduled to commence.

Col. 09: Time that an activity is scheduled to finish.

Title: Project title (short description to identify project).

Contract value: Contract value for total project.

Cost to-date: Actual project cost to-date at report period.

Activity Earliest Dates:

Col. 10: The earliest time that an activity may commence.

Col. 11: The earliest time that an activity can finish.

Activity Latest Dates:

Col. 12: The latest time that an activity may commence.

Col. 13: The latest time that an activity can finish.

Activity Float:

Col. 14: Time activity start may be delayed without extending project duration.

Col. 15: Time activity start may be delayed without delaying start of other activities.

Figure 9.7 Project activities and critical path report

 The Planning Division, taking into consideration actual data being received from the Project Office, is regularly revising the project estimates on a holistic basis. The revised project estimates report is conveyed to the Project Office for onward transmission to the Accounting Division. Figure 9.8 illustrates a sample report regarding the revised project estimates. This report would be issued for a specific period ending date and is divided into three sections:

1. Project details to-date. This shows the estimated percentage complete, actual percentage complete, and the cost to-date;
2. Estimated project cost. This shows the original estimate, estimate now, and the difference between the original estimate and estimate now;
3. Project completion dates. This shows the original estimated project completion date, current estimated project completion date, and the number of work days ahead or behind schedule.

Current Project Details To-Date					Estimated Project Cost			Project Completion Dates		
No.	Title	Est. % Finished	% Now Finished	Cost to Date	Original	Now	Diff.	Original	Current	Ahead Delay
1	2	3	4	5	6	7	8	9	10	11

Project Details:

Column 01: Project number allocated at the project initiation stage.

Column 02: Project title (short description to identify project).

Column 03: Percentage project work that should have been carried out.

Column 04: Percentage project work actually carried out up to the report date.

Column 05: Actual project cost to-date for report period.

Estimated Project Cost:

Column 06: Original estimated project cost.

Column 07: Estimated project cost now (at report period).

Column 08: Estimated project cost variance at report period.

Project Completion Dates:

Column 09: Original project completion date forecast.

Column 10: Current project completion date forecast.

Column 11: Forecast project ahead/delay (work days).

Figure 9.8   Revised projects estimate report

PROJECT OFFICE

The Project Office has a focal information flow function receiving and forwarding information to and from three different sources, Planning Division, Accounting Division and Project Execution Unit(s) as illustrated by Figure 9.9.

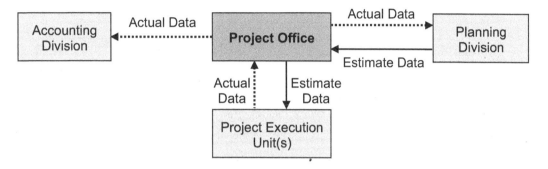

Figure 9.9   Project office information flow

Note that an organization may have a number of projects being implemented and therefore it may have more than one Project Execution Unit. Normally, a single project would have a Project Execution Unit assigned for that specific project. In other words, the Contracts, Planning and Accounting Divisions and the Project Office are a permanent part of the organization. However, the number of Project Execution Unit(s) would vary depending on the number of projects being conducted at any one point in time. Furthermore, a particular Project Execution Unit is temporary, existing only for the duration of the project.

For simplicity, this section will describe the outward information flow from the Project Office to the Planning and Accounting Divisions, and the Project Execution Unit(s). In the previous section, it was highlighted that the Project Office receives estimate data from the Planning Division. This estimate data is in the form of the Project Activities and Critical Path report as shown in Figure 9.7 and the Revised Projects Estimates as seen in Figure 9.8. The Project Activities and Critical Path information (Figure 9.7) is passed on to the Project Manager of the relevant Project Execution Unit that has the responsibility to implement the specific project; and the Revised Projects Estimates information (Figure 9.8) is conveyed to the Accounting Division, namely the Management Accountant. Therefore, the Project Office has a coordinating role and disseminates information to relevant individuals within the divisions.

Two other information sets (or reports) are generated by the Project Office, these are Daily Labour Usage (see Figure 9.10) and Daily Material and Equipment Utilization (see Figure 9.11). Note that the basic data for these two information sets is received from the specific Project Execution Unit. However, this process will be addressed when discussing the information flow within the Project Execution Unit(s).

Current Project Details		Activity Details		Actual Costs
No.	Title	No.	Description	Labour
1	2	3	4	5

Current Project Details:	**Activity Details:**
Column 01: Project number.	Column 03: Project activity number.
Column 02: Project title.	Column 04: Activity description.
Actual Cost:	
Column 05: Actual labour cost.	

Figure 9.10 Daily labour usage report

Current Project Details		Activity Details		Actual Costs	
Project	Title	No.	Description	Material	Equipment
1	2	3	4	5	6

Current Project Details:	**Activity Details:**
Column 01: Project number.	Column 03: Project activity number.
Column 02: Project title.	Column 04: Activity description.
Actual Cost:	
Column 05: Actual material cost.	
Column 06: Actual equipment cost.	

Figure 9.11 Daily material and equipment utilization report

These information sets are provided to the Accounts and Planning Divisions. The Planning Division would use the information to update the project network data and establish a more accurate basis for their revised activity estimates in terms of time and resource schedules and cost. The Accounting Division would use the information to reconcile the salaries and wages calculations and maintain the actual project costing data for the Financial Controller.

ACCOUNTING DIVISION

The Accounting Division is mainly the receiver of information for the purpose of preparing the financial statements, namely, the Profit and Loss Statement and Balance Sheet amongst others. The Accounting Division also prepares the budget for each division and monitors their performance on a division and unit basis (apart from monitoring performance on a project by project basis).

For the purpose of project management, the Accounting Division provides two important information sets. The first is the Project Performance Report (Figure 9.3) that was discussed in the section addressing the CEO. The other is the Overhead Costs Allocation (Figure 9.13) data set. It should be realized that the costs gathered and recorded by the Project Office are mainly direct production costs. However, the organization has also many indirect (or overhead) costs as well. Some of these overhead costs are related specifically to the organization as a whole and therefore are not allocated to projects and appear only in the financial statements. However, there are other overhead costs that are allocated on a project basis. For instance, supervision or management costs for the most part are indirect. Therefore, the Accounting Division must allocate a proportion of this cost type as an overhead cost to specific projects.

In addition, there may be some projects that are supervised by the same resource and it may not be practical to have time sheets for the supervisor that record the time one spends on specific projects. Here again, the Accounting Division would allocate a proportion of the cost to the relevant projects. These overhead costs are utilized by the Accounting Division in preparing the financial statements, but these costs must also be made available to the Planning Division so that they may maintain an accurate cost of the projects being conducted. Figure 9.12 illustrates the information outflow involving the Accounts Division, while Figure 9.13 shows a sample of the Projects Overhead Costs Allocation information set.

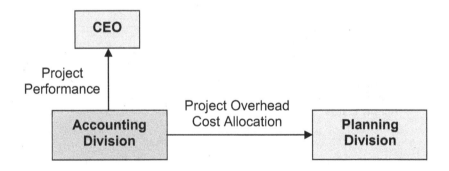

Figure 9.12 Accounts division information outflow

Project No.	Project Title	Overhead Cost

Figure 9.13 Projects overhead costs allocation

PROJECT EXECUTION UNIT(S)

As stated previously, the organization may have a number of Project Execution Units depending on the number of projects that are being implemented. It was also highlighted that a specific Project Execution Unit would normally be a temporary arrangement for the duration of a particular project. A major characteristic of the Project Execution Unit(s) in terms of information flow is the large amount of input data that is gathered about the activities being carried out by the project team members. As shown in Figure 9.14 the information outflow from the Project Execution Unit(s) is definite (actual), whilst the information inflow is related to estimated data regarding costs, resource requirements and time schedules. Hence, the information inflow may be viewed as being the project activity targets to be achieved and the information outflow is what has been accomplished.

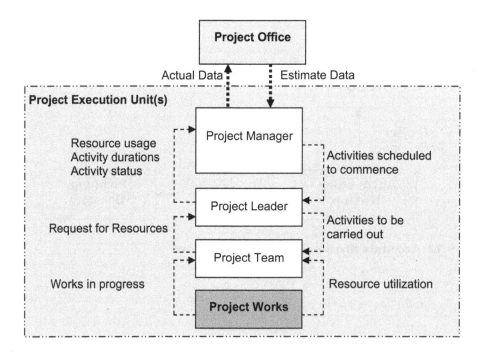

Figure 9.14 Project execution unit(s) information flow

In the context of project management, the Project Execution Unit(s) have a direct information linkage with mainly the Project Office. All other information linkages are of an indirect nature. For instance, the source of the information inflow regarding the estimate data is the Planning Division. However, it is the Project Office that directly conveys this information to the particular Project Execution Unit. Likewise, the detailed information outflow about the activities making up the project is received by the Project Office. However, after the appropriate filtering of the data, the information is disseminated to the Accounts and Planning Divisions. The information flow is mainly of two types, namely, input and output.

Input information

Input information is the raw elementary data that is provided by individual members of the project team, whilst the output information is disclosure data regarding the various activities within a specific project. The input data does not need to be in hard copy format but may use a computer display screen. The input data consists of three types, labour, materials and equipment:

1. *Labour Input Data.* Figure 9.15 is a sample of the Labour Job Details that would be provided daily by every individual noting the time spent on a specific activity within a project. This provides the basis for calculating the labour cost element.

| Name: | | Payroll No.: | Skill Type | Date: /   / |

Start Time	Finish Time	Duration	Project No.	Activity No.	Remarks
1	2	3	4	5	6

| Authorized Person: |

Col. 01: Time work session commenced.	Col. 04: Project being worked on.
Col. 02: Time work session finished.	Col. 05: Activity being worked on.
Col. 03: Duration of work session.	Col. 06: Remarks and observations.

Figure 9.15 Labour job details

2. *Materials Input Data.* Figure 9.16 is a sample of the Daily Material Utilization that is provided by an authorized project team member noting the material consumed by a specific activity within a project. This data provides the basis for calculating the material cost element.

Project No.:	Authorized Person:	Work Day: / /

Activity No.	Material ID	Material Description	Unit of Measure	Qty	Remarks
1	2	3	4	5	6

Col. 01: Activity being worked on.	Col. 04: Unit of measure e.g., metres, kilos.
Col. 02: Material identity number.	Col. 05: Quantity of material used.
Col. 03: Material short description.	Col. 06: Remarks and observations.

Figure 9.16 Daily materials utilization

3. *Equipment Input Data.* Figure 9.17 is a sample of the Daily Equipment Utilization that is provided by an authorized project team member noting the equipment used by specific project activities. This data provides the basis for calculating the equipment cost element.

Project No.:		Authorized Person:				Work Day: / /

Activity No.	Equipment ID	Equipment Description	Start Time	Finish Time	Duration	Remarks
1	2	3	4	5	6	7

Col. 01: Activity being worked on.	Col. 05: Time work session finished.
Col. 02: Equipment identity number.	Col. 06: Duration of work session.
Col. 03: Equipment short description.	Col. 07: Remarks and observations.
Col. 04: Time work session commenced.	

Figure 9.17 Daily equipment utilization

Output information

The output information consists of various types, including works in progress, activities that are to be carried out, activities that are being conducted and the status of various activities within a specific project:

1. *Works in progress.* Figure 9.18 is a typical Daily Works in Progress Report providing information about the critical activities of a specific project. This report would show all the critical activities, including those finished, started and not started.
2. *Activities scheduled to commence.* Figure 9.19 is a sample report of the project activities that are scheduled to commence within five working days. This report would alert the project leader to ensure that the resources required for the itemized activities are made available.
3. *Activities being conducted or to commence.* Figure 9.20 is a sample report of the project activities that are being carried out or are due to commence on that particular work day. This report would allow the project leader to monitor and follow up on the highlighted activities.
4. *Daily project status of all activities being conducted.* Figure 9.21 is a typical report that shows the status of all the project activities that are being carried out on that particular work day detailing the reason for the delay (if applicable). This report would provide the project manager and project leader to follow up on the highlighted activities.

Project No.:	Authorized Person:	Date: / /

Activity				Scheduled		Expected or Actual	
No.	Description	Status	% Complete	Start Date	Finished Date	Finished Date	Reasons for Delay
1	2	3	4	5	6	7	8

Col. 01: Activity number being worked on.	Col. 05: Activity scheduled start date.
Col. 02: Activity short description.	Col. 06: Activity scheduled finished date.
Col. 03: Status - Finished, Started, Not Started	Col. 07: Expected/actual finished date.
Col. 04: % work that has been carried out.	Col. 08: Reasons for delay.

Figure 9.18 Daily works in progress for critical activities report

Project No.:	Authorized Person:	Date: / / to / /

Activity			Scheduled		Resources Required					
No.	Description	Total Float	Start Date	Finished Date	Labour (No./Skills)		Equipment (No./Type)		Material (Qty./Type)	
1	2	3	4	5	6	7	8	9	10	11

Col. 01: Activity number being worked on.	Col. 06: Number of labour needed.
Col. 02: Activity short description.	Col. 07: Type of skill(s) needed(code)
Col. 03: Time an activity start may be delayed without extending project duration.	Col. 08: Number of equipment needed.
	Col. 09: Type of equipment needed (code).
Col. 04: Activity scheduled start date.	Col. 10: Quantity of material needed.
Col. 05: Activity scheduled finished date	Col. 11: Type of material needed (code).

Figure 9.19 Project activities sheduled to commence within five work days

Project No.:		Authorized Person:				Work Day: / /		

Activity					Scheduled		
No.	Description	Status	% Complete	Critical?	Start Date	Finished Date	Remarks
1	2	3	4	5	6	7	8

Col. 01: Activity number being worked on. Col. 05: Whether activity is critical.
Col. 02: Activity short description. Col. 06: Activity scheduled start date.
Col. 03: Status whether "Started", "To Start". Col. 07: Activity scheduled finished date.
Col. 04: % work that has been carried out. Col. 08: Remarks.

Figure 9.20 Activities being conducted or to commence on indicated work day

Project No.:		Authorized Person:			Date: / /

Activity		Status	%	
No.	Short Description	Today	Complete	Reasons for Delay
1	2	3	4	5

Col. 01: Activity number being worked on. Col. 04: % work carried out on activity.
Col. 02: Activity short description. Col. 05: Reasons for delay.
Col. 03: Status: finished today, started today

Figure 9.21 Daily project status of all activities being conducted

5. *Project activity status and resource utilization.* Figure 9.22 provides a typical report that shows the project activity status and resource utilization of all the activities for a specific project. This report would provide the project manager with a comprehensive picture of the full project. The report has two major divisions. The first part provides information about the project in general, such as the overall percentage project completion, contract value, payment received to-date and cost to-date. The second part of the report provides detailed information about the specific activities within the project being reported on. The activity details shown in the report includes:
   a) Activity scheduled start and finish dates;
   b) Estimated and actual to-date activity duration;
   c) Estimated and actual to-date activity cost;
   d) Activity status in terms of whether the activity is normal or critical and the percentage activity complete;
   e) Activity total and free float;
   f) Resource utilization to-date in terms of labour materials and equipment.

It should be noted that the various output reports shown do need to be in hard copy format and are only a small sample of the type of information that may be generated for a given project, provided that the organization has in place the appropriate processes to gather the data required to monitor and control the projects.

Knowledge Management and Critical Data for Project Information Flow

The previous sections covered the information flow processes required between the divisions within a project oriented organization to monitor and control projects. It was shown that information may be classified into three types, namely, input, generated and output information. However, for output information in the form of reports or other suitable media to occur, the project management process must have in place the appropriate systems to store and retrieve input and generated information into and from an information repository. It is important to note that the information repository is a consequence of the information flow processes and consists of estimated and actual data, and knowledge gained from the project review process discussed in Chapter 8, "Project Planning and Control".

Figure 9.23 illustrates that input data is received from various sources, where it is provided to various systems and is further processed and manipulated, thus generating more information and knowledge. Both the input and generated information is stored in a repository where all the relevant data about all the projects is kept. Holistically, the information and knowledge repository (project data warehouse) is the organization's business intelligence instrument that is utilized in the decision-making process. The retrieval of information and knowledge from the repository is also necessary so that various authorized users, such as the CEO, Financial Controller, Management Accountant, Project Managers, Project Leaders, project team members and many other employees may extract information in a format that is meaningful and relevant to them. The information and knowledge retrieval may take the form of paper reports or visual display or some other electronic media.

| Project No: | | Title: | | % Complete: | | Contract Value: | | Payments To-date: | | Cost To-date: | |

Activity Details		Schedule Dates		Activity Duration		Activity Cost		Activity Status		Days Float		Usage Cost To-Date		
No.	Title	Start	Finished	Estimate	Actual To-Date	Estimate	Actual To-Date	% Complete	Critical Normal	Total	Free	Labour	Material	Equip.
1	2	3	4	5	6	7	8	9	10	11	12	13	14	15

Project Information:

Project No. and title.

% Complete: % of project work carried out at report date.

Contract value: Contract value for total project.

Payments To-date: Cash received for conducting project.

Cost to-date: Actual project cost to-date at report period.

Activity Details:

Col. 01: Activity number.

Col. 02: Activity description.

Activity Scheduled Dates:

Col. 03: Date/time an activity is scheduled to commence.

Col. 04: Date/time that an activity is scheduled to finish.

Activity Duration:

Col. 05: Estimated activity duration (work days).

Col. 06: Actual activity duration to-date (work days).

Activity Cost:

Col. 07: Estimated activity cost.

Col. 08: Actual activity cost to-date.

Activity Status:

Col. 09: Actual % activity completion.

Col. 10: Critical or Normal.

Activity Float:

Col. 11: Time activity start may be delayed without extending project duration.

Col. 12: Time activity start may be delayed without delaying start of others.

Activity Resource Usage Cost To-Date:

Col. 13: Actual labour cost to-date.

Col. 14: Actual materials cost to-date.

Col. 15: Actual equipment cost to-date.

Figure 9.22 Project activity status and resource utilization report

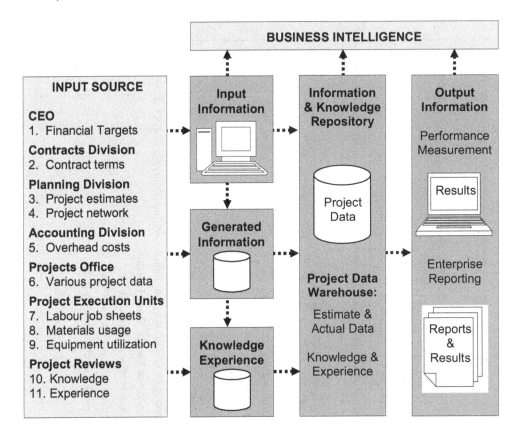

Figure 9.23 Project information and knowledge process cycle

The focus of this section however is the critical data set, in other words the contents of the information repository. The objective of this section is to answer the question: "What project information should be held by the organization to monitor and control all the projects undertaken by the organization?" Figures 9.24 and 9.25 provide the full project information repository required to monitor and control projects. Figure 9.24 depicts the information regarding the data estimates, whereas Figure 9.25 shows the information regarding actual data. It should be noted that in practice there is only one information repository, consisting of a number of databases that contain both project estimates and actual data. However, due to the large variety of data in the repository it was not possible to fit all the information in one diagram.

PROJECT INFORMATION REPOSITORY – ACTIVITY ESTIMATES DATA

The data estimates consist of five categories of information, namely, project activity base estimates, project activity latest revised estimates, labour usage estimate, materials usage estimate and equipment usage estimate. Figure 9.26 shows how each database is created from the project network and the Project Activity Estimate Details.

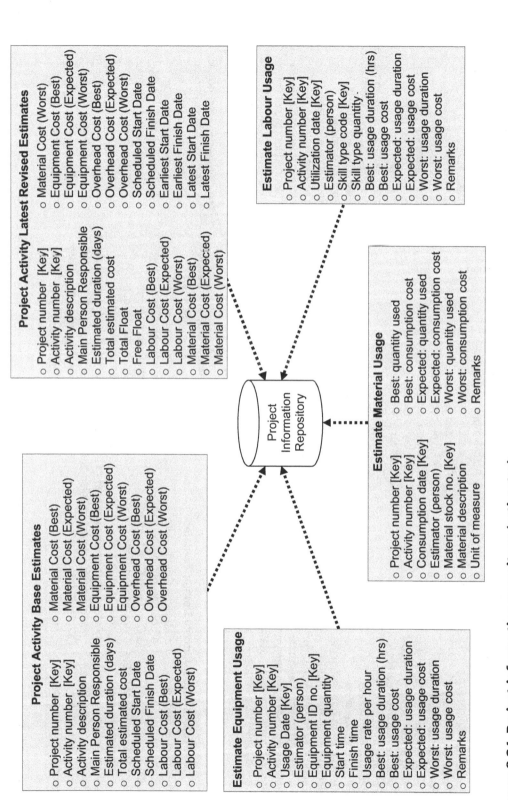

Project Activity Latest Revised Estimates

o Project number [Key]
o Activity number [Key]
o Activity description
o Main Person Responsible
o Estimated duration (days)
o Total estimated cost
o Total Float
o Free Float
o Labour Cost (Best)
o Labour Cost (Expected)
o Labour Cost (Worst)
o Material Cost (Best)
o Material Cost (Expeced)
o Material Cost (Worst)
o Material Cost (Worst)
o Equipment Cost (Best)
o Equipment Cost (Expected)
o Equipment Cost (Worst)
o Overhead Cost (Best)
o Overhead Cost (Expected)
o Overhead Cost (Worst)
o Scheduled Start Date
o Scheduled Finish Date
o Earliest Start Date
o Earliest Finish Date
o Latest Start Date
o Latest Finish Date

Estimate Labour Usage

o Project number [Key]
o Activity number [Key]
o Utilization date [Key]
o Estimator (person)
o Skill type code [Key]
o Skill type quantity.
o Best: usage duration (hrs)
o Best: usage cost
o Expected: usage duration
o Expected: usage cost
o Worst: usage duration
o Worst: usage cost
o Remarks

Project Activity Base Estimates

o Project number [Key]
o Activity number [Key]
o Activity description
o Main Person Responsible
o Estimated duration (days)
o Total estimated cost
o Scheduled Start Date
o Scheduled Finish Date
o Labour Cost (Best)
o Labour Cost (Expected)
o Labour Cost (Worst)
o Material Cost (Best)
o Material Cost (Expected)
o Material Cost (Worst)
o Equipment Cost (Best)
o Equipment Cost (Expected)
o Equipment Cost (Worst)
o Overhead Cost (Best)
o Overhead Cost (Expected)
o Overhead Cost (Worst)

Project Information Repository

Estimate Material Usage

o Project number [Key]
o Activity number [Key]
o Consumption date [Key]
o Estimator (person)
o Material stock no. [Key]
o Material description
o Unit of measure
o Best: quantity used
o Best: consumption cost
o Expected: quantity used
o Expected: consumption cost
o Worst: quantity used
o Worst: consumption cost
o Remarks

Estimate Equipment Usage

o Project number [Key]
o Activity number [Key]
o Usage Date [Key]
o Estimator (person)
o Equipment ID no. [Key]
o Equipment quantity
o Start time
o Finish time
o Usage rate per hour
o Best: usage duration (hrs)
o Best: usage cost
o Expected: usage duration
o Expected: usage cost
o Worst: usage duration
o Worst: usage cost
o Remarks

Figure 9.24 Project information repository (estimates)

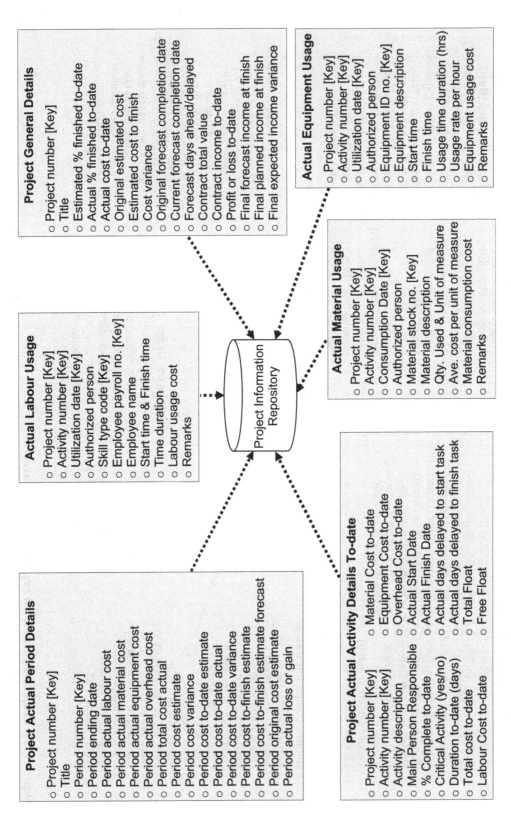

Project General Details
- o Project number [Key]
- o Title
- o Estimated % finished to-date
- o Actual % finished to-date
- o Actual cost to-date
- o Original estimated cost
- o Estimated cost to finish
- o Cost variance
- o Original forecast completion date
- o Current forecast completion date
- o Forecast days ahead/delayed
- o Contract total value
- o Contract income to-date
- o Profit or loss to-date
- o Final forecast income at finish
- o Final planned income at finish
- o Final expected income variance

Actual Equipment Usage
- o Project number [Key]
- o Activity number [Key]
- o Utilization date [Key]
- o Authorized person
- o Equipment ID no. [Key]
- o Equipment description
- o Start time
- o Finish time
- o Usage time duration (hrs)
- o Usage rate per hour
- o Equipment usage cost
- o Remarks

Actual Labour Usage
- o Project number [Key]
- o Activity number [Key]
- o Utilization date [Key]
- o Authorized person
- o Skill type code [Key]
- o Employee payroll no. [Key]
- o Employee name
- o Start time & Finish time
- o Time duration
- o Labour usage cost
- o Remarks

Project Information Repository

Actual Material Usage
- o Project number [Key]
- o Activity number [Key]
- o Consumption Date [Key]
- o Authorized person
- o Material stock no. [Key]
- o Material description
- o Qty. Used & Unit of measure
- o Ave. cost per unit of measure
- o Material consumption cost
- o Remarks

Project Actual Period Details
- o Project number [Key]
- o Title
- o Period number [Key]
- o Period ending date
- o Period actual labour cost
- o Period actual material cost
- o Period actual equipment cost
- o Period actual overhead cost
- o Period total cost actual
- o Period cost estimate
- o Period cost variance
- o Period cost to-date estimate
- o Period cost to-date actual
- o Period cost to-date variance
- o Period cost to-finish estimate
- o Period cost to-finish estimate forecast
- o Period original cost estimate
- o Period actual loss or gain

Project Actual Activity Details To-date
- o Project number [Key]
- o Activity number [Key]
- o Activity description
- o Main Person Responsible
- o % Complete to-date
- o Critical Activity (yes/no)
- o Duration to-date (days)
- o Total cost to-date
- o Labour Cost to-date
- o Material Cost to-date
- o Equipment Cost to-date
- o Overhead Cost to-date
- o Actual Start Date
- o Actual Finish Date
- o Actual days delayed to start task
- o Actual days delayed to finish task
- o Total Float
- o Free Float

Figure 9.25 Project information repository (actual)

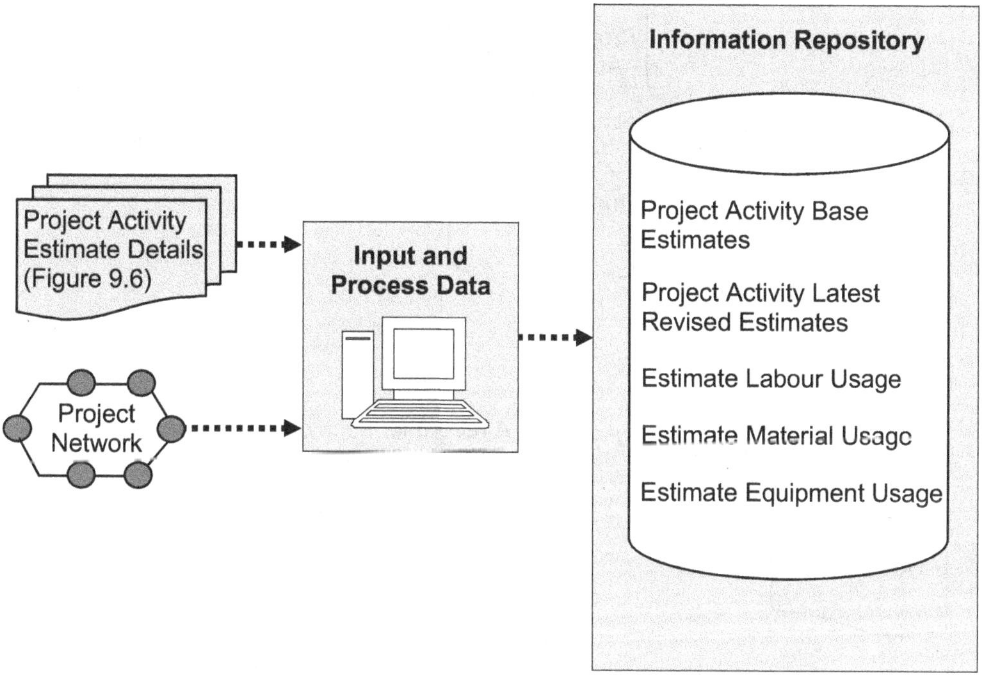

Figure 9.26 Project estimates information repository generation

Project activity base estimates

The Project Activity Base Estimates database consists of information regarding specific activities within a particular project. Hence, if a project has 250 activities, then there will be 250 database records, one record for every activity as shown in Figure 9.27. The Project Activity Base Estimates database contains the original project estimates and is a summary of the input information from Figure 9.6 (Project Activity Estimate Details) and the scheduled start and finish date calculations from the initial project network.

Project activity latest revised estimates

This database is structured in a similar manner to the Project Activity Base Estimates database. However, it contains the latest activity revised estimates data. Apart from having the scheduled start and finish dates, this database also contains the earliest and latest start dates, earliest and latest finish dates, total float and free float.

Labour Usage Estimate

This database consists of information regarding each labour skill type for every activity within a project. Note that the estimate databases regarding labour, material and equipment usage are structured in a similar manner as shown by Figure 9.28. For instance, if a specific activity utilizes three labour skill types, for example, carpenter, painter and handyman, then three separate records are created, one for every skill type for the specific activity for the project.

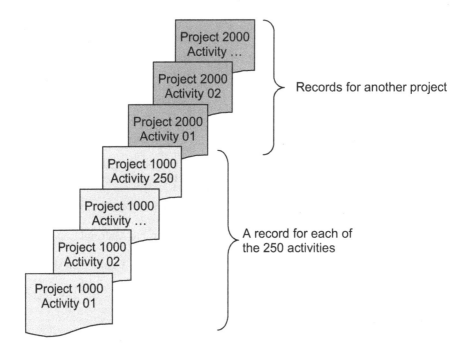

Figure 9.27 Activity base estimates database structure

Materials Usage Estimate

The Materials Usage Estimate database consists of information regarding each material type that is estimated to be utilized for every activity within a project. Hence, if an activity is envisaged to use four types of material, for example, steel mesh, paint, cement and gravel, then four separate records are created, one for every material type for the activity within the project as shown by Figure 9.28.

Equipment Usage Estimate

This database contains information about the equipment that is to be used for every activity within a project and has a similar structure to the Labour Usage Estimate and Materials Usage Estimate databases. Hence, if an activity is estimated to use two types of equipment, for example, one front-end loader and two tip-trucks, then two separate records are created, one for every equipment type for the activity within the project as shown by Figure 9.28. Although two tip-trucks are to be utilized on the project, one record is created for this equipment.

PROJECT INFORMATION REPOSITORY – ACTIVITY ACTUAL DATA

Actual data consists of six categories of information, namely, project general details, project period details, project actual activity details to-date, actual labour usage, actual materials usage and actual equipment usage. This repository is created in a similar manner as the estimates. However, the input sources are different as illustrated by Figure 9.29.

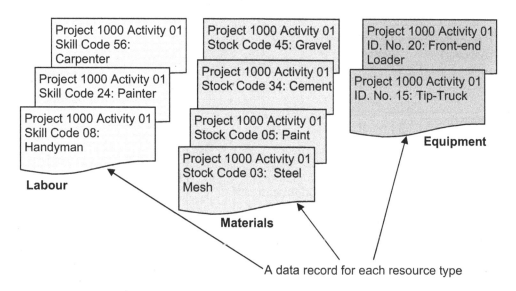

Figure 9.28 Estimated labour, materials and equipment usage DB structure

The input sources for actual data include the project network, Overhead Costs Allocation (Figure 9.13), Labour Job Details (Figure 9.15), Daily Materials Utilization (Figure 9.16) and Daily Equipment Utilization (Figure 9.17).

Project General Details

This database consists of information regarding specific projects. Therefore, the database would contain only one record for each project undertaken by the organization. There would be no reference to any project activities. Figure 9.30 illustrates the record structure of this database. Note that the information about the project is of a general nature and provides summary details, hence providing the holistic project status.

Project Period Details

The Project Period Details database also stores information about a specific project and does not hold details at activity level. However, unlike the Project General Details database which only has one record for every project, this database has a record for every accounting period. An accounting period normally consists of four weeks. Hence there would be 13 periods within a year. Therefore, the project would have a record for every accounting period until its completion. For example, if a project took twenty weeks to complete, this database would have five records for the particular project (one for every four weeks) as illustrated in Figure 9.31.

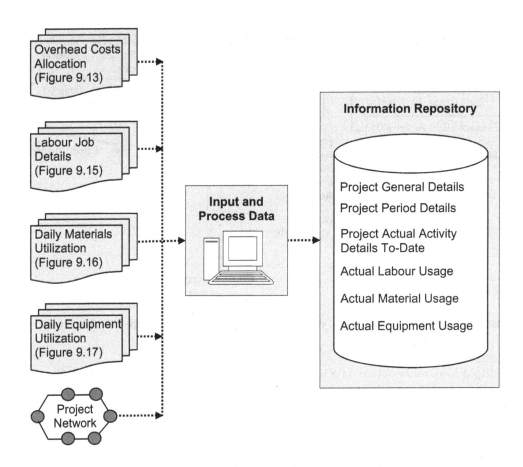

Figure 9.29 Project actual information repository generation

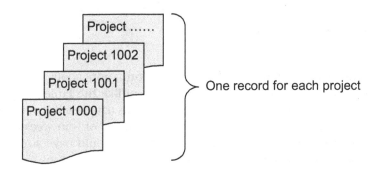

Figure 9.30 Project general details database structure

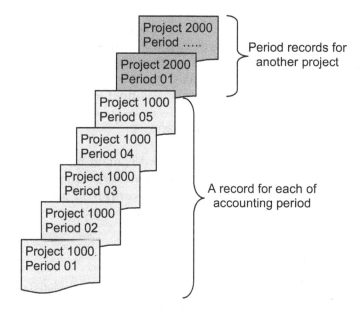

Figure 9.31 Project period details database structure

Project actual activity details to-date

This database would contain information about the activities within a project as the project is being implemented. Hence, the information does not refer to estimates (targets) but to actual data (achievement). Therefore, a project may have many activities but

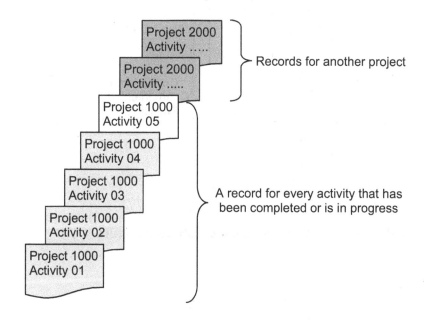

Figure 9.32 Project actual activity details to-date database structure

only the activities that are complete or are in progress would appear in this database. For example, a project may have 50 activities, but only activities 01 to 04 have been completed and activity 05 is being conducted, then the database structure would be as shown in Figure 9.32. Similar to the Project General Details and Project Period Details databases, this database would contain summarized input information.

Actual labour, materials and equipment usage

These three databases have a similar structure and contain information regarding the actual utilization of labour, materials and equipment. Furthermore, these databases are very detailed, for example, the labour utilization records hold information about each individual employee working on a particular activity within a project on a specific date, including the skill type as shown at Figure 9.33.

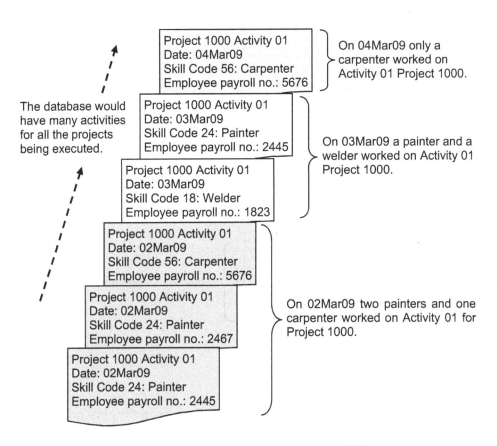

Figure 9.33 Project actual labour usage database structure

Similar detailed information is recorded about materials and equipment utilization, using the material stock number and equipment identity number respectively. Note that the information about the overhead costs is directly inputted as part of the Project Period Details database since there is no detailed information applicable except for the value allocated to a specific project for the related period.

PROJECT CRITICAL DATA SET

The data repository as illustrated in the above sections is basically a database of critical project data acting as an information storage facility. It is important to remember that information consists of data that is transformed into a meaningful pattern. However, knowledge is the ability to use that information. What is more, knowledge and lessons learnt about a project can be stored and retrieved when required. Hence, having the project critical data set supported by the proper processes is essential, but these together with the related information processing systems must be seen as being merely a precision tool. It is the skilled managers within the organization, collaborating and working as a well-synchronized team that will transform information into knowledge, so that the critical data set may be extensively utilized like every other organizational resource, to make the proper judgements and decisions for the benefit of the organization and clients.

Conclusion

It is not enough to have clearly defined and unambiguous milestones with excellent channels of communication to monitor and control projects. Management must also have adequate information and the appropriate information flow processes to facilitate the communication and dissemination of information to the relevant people. For information to be of value in the execution of a project it must meet three basic criteria. It must be accurate and complete, timely and meaningful. Having the proper processes in place will help the organization to achieve these basic criteria. However, the processes must be simple, but at the same time, the information flow must also be comprehensive enough to ensure that every relevant individual receives the information needed for making specific decisions related to their particular job function.

Information may be classified into three types, namely input, generated and output information. Input information is the raw elementary data that is provided by individuals. For instance, employees working in the Planning Division would provide the input details regarding the various activities and their respective time and resource utilization estimates. Generated information refers to information that is provided automatically by the application Management Information System (MIS). For instance, the input estimate information provided by the Planning Division would be utilized by the critical path method application to calculate the scheduled activity start and finish dates, and their respective total float duration would indicate whether the activities are critical to the project. Output information refers to the reports that are produced from the input and generated information. For instance, the project manager may want to know the project activities that have fallen behind schedule.

Furthermore, information may be transformed into knowledge. This may be achieved through regular project reviews and the application of Decision Support Systems (DSS) and Executive Information Systems (EIS). For example, project reviews must be documented so that lessons learnt from the project are not lost. Moreover, this documented knowledge must be stored in a meaningful manner so that it may be retrieved when required. Therefore, an organization's data warehouse or data repository would contain an accumulation of raw data, information and knowledge about current and previously executed projects. This data warehouse must be well managed and utilized in the decision-making process to ensure repeatable project management success.

In an organization there are several information flow divisions which are all linked with each other and all require information in varying degrees of detail and for different purposes. Moreover, information flow in projects tends to move in a cyclical pattern. For instance, projects normally start off with estimates, then as the project is being conducted, actual data is collected and this actual data is inputted into the project network and utilized to revise the various estimates. This estimate–actual–estimate cycle is continuous for the full duration of the project until the project is fully executed, thus the information at completion would reflect the actual project position.

Identifying the critical data set is essential for monitoring and controlling a project. For output information in the form of reports or other suitable media to occur, the project management process must have in place the appropriate systems to store and retrieve input data, generated information and knowledge into and from a data warehouse. The data warehouse is basically a database of critical project data acting as an information storage repository. It is important to note that the information repository is a consequence of the information flow processes. It consists of both estimates and actual data and project knowledge gained in the project implementation process. An information repository permits data, information and knowledge to be retrieved so that various authorized users may extract its contents in a format that is meaningful and relevant to them.

However, the major issue is: What project data, information and knowledge should be held by the organization to monitor and control all the projects undertaken by the organization? Figures 9.24 and Figure 9.25 provide a general response to this question. The question as to what knowledge should be stored about a project is difficult to answer because there is no set pattern. However, one should document and store what went right and/or wrong with the project and the exceptional functional occurrences that need to be emulated or avoided in future projects. The information repository may include the following critical data sets:

1. Project Data Estimates:
   • Project Activity Base Estimates;
   • Project Activity Latest Revised Estimates;
   • Labour, Materials and Equipment Usage Estimate.
2. Project Actual Data:
   • Project General Details;
   • Project Period Details;
   • Project Actual Activity Details To-Date;
   • Actual Labour, Materials and Equipment Usage.

Finally, it is important to note that information is about taking data and transforming it into a meaningful pattern. However, knowledge is the ability to use that information. Hence, it is the skilled managers within the organization collaborating and working as a well-synchronized team that will turn the available information into knowledge so that the critical data set is extensively utilized like every other organizational resource to make the proper judgements and decisions for the benefit of the organization and clients.

References

Bocij, P., Chaffey, D., Greasley, A. and Hickie, S. 1999. *Business Information Systems: Technology, Development and Management*. London: Prentice Hall.

Kerr, J.M. 1991. *The IRM Imperative: Strategies for Managing Information Resources*. New York: John Wiley & Sons Inc.

Laudon, K.C. and Laudon, J.P. 1995. *Information Systems: A Problem Solving Approach*. Fort Worth: Dryden Press, Harcourt Brace College Publishers.

Rothstein, M.F. and Rosner, B. 1990. *The Professional's Guide to Database Systems Project Management*. New York: John Wiley & Sons Inc.

Nissen, M.E. 2000. An extended model of knowledge-flow dynamics. *Communications of the Association for Information Systems*, 8, 251–66.

10 *Project Risk Management*

*Living at risk is jumping off the cliff and building your wings on
the way down.*

Ray Bradbury, author (1920)

All projects carry a certain magnitude of risk. However, frequent and thorough risk analysis and risk management techniques can help to resolve concerns before they arise or become serious. A risk is often viewed as an event that may happen and if it occurs, it may have a favourable or unfavourable impact on the project. Examples of unfavourable effects include delays in project delivery dates and budget overruns, resulting in the demoralization of project team members and harming the reputation of the project manager. Hence, a risk (of an event) has a probability attached to it and the consequence of it happening may have a positive or negative effect on the project.

Project risk management endeavours to foresee and deal with uncertainties that jeopardize the project objectives and the time and cost schedules of a project. There are many sources of uncertainties or risks. These may include delays in the delivery of adequate materials, quality levels of procured items that are essential for the project, high turnover of project team members, adverse weather conditions and industrial disputes. Risk management is a systematic process to identify, quantify, respond to and monitor and control project risk.

An important point to remember is that risk is not always bad. There are both opportunities and threats. The opportunities represent the beneficial risks, whereas the threats are the adverse risks. Therefore, project risk management consists of processes, tools and methods that will aid the project management team to increase the likelihood and impact of positive events and to decrease the probability and impact of negative events. Project risk management, therefore, is a continuous process to be conducted during the entire project and should particularly be commenced early in the project.

Project Risk Concepts

A risk is an event that is uncertain and has a negative or positive impact on some undertaking. For example, to a car insurance company the event of accidents to any of its policyholders are considered to be the risks. The company does not know who of its policyholders will have an accident in a given time period (uncertainty) and every accident costs the company a payout equal to the value of repairing the damage that does not exceed the vehicle's insured value (adverse effect on profitability). On the other hand, risk analysis is the process of assessing risks through qualitative or quantitative methodology.

Risk analysis requires an estimation of both the uncertainty of the risk and its impact or effect. For example, the car insurance company may estimate the number of accidents in a particular time period based on historical data related to its policyholders. This estimate, together with information about its policies, will in turn allow the car insurance company to estimate the value they will have to pay out during the time period in question. Generally, these estimates will not be equal to the precise amount of money paid out, but they permit the car insurance company to have a good idea of how likely the different claims will materialize and the value of their payouts.

Project risk may be viewed as a combination of the probability of an event and its consequences. If an event is anticipated but its impact insignificant, it does not represent a risk, because it has no impact or influence on the outcome. Likewise, an unlikely event with significant consequences may not be a high risk either. Therefore, the combination of the likelihood and consequence of an event provide the possibility of loss or gain, or success or failure.

Hence, the risk of an event is its probability of occurring times its consequence in terms of value. For example, an event such as a dispute with a Workers Union may have a probability of 0.02 (2 per cent chance of occurring) and if this event occurs, the cost to the organization may be 100,000 units. Therefore, the risk of this event (dispute with a Workers Union) is 2,000 units (0.02 times 100,000 units). Project consequential risk is simply the summation of all the events' risk consequences in a project.

Example – project risk

Let's assume that management have identified three risk events in a construction project being undertaken by the organization:

1. Dispute with a Workers Union. Probability of occurring is 0.02 and if this event occurs the cost to the organization may be 100,000 units. The consequence arising from the risk of this event is 2,000 units.
2. Late delivery of materials. Probability of occurring is 0.05 and if this event occurs the cost to the organization may be 150,000 units. The consequence arising from the risk of this event is 7,500 units.
3. Work accidents (safety issues). Probability of occurring is 0.03 and if this event occurs the cost to the organization may be 500,000 units. The consequence arising from the risk of this event is 15,000 units.

Therefore, total project consequential risk is the summation of all the events' risk consequences in a project, which amounts to 24,500 units. Once all the risks are evaluated, an appropriate risk strategy may be identified. Hence, if project managers understand the project risks involved, they are in a position to determine which risks are acceptable and then take the appropriate action to mitigate or forestall the adverse risks.

Furthermore, if the project risk evaluation reveals excessive risks, the project manager may decide to restructure the project within acceptable risk and project parameters. For instance, a simple means to reduce risk is to streamline the project or to have lower project objectives. However, such action would depend on the authority level of the project manager.

Project risk may be viewed as a combination of the project domain and the vagueness of knowledge of the project domain, which is transformed to uncertainty. These two factors have a negative relationship, in that uncertainty is reduced when more is known about the project domain parameters. This relationship is illustrated by Figure 10.1. Projects will always have a level of uncertainty due to the number of independent activities that utilize a variety of resources, therefore projects are always confined by the domain parameters. Hence, the relationship between these two variables is not linear since they will never be negative or zero. Moreover, the acceptable risk level is a point somewhere between the project domain parameters and the uncertainty level, where both factors are at their optimum level.

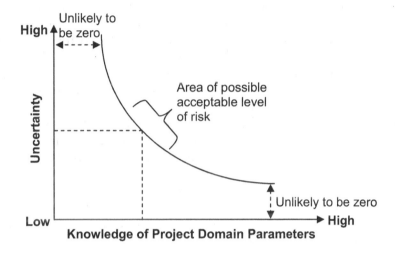

Figure 10.1 Acceptable level of project risk

Project risk may be minimized by lessening the project limitations defined by the project domain parameters and by identifying and decreasing uncertainty through the increase in knowledge of the project activities. Lessening the project domain parameters is difficult to attain because these are not normally under the control of the project manager and are likely to be determined by individuals external to the project team. Therefore, most project managers tend to focus on reducing uncertainty. Project risks that have a chance of a beneficial return should be pursued, otherwise they should be avoided. Hence, risks that have a potential for gain should be proactively managed.

Uncertainty may result due to vagueness or ambiguity of events, therefore a possible means of reducing risk is to collate information about the event and its relevant concerns to reduce its uncertainty. Hence, through information gathering, a process may be initiated to decrease probabilities of failures and/or to reduce their consequences. The concept of acceptable or unacceptable risk is difficult to portray because what may be considered as an unacceptable risk to one person may be deemed as an opportunity to another. Thus, the foresight and general behavioural personality of a project manager makes a significant difference in the way one views risk taking.

The project manager should examine tasks within the project plan closely to determine the extent of their impact and likelihood of successful completion. Activities on the critical path that have a high project impact and their achievement is uncertain should be viewed as risk areas and given special attention by the project manager.

Project management experience suggests that risk is usually linked with project segments that do not have a well-defined scope or are subject to change. The general rule to keep in mind is that project risk is generated when things are not well documented or understood or can change or have not been adequately examined.

Some common features that increase project risk are ambitious goals, lack of adequate experience of some or all project team members, untested technical methods, design complexity of the project outcome and deficient planning or unduly optimistic time and cost schedules. Moreover, the less that is known about the path towards the project outcome increases risk. For instance, a construction firm building domestic housing to standard plans has little risk. However, undertaking a project that has never been conducted before, such the building of the English Channel Euro Tunnel or launching a manned mission to Mars have a much higher risk and will normally have political (not necessarily commercial) implications linked to them.

External project interfaces are also a common source of risk because they may change at some point in the duration of the project or the requirement specifications are not accurately defined. These external interfaces also represent project areas over which the project manager has very little or no control over. It is emphasized that any project area over which a project manager does not have full control may evolve into a serious project risk. For instance, imagine the impact on an information system development project if a vital hardware vendor files for bankruptcy. Risk is also always high if the customer or the eventual recipient of the project is not adequately involved. For example, consider the risk repercussion if a medical clinic is designed without adequate consultations being held with medical practitioners.

Project managers should look to themselves and to the past to identify and take precautions to reduce risk. It is more likely that project managers will have problems from known risk areas than be surprised by things completely unforeseen. This means that a project manager must develop an instinct to feel and detect risk. Admittedly this takes experience and is developed by conducting post-project reviews to determine what went right and/or wrong with a project. Hence, the project manager must create an internal repository of experience and develop this into a personal and organizational knowledge base.

Finally, the project manager must look to the past and holistically understand what went wrong (and right) with the projects undertaken by the organization with the objective of finding ways to mitigate risk and taking action to avoid past mistakes.

The above all contribute towards the concept of risk management. Risk management is the procedure of using risk analysis to develop management strategies to mitigate or ameliorate risk. In this chapter we are concerned with the use of techniques in managing projects, where some of the important questions that need to be addressed are: "How long will this project eventually take?" "How much will it finally cost?" "Will its product perform according to specifications?"

These questions can never be answered with certainty either before the commencement of a project or while the project is in progress. Hence, project managers and clients are concerned with both the uncertainty these questions pose and their potential impact or consequences. Risk analysis and risk management techniques are designed to provide a probable answer to these questions.

It is important to note that project risk management consists of two major phases. The first phase is related to preparing a project risk management plan. This basically consists of risk analysis and should be undertaken at the very early stages of the project, preferably at the project initiation stage. However, it should be noted that risk management planning may be considered as being a continuous process and should be regularly reviewed. The second phase is related to risk monitoring and control which depends upon having conducted a thorough risk analysis.

Project Risk Management Planning

Project risk management planning consists of four components, namely risk identification, risk quantification in terms of analysing and prioritizing risk, risk response, and risk monitoring and control. Together these four components provide a road map for the project management team in the eventuality that the risk occurs, by giving them the ability to decide what to do, when to do it and then decide whether enough has been done.

The risk management plan may also be viewed as a major feature of project quality that enables the project team to respond adequately to risk situations. Figure 10.2 illustrates the project risk management planning process. It shows that the inputs to the plan are the external and internal organizational environmental factors. The external environment provides the greatest source of risk, since the external factors are normally outside the control of the organization, particularly the project manager. The risk management plan consists of four major processes with each process having a specific deliverable.

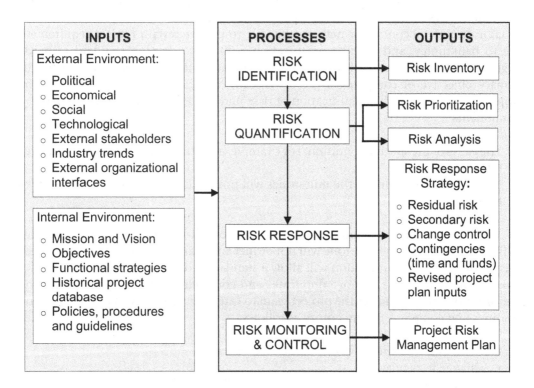

Figure 10.2 Project risk management planning process

PROJECT RISK IDENTIFICATION

Project risk identification basically addresses the question: "What might go wrong?" Hence, it identifies and names the project risks and their characteristics. This process provides the warning signs that indicate whether the identified risks are likely to occur and also gives the project team an opportunity to find better methods for achieving the project's specific requirements and objectives. Information for the identification of project risk may be obtained from various sources. However, a common approach is to conduct a workshop where key project stakeholders, through brainstorming sessions, identify and review standard risk lists.

To compile a risk inventory, the entire project plan is examined closely and meticulously looking for areas of uncertainty. For example, "the project will be behind schedule" is not a risk but the consequence of risk. Therefore, the objective of the brainstorming sessions would be to examine the plans to search for issues that could cause the project to be behind schedule.

There are various types of risks that are associated with a variety of different projects. Therefore, in a multi-project environment it is important to identify risk and decide on a project by project basis what to do about each type of risk. For instance, business risks are ongoing risks that are best resolved by the organization's Financial Division. For example, if the project is seen as not meeting the cash-inflow financial targets, the financial division may need to examine the possibility of obtaining or extending the bank overdraft facilities. The response is likely to be a contingency plan developed by the financial division to acquire bank overdraft arrangements for a specified period.

Generic risks are applicable to all types of projects. For example, there is the risk that a major project subcontractor may not be able to deliver certain project requirements due to bankruptcy, and so each organization is likely to develop standard responses to generic risks. Figure 10.3 illustrates the risk identification procedure, which has the primary objective of compiling a project risk inventory and assigning each risk to a project team member. The identification of risks may be viewed as being made up of two components:

1. The cause of the specific condition. For example, a contractor not meeting the delivery schedule;
2. The impact. For example, the milestones will not be achieved and/or the budget will be exceeded.

Thus, a risk might be defined as: "The contractor not meeting the defined schedule will imply that a primary milestone will not be met and that the budget will be exceeded." This method of risk identification will allow a standardized definition approach that will make it simple to define, remove duplicates and comprehend the risk. The project risk identification process enables the project team to categorize risk under a number of major headings and compile a risk inventory as follows:

1. *Ecological Risks.* Examples of ecological risks include:
   - Change in regulations;
   - Coastal zone projects;
   - Delay in issuance of permits;

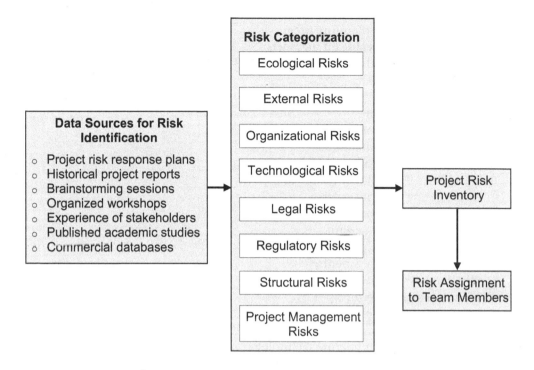

Figure 10.3 Project risk identification process

- Emission control conditions;
- Environmental controversy;
- Formal consultation process;
- Hazardous waste conditions;
- Archaeological sites or green areas;
- Impact assessments needs;
- Lack of specialized staff;
- Negative community impact.
2. *External Risks.* Examples of external risks include:
   - Bankruptcy of key supplier;
   - Change in organization's project implementation priorities;
   - Change in political priorities;
   - Change to funding schedule;
   - Inconsistent project aims;
   - Lobby group pressure;
   - Objections from general public or community groups;
   - Priority to cost over quality;
   - Stakeholder initiated change;
   - Threat of litigation;
   - Unclear external interfaces.
3. *Organizational Risks.* Examples of organizational risks include:
   - Frequent changes in project or tasks priorities;
   - High project team turnover rate or loss of critical team members;

- Inadequate project planning time;
- Inexperienced project team members;
- Insufficient internal support;
- Insufficient resources;
- Internal bureaucracy delays;
- Lack of commitment;
- Lack of internal coordination;
- Overloaded functional units;
- Unexpected injury and sick time.

4. *Technical Risks.* Examples of technical risks include:
   - Errors in raw material orders;
   - Inaccurate assumptions;
   - Incomplete project design;
   - Lack of technical expertise;
   - Late or errors in assessments;
   - Structural design errors;
   - Technical analysis errors;
   - Unexpected technical issues;
   - Unreliable technology;
   - Use of untested or immature technology.

5. *Legal Risks.* Examples of legal risks include:
   - Faulty legal contracts;
   - Property expropriation rights;
   - Objections to right of way;
   - Obscure legal agreements.

6. *Regulatory Risks.* Examples of regulatory risks include:
   - Financial regulations;
   - Incomplete application forms;
   - Lack of financial approval;
   - Lack of legal authorization;
   - New permits required.

7. *Structural Risks.* Examples of structural risks include:
   - Faulty or incomplete design;
   - High incidents of occupation safety issues or job injury;
   - Inaccurate estimates;
   - Industrial disputes;
   - Lack of full or proper permits;
   - Unexpected ecological site;
   - Unexpected geographical conditions.

8. *Project Management Risks.* Examples of project management risks include:
   - Ambiguous project scope;
   - Contractor delays;
   - High project staff turnover;
   - Inaccurate estimates;
   - Lack of communication;
   - Poorly defined project aims;
   - Unclear staff priorities;

- Unreasonable targets;
- Unscheduled works.

PROJECT RISK QUANTIFICATION

Project risk quantification consists of two stages, namely qualitative and quantitative risk analysis as depicted by Figure 10.4. Both methods help the project manager to assess the risk in the planning and execution of a project.

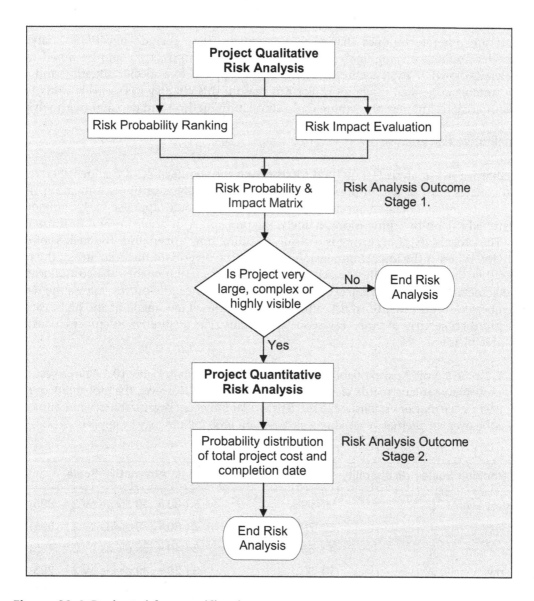

Figure 10.4 Project risk quantification process

Figure 10.4 illustrates that risk analysis consists of two stages. The first stage is the qualitative risk analysis which provides the prioritization of the risks and their respective impact. The outcome from this stage is the risk probability and impact matrix. The second stage consists of conducting a project quantitative risk analysis. However, a quantitative risk analysis is usually only carried out if the project is very large or is very complex or is highly visible. Quantitative risk analysis normally requires specialized computer software for the analysis. The outcome from this stage is the probability distribution of the holistic project in terms of cost and completion date.

Furthermore, the Monte Carlo simulation methodology using a project model is the most common and practical tool that is used in quantitative risk analysis. However, there are other techniques that may be applied. These include sensitivity analysis, expected monetary value analysis and decision tree analysis. It should be noted that these additional analysis techniques are as a rule applied to a specific situation and are not suitable as general usage tools. For this reason, this chapter will consider only two quantitative techniques, the Monte Carlo simulation method and decision tree analysis.

Qualitative risk analysis

Qualitative risk analysis is a method for assessing the significance of the identified risks and collates a list of risk in priority order for further analysis or direct mitigation. The project team members or specialist functional units would appraise each individual identified risk on two dimensions, namely, the probability of occurring and its impact.

The probability of occurring is basically deciding how uncertain is the success of the activity. Whereas the impact dimension measures the severity of the influence of the risk on either the project's ability to achieve the recipient's requirements, the cost allocated and achieving the agreed project completion period. Hence, the process allows the team members to sort the identified risks into three categories of low, medium and high risk for the project objectives of time, cost, scope and quality. The qualitative risk process consists of three phases:

1. Establish a project risk probability ranking matrix as shown in Figure 10.5. The project risk probability ranking matrix classifies risk into five scales. However, the probability of risk occurrence may be established to suit a particular project or organizational environment. Moreover, an alternative ranking scale based on probabilities may be applied.

Ranking Scale		Probability of Risk Occurrence	Alternative Scale
Very High	5	80–99%	.9 (.80 + .99 divide by 2 = .895)
High	4	60–79%	.7 (.60 + .79 divide by 2 = .695)
Medium	3	40–59%	.5 (.40 + .59 divide by 2 = .495)
Low	2	20–39%	.3 (.20 + .39 divide by 2 = .295)
Very Low	1	1–19%	.1 (.01 + .19 divide by 2 = .100)

Figure 10.5 Project risk probability ranking matrix

2. Establish a project risk impact matrix as shown in Figure 10.6. This matrix has two dimensions to match the project objective of time, cost, scope and quality to a defined impact. The impact definition may be established according to the particular requirements of the project or organization. In the example shown, the impact has five scales, with each scale being assigned the indicated value.

Project Goals	Risk Impact on Major Project Objectives				
	1 (very low)	2 (low)	4 (medium)	8 (high)	16 (very high)
Time	Slight time increase	<5% increase in time	5–10% increase in time	11–20% increase in time	>20% increase in time
Cost	Minor cost escalation	<10% cost escalation	10–20% cost escalation	21–40% cost escalation	>40% cost escalation
Scope	Scope shrinkage barely evident	Small sections of scope affected	Key sections of scope affected	Scope cutback objectionable to sponsor	Project outcome is ineffective
Quality	Quality decline scarcely evident	Only very rigorous items affected	Sponsor consent needed for lower quality	Quality cutback objectionable to sponsor	Project outcome is ineffective

Figure 10.6 Project risk impact evaluation matrix

3. The risk probability ranking matrix (Figure 10.5) and the risk impact matrix (Figure 10.6) are combined in a two-dimensional matrix that establishes whether each risk is low, medium or high as illustrated by Figure 10.7.

   The contents of the matrix are calculated by multiplying the impact scale by the probability scale across all rows and columns. For instance, probability scale 5 (Row 1) times impact scale 1, 2, 4, 8, and 16 would give a value of 5, 10, 20, 40, and 80 respectively. This combined risk probability–impact matrix is applied by assessing a specific event, for example, "Industrial dispute". If the probability of an event occurring is very high and the impact is low then the risk is medium (score value of 10). Therefore, those events that have a score of 1 to 6 would be considered as low risk; those with a score of 7 to 14 are viewed as medium risk; and a score greater than 14 would be classified as high risk.

   The above process provides a simple method of classifying events according to the probability of occurrence and impact on the project. This permits the project team members to review the risk analysis during the project lifecycle.

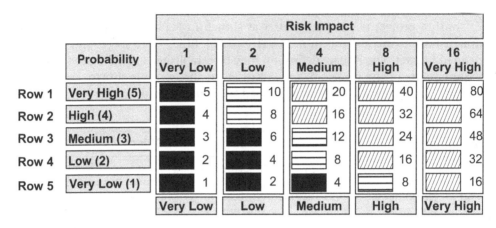

Figure 10.7 Project risk probability and impact matrix

Quantitative risk analysis – Monte Carlo simulation

Quantitative risk analysis is normally applied to the planning and execution of very large, complex or highly visible projects or those projects which propose to utilize new and untried technologies. Hence, this technique is normally applied in exceptional circumstances. Quantitative risk analysis is a method for estimating the chance that a project will achieve the established objectives of time, cost and performance. The three major concerns for both the project sponsor and project manager are:

1. *Time schedule.* Will the project extend over the schedule?
2. *Cost.* Will the project expenditure be greater than its budget allocation?
3. *Performance.* Will the project outcome satisfy the purpose of the project?

Quantitative risk analysis has the objective of providing answers to questions that cannot be addressed with deterministic project management methods, these are:

1. What is the probability of meeting the project scope, taking into account all known and quantified risks?
2. By how much will the project be delayed?
3. What level of contingency does the organization need to allocate in terms of both time and cost to meet the desired level of certainty taking into consideration the predicted project delay?
4. Where in the project is the most risk, taking into consideration the project model and all the identified and quantified risks?

It should be noted that qualitative risk analysis addresses only the last question. However, the qualitative approach cannot estimate the total project risk since it examines each risk one at a time. On the other hand, quantitative risk analysis applies statistical methods to appraise simultaneously the impact of all identified and quantified risks. The outcome of the analysis is a probability distribution of the project's cost and completion date based on the project risks. Therefore, the quantitative methodology estimates both schedule risk and cost risk as illustrated by the conceptual graphs shown at Figures 10.8 and 10.9.

Project time schedule risk is the probability that a project will go beyond its calculated schedule. Figure 10.8 illustrates that if the project closing date is 46 months the analysis would suggest an 80 per cent probability of completing the project in that time. Furthermore, there is a 50 per cent chance of the project being completed in 41 months, and there is very high certainty that the project will be completed in 65 months.

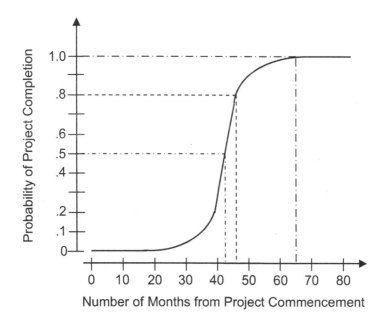

Figure 10.8 Project time schedule risk

Similarly, project cost risk is the probability that a project will go beyond its calculated cost estimate. Figure 10.9 illustrates that there is an 80 per cent probability that the project will be completed within the estimated cost of 20 million, with a 50 per cent chance of the project being completed at a cost of 18 million, and there is very high certainty that the project will not cost more than 40 million.

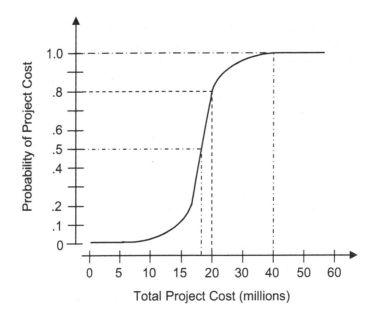

Figure 10.9 Project cost risk

These conceptual curves vary according to the project stage. For example, during the planning phase both curves will most likely have a mild slope, indicating that there is significant uncertainty regarding the project period length or its total cost. For instance, there is higher probability of going past 60 months in duration. As the project progresses the curves may change in either direction as events occur that increase or reduce time or cost schedules. Finally, as the project approaches completion, the curve will most likely become steeper as the project team becomes more certain about the final completion date and cost. The curves summarize the risk appraisal of the cost and time schedules. However, generating these curves in a meticulous and realistic manner is not an easy task for large and complex projects and requires specialized computer software to enable a proper project model to be defined.

The above illustrate that quantitative risk analysis appraises the consequences of all the identified and quantified risks concurrently for the project model as defined by the Critical Path Method (CPM) schedule for time and respective cost estimates. However, the CPM model is just one major input to the quantitative risk analysis method. The other major input is related to the probability distributions of the activity durations and cost elements. These are normally continuous distributions depicting the possible values of the activity durations or cost elements that are formulated through historical project data and intensive interviews of those involved in the respective activities. These mathematical distributions together with the CPM data form the basis for a simulation model.

A Monte Carlo simulation approach of the CPM cost or time schedule model is often utilized. This approach brings together the distributions according to the relationships in the models by seeking many combinations of costs or durations and storing these results for eventual display. The simulation outcomes are often graphs of probability distributions or cumulative probability distributions of the total cost or dates of project completion. Other useful outputs include a list of cost components that contain the greatest risk which have the highest contingency contribution to the total cost mean or schedule activities.

Common distributions that are normally used for the simulation model include the beta, triangular, uniform and normal distributions. The input for these distributions is usually based on a three parameter estimating method in which the cost or duration is represented by:

1. *The most optimistic value.* This is an estimate of the minimum time (and cost) required to complete an activity if outstandingly good conditions are experienced in the execution of the activity. This estimate is not the expedited solution unless all the three parameter estimates are targeted to expedite an activity.
2. *The most likely value.* This is based on previous experience or the project manager's personal judgement. It is basically the time (and cost) that one would expect to complete the activity if it were repeated on a number of occasions under similar conditions.
3. *The pessimistic value.* This is the highest or worst estimate possible if abnormally bad circumstances are encountered in the execution of the activity.

There are two major concerns with quantitative risk analysis, namely the reliability of the CPM project model and the realism of the three parameter estimates and respective distribution selected. The CPM project model must have an accurate project network representation and resultant project schedule. This requires robust network logic that would calculate a proper critical path and respective activity schedule dates when durations change. In addition, the mathematical distribution selected must approximate as much as possible the true and accurate time and cost behaviour.

The first concern related to the CPM model reliability requires a careful analysis of the project outcomes and the respective processes to achieve them. Hence, the CPM network logic (sequence and relationships between activities) needs to be discussed with the relevant persons who understand the process and are experts in their respective fields. The second concern is related to the realism of the distributions selected. Realism is achieved by collating and analysing relevant and accurate data. Data must be free from personal and institutional biases. Hence, this frequently requires focused interviews of project participants and other specialists.

Quantitative risk analysis is carried out after qualitative risk analysis. The major reason for this is the fact that quantitative risk analysis is not generally applicable to all projects. If a project requires a quantitative risk analysis it is important to identify and include all the major project risks in the project model and resultant cost and time schedules. It should be noted that project risk analysis is a strategic tool to help in the management of a project. Hence, quantitative risk analysis applies the time and cost distribution models at a strategic level. Therefore, if data is difficult or impractical to collect at a detailed level, it is still possible to conduct quantitative risk analysis at a higher level, thus data collection at a detailed day-to-day activity level is avoided.

For example, a CPM network of a large and complex project may contain thousands of activities. This may result in too much detail and would be unmanageable for the purpose of risk analysis. It would be very difficult to verify the network logic of projects having hundreds (if not thousands) of activities. Likewise, data collection at an activity level for such large project networks would become impractical. Moreover, the simulation process may also underestimate the risk, particularly when having many short uncorrelated activities. To overcome this difficulty it is recommended that a concise schedule, based on milestones, is generated for time-based simulations and applying cost sub-totals for the simulation of cost models.

The discussion regarding quantitative risk analysis revealed that it consists of three major processes, namely project modelling, data gathering, and simulation.

Project modelling. Project modelling is based on standard project management tools. However, the project model will need to be compatible with the quantitative risk analysis approach. The schedule risk model analysis will utilize the CPM, whereas the cost risk model analysis will use the cost estimates found at the Work Breakdown Structure (WBS) or the Cost Breakdown Structure (CBS). The CPM model must be viewed as being dynamic where durations are not static but tend to change as a project is being executed.

This is sometimes referred to as "dynamic scheduling". Moreover, CPM models are based on logic, in other words, activities are conducted in a specific sequence and have a logical relationship with other activities. Therefore, CPM models are not mere lists of tasks with dates and durations, but are linked together by a logical process. Cost estimates are easier to understand because they are represented through the WBS or CBS. However, their basis is still the underlying CPM network model.

Data gathering. Data gathering is generally based on intensive and focused interviews. The interview process is conducted by a risk analyst or risk facilitator to a focus group of employees who possess expert knowledge of a particular project segment. The employees participating in the focus group interviews do not necessarily need to be part of the project team. The risk interview facilitator must isolate motivational and cognitive bias so that the true risks are identified and assessed.

Motivational bias occurs when individuals or organizations have the aim of routing the inputs and resultant conclusions on a particular track. At times, project supporters tend to understate the risk so that the project looks more feasible than it actually is. This practice is intentional and very common in organizations. Hence the risk facilitator needs to be aware of any biased data. Cognitive bias is unintentional and usually results in underestimating the maximum ranges of the pessimistic and optimistic estimate. Therefore, the risk facilitator must continuously question the data during the interview to obtain more realistic estimate values.

Model simulation. Model simulation may be carried out using two basic methods. The first method utilizes simulation tools that are add-ons to Excel spreadsheets for cost risk analysis using a selection of probability distributions. The second method is the use of simulation tools that integrate with project management packages used to carry out schedule risk analysis.

As stated previously the Monte Carlo simulation methodology using a project model is the most common and practical tool that is used in quantitative risk analysis. The next two sections will examine decision tree analysis and the application of the simulation method to a Project Evaluation Review Technique (PERT) project network.

Quantitative risk analysis – decision tree analysis

Decision tree analysis is a tool that helps the project team to select the best strategy from various alternatives. The method provides a means whereby alternative strategic options are identified and structured in a way that permits the project team to examine the possible outcomes for each strategy. Hence, the technique provides a way of presenting a balanced view of the risks and pay-outs associated with each possible strategy.

The best way to illustrate the use of decision tree analysis is through an example. Assume that a computer manufacturer has to decide between developing a new product or to strengthen its existing product line. Such a decision may be represented by a decision tree as shown by Figure 10.10. Note that the basis of a decision tree is the decision that needs to be determined.

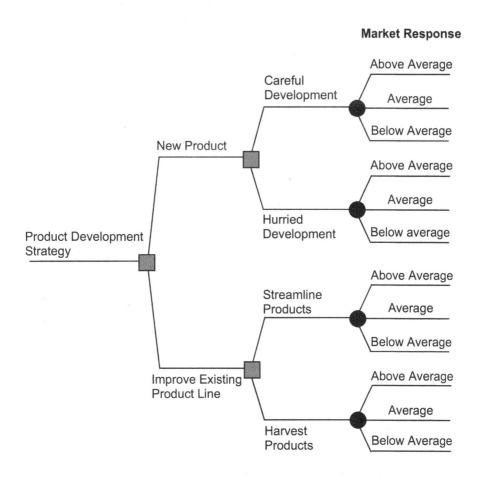

Figure 10.10   Decision tree for product development strategy

In the example the object of the decision is to choose the product development strategy, in other words: Should the company develop a new product or strengthen its existing product line? The squares on the diagram represent decisions and the circles represent uncertain outcomes. The decision tree moves from left to right. Therefore, in the example, the management team has two options, to develop a new product or to improve the existing product line. Each of these two options has two other alternative decisions:

1. For the development of a new product, the company can adopt a very meticulous approach or it can adopt a hurried development procedure to shorten the process;
2. For the improvement of the existing product lines, the company can either streamline its existing product line or continue as is and harvest the potential of its existing product line.

Note that the branches of the decision tree for these choices are depicted with squares, because they represent decisions. However, the branch from each of the decision is represented by a circle which indicates uncertain outcomes regarding how the market will respond to each decision taken. Like many other modelling techniques, obtaining an accurate representation of the model is an iterative process. Therefore, once the first version of the decision tree is achieved it must be reviewed by questioning each square and circle to determine whether there are any other solutions or outcomes that have not been considered. This process is repeated until a satisfactory decision tree is obtained.

The next step is to generate a probability–payoff matrix as shown by Figure 10.11 for every option represented by the decision tree depicted in Figure 10.10. This matrix will indicate the option that has the greatest value for the organization. The probabilities and values for the matrix are estimates based on historical data and market research. Note that the branches stemming from each circle in the decision tree shown in Figure 10.10 represent an uncertainty and will require a probability and the estimated outcome worth to be assigned to them. Furthermore, the probabilities of the branches stemming from a specific circle must add up to 1 (100 per cent).

The computation of the decision outcomes is calculated by using the decision tree and the probability–payoff matrix. Starting from the right of the decision tree and moving towards the left, multiply the value of the outcomes by their probability on every node (decision square or uncertainty circle). The full decision tree calculation process is shown in Figure 10.12. The results of the decision outcomes are also shown in Figure 10.11 (Outcome column).

Let us assume that the various options have the following costs:

- New product – Careful development costs 82,500;
- New product – Hurried development costs 44,500;
- Improve existing product line – Streamline products costs 16,500;
- Improve existing product line – Harvest products option has no costs.

Note that the costs do not represent past or historical expenditure but are new costs that would be spent if a specific decision is undertaken. The next step is to assess the decision node by subtracting the decision option cost from the calculated decision outcomes to provide the benefit of the particular decision as shown by Figure 10.13.

For example, the cost for "New Product – Careful Development" is estimated at 82,500 and the decision outcome as previously calculated is 241,730. Hence, the net decision benefit would be 159,230 (that is 241,730 minus 82,500). Therefore, the complete

Product Development Strategy		Market Response						Outcome
		Above Ave.		Average		Below Ave.		
		Pr	Value	Pr	Value	Pr	Value	
New Product	Careful development	0.4	575,000	0.4	28,750	0.2	1,150	241,730
	Hurried development	0.1	575,000	0.2	28,750	0.7	1,150	64,055
Improve Existing Products	Streamline products	0.3	230,000	0.4	11,500	0.3	3,450	74,635
	Harvest products	0.4	17,250	0.2	11,500	0.4	1,150	9,000

Example: Calculation of decision outcome for "new product – careful development"

0.4	(probability for above average)	×	575,000 (value) =	230,000
0.4	(probability for average)	×	28,750 (value) =	11,500
0.2	(probability for below average)	×	1,150 (value) =	230
1.0				241,730

Figure 10.11   Product development strategy – probability and payoff matrix

decision tree analysis process computes the best option and shows that the "new product with careful development" option is the optimum alternative.

Then again, the decision tree analysis suggests that a better financial return would result if the company meticulously plans and develops a new product and does not rush to release a new product on the market place. Moreover, it is also better to streamline the existing product line than to develop a new product badly even though it may cost the company less. The example illustrates that decision tree analyses are beneficial because they:

• Visibly and unambiguously define the decision to be resolved by showing all the options, so that they may be systematically computed in terms of costs;
• Allow management to fully assess all the likely consequences of a decision;
• Offer a feasible framework for calculating the outcome values and the respective probabilities of achieving them.

Finally, decision tree analysis helps management to evaluate the estimates and available information to arrive at the best decisions by selecting the better alternative. However, like every other management tool, it takes experience and a rational approach in applying the method.

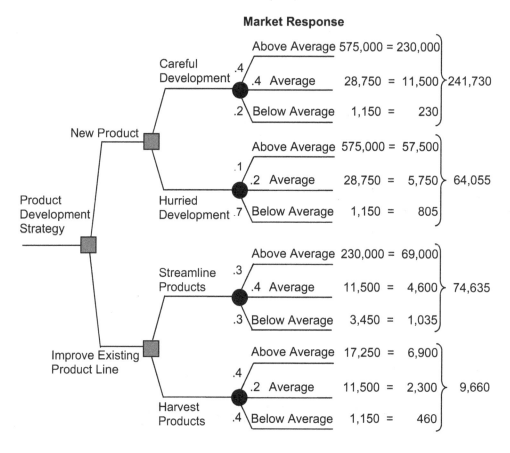

Figure 10.12 Product development strategy – decision outcome calculations

Quantitative risk analysis – using the PERT approach

PERT (Project Evaluation and Review Technique) is a technique that utilizes a three-parameter estimate approach similar to the Monte Carlo simulation method that was described previously. PERT is normally used in projects with high uncertainty and was developed by the US Navy to control contracts for its Polaris Missile program in the late 1950s. Hence, PERT has been developed for environments where there is either inadequate intrinsic information to accurately define and estimate time and cost data or where project activities require extensive research and development.

The Monte Carlo simulation approach for the CPM cost or time project schedule model utilizes a number of common mathematical distributions. These mathematical distributions include the beta, triangular, uniform and normal distributions. However, PERT considers only the beta-distribution but it still applies the three-parameter estimate through the equation as shown in Figure 10.14.

PERT uses the expected mean time (t_e) concurrently with an associated uncertainty measure of the activity duration. The uncertainty measure is expressed by either the standard deviation (σ) or the variance (σ^2) of the duration. Therefore, PERT assumes a beta distribution with the input for this distribution being represented by the most

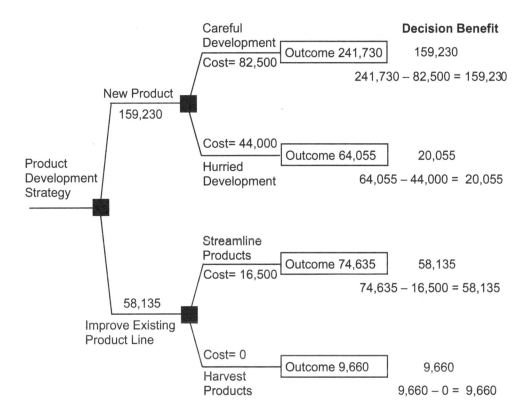

Figure 10.13 Product development strategy – decision benefits calculations

optimistic value, most likely value and pessimistic value. The beta-distribution is depicted by Figure 10.14.

Hence, the essential characteristic of PERT analysis is to determine the expected time for each activity by using the weighted average of the best, worst and most likely time estimates. When the expected times have been determined for all the activities on the critical path, these can be accumulated to ascertain the expected time and cost for the total project. Moreover, the standard deviation and variance, which represent the magnitude of uncertainty and measure the dispersion of the distribution curve about the mean value, are also computed (refer to Figure 10.14).

The project duration is calculated by accumulating the activity expected mean times of all the activities along the critical path. This calculation will provide the expected mean duration for the total project. It should be noted that the critical path activities are independent of each other. Hence, according to statistical theory, the variance of the project duration is the sum of the individual variances of the activities on the critical path. Therefore, the standard deviation for the total project is the square root of the variance of the project duration. If the project has more than one critical path, calculate the project duration variance of each individual critical path and choose the maximum project duration variance. Again, the variance of the expected mean time of any event is the summation of the variances of those activities along the longest (time-consuming) path leading to that event.

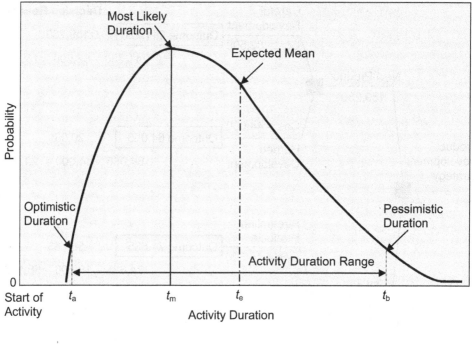

Figure 10.14   Activity duration probability beta distribution

Therefore, from the calculated expected mean time for an event and its standard deviation, the probability of achieving a specific event scheduled time may be determined through the use of probability theory by applying the normal probability distribution. Figure 10.15 shows an abridged table of probabilities for the respective normal distribution Z-value. The probability of an event (Z-value) is obtained by using the equation shown at Figure 10.15.

The probability of an event is obtained by using the Z-value and finding the corresponding probability from Figure 10.15. The Event Scheduled Time for a given probability (risk level) acceptable to management is calculated as follows:

Event Scheduled Time = Expected mean time for an event + (Std. Deviation × Z)

The value for Z is obtained from Figure 10.15 for a specified probability of an event. Note that time is an essential element with the PERT method, because the cost estimates are based on the determined time forecasts. The PERT concept, even though catering for high uncertainty, is normally used in practice for projects with often repeated

Z-Value	Pr.	Z-Value	Pr.	Z-Value	Pr.	Z-Value	Pr.
-3.0	0.00	-1.5	0.07	0.1	0.54	1.6	0.95
-2.9	0.00	-1.4	0.08	0.2	0.58	1.7	0.96
-2.8	0.00	-1.3	0.10	0.3	0.62	1.8	0.96
-2.7	0.00	-1.2	0.12	0.4	0.66	1.9	0.97
-2.6	0.00	-1.1	0.14	0.5	0.69	2.0	0.98
-2.5	0.01	-1.0	0.16	0.6	0.73	2.1	0.98
-2.4	0.01	-0.9	0.18	0.7	0.76	2.2	0.99
-2.3	0.01	-0.8	0.21	0.8	0.79	2.3	0.99
-2.2	0.01	-0.7	0.24	0.9	0.82	2.4	0.99
-2.1	0.02	-0.6	0.27	1.0	0.84	2.5	0.99
-2.0	0.02	-0.5	0.31	1.1	0.86	2.6	1.00
-1.9	0.03	-0.4	0.34	1.2	0.88	2.7	1.00
-1.8	0.04	-0.3	0.38	1.3	0.90	2.8	1.00
-1.7	0.04	-0.2	0.42	1.4	0.92	2.9	1.00
-1.6	0.05	-0.1	0.46	1.5	0.93	3.0	1.00
		0.0	0.50				

To obtain the probability of an *event*, the following equation is necessary:

Z = (Event Scheduled Time – Expected mean time for an event) ÷ (Event Std Deviation)

Figure 10.15 Standard normal distribution values and probabilities (estimated)

tasks and highly standardized methodologies, for instance, construction, new product development and system development projects. Moreover, PERT may not be sensitive enough to cater for the many unknowns, uncertainties and instabilities that may be relevant issues driving the schedule risk, because unlike Monte Carlo Simulation it does not utilize random simulation techniques in conjunction with a variety of mathematical distribution functions.

Example using PERT analysis

Let us assume that a construction company has been awarded a contract to build a steel frame for a warehouse. The project scope includes the preparation of the construction site to the assembly of the steel frame for the warehouse. Figure 10.16 provides the project network showing the critical path and the respective network data.

Note that the optimistic, most likely and pessimistic estimates are provided by the Project Management Team. The expected mean time, standard deviation and variance are calculated by the following three equations:

Expected Mean Time = [Optimistic + (4 × Most-Likely) + Pessimistic] ÷ 6

Standard Deviation (σ) = (Pessimistic - Optimistic) ÷ 6

Variance (σ²) = ((Pessimistic - Optimistic) ÷ 6)²

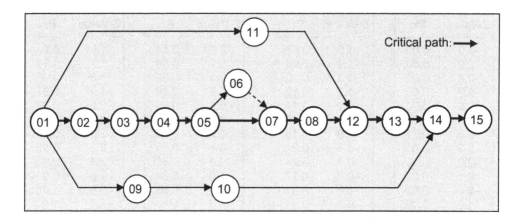

Time Estimates		Estimated Durations (Days)					
		t_a	t_m	t_b	t_e	σ	σ^2
Activity	Description	O	ML	P	Expected Mean	S.D	V
01-02*	Prepare Site	3	5	10	6	1.17	1.36
01-09	Fabricate steel frame	25	35	60	38	5.83	34.03
01-11	Procure concrete	3	5	8	5	0.83	0.69
02-03*	Fence Site	5	8	15	9	1.67	2.78
03-04*	Erect site workshop	4	8	13	8	1.50	2.25
04-05*	Survey excavation site	2	4	7	4	0.83	0.69
05-06	Bend re-enforcement steel	5	10	18	11	2.17	4.69
05-07*	Excavate site	10	16	25	17	2.50	6.25
06-07	Dummy	0	0	0	0	0.00	0.00
07-08*	Assemble formwork	6	10	17	11	1.83	3.36
08-12*	Place re-enforcement steel	5	7	10	7	0.83	0.69
09-10	Paint fabricated steel frame	11	15	23	16	2.00	4.00
10-14	Transport fabricated steel frame	3	5	9	5	1.00	1.00
11-12	Pour concrete in foundation	5	5	5	5	0.00	0.00
12-13*	Cure & set concrete	28	28	28	28	0.00	0.00
13-14*	Dismantle formwork	4	9	12	9	1.33	1.78
14-15*	Assemble warehouse frame	15	24	38	25	3.83	14.69

(* = Activities on critical path which total to 124 days)
O = Optimistic; ML = Most Likely; P = Pessimistic

Figure 10.16   Standard normal distribution values and probabilities (estimated)

The project duration is 124 days, which is obtained by the summation of the expected mean times of all the activities along the critical path, thus giving the expected mean duration for the total project. Note that there is only one critical path therefore the variance (σ^2) of the project duration is 33.85 days, which is obtained by adding the individual variances of the activities on the critical path. Furthermore, the standard deviation (σ) for the project duration is 5.82 days (√33.85). By using the equation below for a range of project durations the value of Z may be computed:

$$Z = (Project\ Scheduled\ Time - Project\ Expected\ Mean\ Time) \div (Event\ Std.\ Deviation)$$

Knowing Z will provide, by reading the values from Figure 10.15, the probability of achieving a particular project duration. Figure 10.17 provides the probabilities of achieving

Project Durations	Project Expected Mean Time	Z	Pr
113	124	-1.9	0.00
114	124	-1.7	0.04
115	124	-1.5	0.07
116	124	-1.4	0.08
117	124	-1.2	0.12
118	124	-1.0	0.16
119	124	-0.9	0.18
120	124	-0.7	0.24
121	124	-0.5	0.31
122	124	-0.3	0.38
123	124	-0.2	0.42
124	124	-0.0	0.50
125	124	0.2	0.58
126	124	0.3	0.62
127	124	0.5	0.69
128	124	0.7	0.76
129	124	0.9	0.82
130	124	1.0	0.84
131	124	1.2	0.88
132	124	1.4	0.92
133	124	1.5	0.93
134	124	1.7	0.96
135	124	1.9	0.97

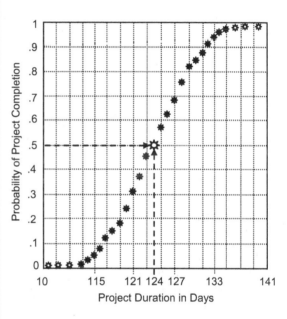

Figure 10.17   Project schedule risk for building steel warehouse frame

various project durations, ranging from 113 to 135 days. The graph at Figure 10.17 shows the probability distribution obtained by plotting each project duration probability. This provides a pictorial version of the project schedule risk.

It is worth remembering that a node (circle) in a PERT network (see Figure 10.16) represents an event. As we have illustrated, event 15 represents the completion of the project. By applying the same method as shown above, the probability of achieving any particular event stage for a given event schedule time may be computed. Note that the variance of the expected mean time of any event is the summation of the variances of those activities along the longest path leading to that event. For example, event 7 has two paths:

1. Path one has activities 01–02, 02–03, 03–04, 04–05, 05–06 and 06–07;
2. Path two has the activities 01–02, 02–03, 03–04, 04–05, and 05–07.

The variance of the event is obtained by accumulating the variances of the activities on each path. For instance path one has a variance of 11.77 and path two has a variance of 13.33. Hence, the greatest variance of 13.33 is selected. Thus, the standard deviation is the square root of the variance. Hence, the standard deviation of event 7 is 3.65. Similarly, the expected mean up to a particular event is obtained by summating the activity expected mean times of all the activities along the longest path leading to that event. Hence, the expected mean up to event 7 is 38 or 44 days, with the longest being 44 days.

The event scheduled times for all events may be calculated for specific probability values (as shown by Figure 10.18) using the equation: Event Scheduled Time = Expected mean time for an event + (Std. Deviation × Z). Where: Z is obtained from Figure 10.15 for a specified probability of an event.

Note that the specific probabilities have been selected and the equation is applied to calculate the event scheduled time. For example, Figure 10.18 shows that event 7 has a probability of 16 per cent of being achieved by day 40 (40.3), 31 per cent by day 42 (42.2), 50 per cent by day 44, 70 per cent by day 45 (45.8), and 84 per cent by day 47 (47.7).

Event & Project Stage	Event (Earliest Start)			Approx. Event Scheduled Time for Z Values & Corresponding Probabilities				
	Exp. Mean	V (σ^2)	S.D (σ)	Z -1.0 P 0.16	-0.50 0.31	0.00* 0.50*	0.50 0.70	1.00 0.84
1 PROJECT START								
2 Preparation of site	6	1.36	1.17	4.8	5.4	6.0	6.6	7.2
3 Fencing of site	15	4.14	2.03	13.0	14.0	15.0	16.0	17.0
4 Erecting site workshop	23	6.39	2.53	20.5	21.7	23.0	24.3	25.5
5 Survey excavation site	27	7.08	2.66	24.3	25.7	27.0	28.3	29.7
6 Bend reinforced steel	38	11.77	3.43	34.6	36.3	38.0	39.7	41.4
7 Site excavation	44	13.33	3.65	40.3	42.2	44.0	45.8	47.7
8 Assembling formwork	55	16.69	4.09	50.9	53.0	55.0	57.0	59.1
9 Fabricating steel frame	38	34.03	5.83	32.2	35.1	38.0	40.9	43.8
10 Paint fabricated frame	54	38.03	6.17	47.8	50.9	54.0	57.1	60.2
11 Procuring concrete	5	0.69	0.83	4.2	4.6	5.0	5.4	5.8
12 Pouring concrete	62	17.38	4.17	57.8	59.9	62.0	64.1	66.2
13 Cure & set concrete	90	17.38	4.17	85.8	87.9	90.0	92.1	94.2
14 Transport steel frame	99	19.16	4.38	94.6	96.8	99.0	101.2	103.4
15 Assemble frame	124	33.85	5.82	118.2	121.1	124.0	126.9	129.8

* This would be equal to the expected mean of the event.

Figure 10.18   Probability of achieving project events – steel warehouse frame

The above technique has focused on the time aspect because cost would be computed by the method shown in Chapter 8 that dealt with activity utility data (see pp. 113–55). The cost would depend on the time, whether the activity would be executed using the all normal solution or expedited.

PROJECT RISK RESPONSE

Basically, project risk response has the objective of identifying the options available and defining the appropriate actions to enhance the opportunities and minimize the threats. The project risk response phase takes into consideration all the identified risks and their quantification to determine the appropriate strategy for addressing the risks. It should be noted that the project risk response addresses only the high risk items that were assessed and examined in the qualitative (and quantitative, if conducted) risk analysis and has the added objective of assigning an owner to each risk requiring a response. Therefore, the project risk response process identifies and assigns responsibility to an individual or group for each risk response. When dealing with risk there are basically four strategic options that are available to the project manager, these are:

1. Risk avoidance;
2. Risk transference;
3. Risk mitigation;
4. Risk acceptance.

Risk avoidance. The risk avoidance strategy is based on the principle of doing something to remove the risk. The project team would modify the project plan to eliminate the risk or to safeguard the project objectives from the consequences of the risk. For example, depending on the risk item, the project team may change a subcontractor or provide additional resources or simply allocating more time.

Risk transference. This strategy shifts the responsibility of the risk from the project team to someone else. For example, a risky segment of the project may be outsourced. In this case, the project team would transfer the financial impact of the risk to the contractor. However, this strategy would lessen the risk only if the party taking on the responsibility for the risk is better geared to take the necessary measures for the reduction of the risk.

Risk mitigation. This strategy takes the appropriate steps to lessen the probability of the risk occurring or lowering the consequences of the risk if it occurs. For instance, if the risk is associated with the availability of a specific resource type or expertise, the project manager would enter into a formal agreement ensuring that the resource would be made available when needed.

Risk acceptance. There are situations where the project manager may decide to accept certain risks, thus reacting to the specific risk if and when it occurs. This strategy is usually applicable when the risks involved (or their impact) are not significant to warrant the effort needed to address them proactively.

The aim of the project manager when dealing with project risk response is to select the best strategy to address each risk (that merits attention) and propose particular actions for implementing the selected strategy. Hence, the project risk response stage identifies and defines the risk related tasks that need to be carried out, the individual (or collective unit) responsible for executing the tasks and the schedule for the completion of the tasks.

PROJECT RISK MONITORING AND CONTROL

Risk monitoring and control keep a close watch on the identified risk, outstanding risk and any new emerging risks. In addition, the process ensures that the risk response plans are implemented effectively. The continuous monitoring of risks will identify any change in the risk status or if a particular risk has developed into an issue. Hence, the risk monitoring and control process regularly assesses the effectiveness of the risk response plans.

As one may appreciate, the inventory of project risk is not static and continually changes as the project is being implemented, thus new risks evolve and other risks disappear. The risk monitoring and control stage is best achieved by having frequent risk reviews to:

- Identify any outstanding actions;
- Update risk probability and respective impact;
- Remove risks that are no long current;
- Identify new risks.

Risk reviews allow the project manager to reassess and modify the risk ratings and prioritization throughout the project life cycle. However, the project manager may need to perform further risk response planning to control risk when an unforeseen risk becomes known or in the event that the risk impact is greater than anticipated. Note that the individual or unit assigned responsibility for a particular risk must report regularly to the project manager highlighting the effectiveness of the response plan, any unforeseen affects and the course of action that must be taken to mitigate the risk.

PROJECT RISK MANAGEMENT PLAN

Risk management need not be a complex task. As has been illustrated in the previous sections, project risk management planning consists of four components:

1. Risk identification;
2. Risk quantification in terms of analysing and prioritizing risk;
3. Risk response;
4. Risk monitoring and control.

Figure 10.19 provides a project risk management plan template that may be adapted to a particular organizational project management environment. The sample risk management plan consists of five segments.

The first segment describes the project and the project manager implying that the report is prepared for a specific project by the individual who has the overall responsibility for that project. The four remaining report segments reflect the components that make up the project risk management process.

The first column, entitled "Risk Rating" can be one of three rates, namely, low, medium or high. The risk rating is obtained from the qualitative risk analysis (refer to Figure 10.7) and establishes the risk priority, hence the reason why this column for visual display purposes is shown as the first information item.

The segment headed "Risk Identification" essentially describes each risk and its association with the project phase (and WBS element). The column headed "Threat or Opportunity" provides information regarding how the particular risk affects the defined project objectives (or outcomes), while the column headed "Causes of Risk" describes the

Risk Rate	ID	Risk Identification						Qualitative Analysis		Quantitative Analysis			Risk Response Strategy		Risk Monitoring and Control		
		Category & Description	Date	Project Area	Threat or Opp.	Causes of Risk	Risk Type	Pr.	Impact	Pr.	Impact	Result	Strategy	Measures	Task Manager	Status Period	Remarks
1	2	3	4	5	6	7	8	9	10	11	12	13	14	15	16	17	18

Col 01: Risk Rating (High=1; Medium=2; Low=3.)
Project Risk Identification:
Col 02: Risk Identity Number (reference number)
Col 03: Risk category and description (refer to risk inventory)
Col 04: Date (date risk identified)
Col 05: Project area affected (milestone and/or WBS element)
Col 06: Threat or Opportunity (effect on project objectives)
Col 07: Cause of risk (the factors that may trigger the risk)
Project Risk Qualitative Risk Analysis:
Col 08: Risk type (Time, Cost, Scope or Quality)
Col 09: Probability (Very high, High, Medium, Low, Very low.)
Col 10: Impact (Very high, High, Medium, Low, Very low.)

Project Risk Quantitative Risk Analysis (only if necessary):
Col 11: Pr. (Probability range from +1 to -1)
Col 12: Impact (In terms of money or time)
Col 13: Result in terms of money or time (Col 11 × Col. 12)
Project Risk Response Strategy:
Col 14: Strategy (avoidance, transference, mitigation, acceptance)
Col 15: Measures (response actions, benefits and shortcomings)
Project Risk Monitoring and Control:
Col 16: Task Manager (person responsible i.e., risk owner)
Col 17: Status Period (interval period for checking milestone at risk)
Col 18: Remarks (any relevant comments)

Figure 10.19 Project risk management plan template

factor(s) that would trigger the risk. For example, "risk is occurring if the contractor files for bankruptcy".

The information for the segment headed "Qualitative Analysis" is obtained from the qualitative risk analysis as illustrated by Figure 10.7. The risk type may be time, cost, scope and quality. The probability and impact columns both contain one of the following classifications, very low, low, medium, high or very high.

The "Quantitative Analysis" is only conducted when the risk is very high. Therefore, this report segment may not always have information pertaining to a particular project. If present, the information will describe the:

- Probability of the risk occurring expressed as a range from one to minus one;
- Impact in terms of delay or gain in time or monetary value;
- Result or end effect which is calculated by the multiplication of the impact by the probability.

The "Risk Response" segment itemizes the selected risk strategy option and the response actions to be taken (including the benefits and shortcomings of the response action). Note that the risk strategy options may include one of the following:

- Risk avoidance;
- Risk transference;
- Risk mitigation;
- Risk acceptance.

The final report segment is "Risk Monitoring and Control". This provides the details of the individual (or unit) directly responsible for the risk, the status interval period for reviewing the risk and any relevant remarks regarding the response action.

Note that Figure 10.19 is meant to provide a sample template of a risk management plan. Therefore the space allocated to each column will need to be adjusted to reflect a realistic and practical situation. It is worth remembering that without a risk management plan, the success of the project and the credibility of both the organization and project manager are at stake. The project risk management process has the objective of increasing the chances of success for both the project and the individuals who have the responsibility for its implementation.

Conclusion

Project risk management strives to foresee and deal with uncertainties that threaten the objectives, and the time and cost schedules of a project. However, risk is not always bad. There are both opportunities and threats. Project risk management is defined as a succession of processes, tools and methods that will aid the project management team to increase the likelihood and impact of positive events and to decrease the probability and impact of negative events. This chapter has shown that project risk management planning consists of four components:

1. Risk identification;
2. Risk quantification;
3. Risk response;
4. Risk monitoring and control.

Risk identification

Project risk identification basically addresses the question: What might go wrong? It identifies and names the project risks and their characteristics. The outcome of this phase is an itemized risk inventory. A risk inventory is generated by examining in detail the entire project plan, systematically seeking areas of uncertainty and categorizing risk under major sub-headings.

Risk quantification

Project risk quantification assesses the magnitude of risk and its impact. It consists of two distinct methods, namely qualitative and quantitative risk analysis. The latter approach is usually used for projects that are considered to have extremely high risks associated with them. Qualitative risk analysis provides the prioritization of the risks and their respective impact so that all major risks are included. The outcome from this stage is the risk probability and impact matrix.

The quantitative approach normally uses mathematical distributions for defining a project model and applies simulation techniques to determine the overall project cost and completion date. Other techniques that may be applied include sensitivity analysis, expected monetary value analysis and decision tree analysis.

Quantitative risk analysis has the aim of providing answers to questions that cannot be addressed with deterministic project management methodologies, these are:

• What is the probability of meeting the project scope, taking into account all known and quantified risks?
• By how much will the project be delayed?
• What level of contingency does the organization need to allocate in terms of both time and cost to meet the desired level of certainty, taking into consideration the predicted project delay?
• Where in the project are the most risks, taking into consideration the project model and all the identified and quantified risks?

Risk response

Project risk response has the objective of identifying the options available and defining the appropriate actions to enhance the opportunities and minimize the threats. Thus, the process identifies and assigns responsibility to an individual or group for each risk response. Generally, there are four strategic risk options that a project manager may choose from:

1. *Risk avoidance.* Doing something to remove the risk;
2. *Risk transference.* Shifting the responsibility of the risk from the project team to someone else who is better at doing that activity;
3. *Risk mitigation.* Lessening the probability of the risk occurring or lowering the consequences of the risk if it occurs;
4. *Risk acceptance.* To accept certain risks, thus reacting to the specific risk if and when it occurs.

The objective of the project manager when dealing with project risk response is to select the best strategy for addressing each risk and propose particular actions for implementing the selected strategy.

Risk monitoring and control

Risk monitoring and control keeps a close watch on the identified risk, outstanding risk and new arising risks. Risk monitoring and control ensures that the risk response plans are implemented effectively. The risk monitoring and control process regularly assesses the effectiveness of the risk response plans and is best achieved by having frequent risk reviews to identify any outstanding actions, update risk probability and impact, remove risks that are no long relevant and identify new risks.

One should note that the risk management plan is the product of the above four components. The project risk management plan template provided at Figure 10.19 consists of five segments. The first part describes the project and the project manager, therefore the report is prepared for a specific project by the individual who has the overall responsibility for that project. The four remaining report segments reflect the components that make up the project risk management process. Without a realistic and reliable project risk management plan, the success of a project and the credibility of the organization and project manager are at stake. The proper application of project risk management will increase the chances of success for both the project and the individuals who have the responsibility for the project.

References

Anderson D.R., Sweeney, D.J. and Williams, T.A. 2000. *An Introduction to Management Science: Quantitative Approaches to Decision Making*. London: South-Western College Publishing.

Bocij, P., Chaffey, D., Greasley, A. and Hickie, S. 1999. *Business Information Systems: Technology, Development and Management*. London: Prentice Hall.

Caltrans, Office of Project Management Process Improvement. 2007. *Project Risk Management Handbook* (5th Edition.). Sacramento, CA, USA: Office of Project Management Process Improvement.

Kerr, J.M. 1991. *The IRM Imperative: Strategies for Managing Information Resources*. New York: John Wiley & Sons Inc.

The Project Management Institute Standards Committee. 2004. *A Guide to the Project Management Body of Knowledge*. Upper Darby, PA, USA: Project Management Institute.

Wagner, H.M. 1969. *Principles of Operations Research with Applications to Managerial Decisions*. Englewood Cliffs, New Jersey: Prentice-Hall, Inc.

11 *Project Competency Development*

Training is everything. The peach was once a bitter almond; cauliflower is nothing, but cabbage with a college education.
                                        Mark Twain, writer (1835–1910)

Project competency development facilitates the ability of employees to become more efficient and flexible in carrying out their respective functions. Hence, in a project management environment, having skilled, knowledgeable and flexible employees is an important factor for organizations to increase their competitiveness and succeed in being awarded lucrative contracts. Organizations must therefore develop creative ways to help employees make the most of their individual development by focusing on the project management process and the competencies required to execute this process effectively.

An important objective of training is to help employees fully develop their potential in their chosen profession. However, one should note that this objective is not something that can be achieved completely because the development of employees is a continuous process and the competencies required by an organization are also in an ever-changing mode. Therefore, both employees and organizations are confronted with a situation where the organizational needs and the employee development goal posts are always in motion. Organizations must recognize this condition and continually seek feasible opportunities to be effective in the training activities undertaken.

All too often, employee development training programmes in organizations fail to achieve their objectives. It is not uncommon for many to proclaim that training does not work and to some extent this may be true. If training is seen to be disjointed because it does not form part of an overall strategy then it will not provide the optimum return and at times may turn out to be a waste of effort.

Training has been identified as one of the critical success factors for project management. Therefore, the objective of this chapter is to provide guidance about defining the employee development training programmes that would benefit both the organization and its employees. From an organizational prospective, an employee development training programme must support the organization's strategic direction and address the following questions:

- What competencies does the organization currently possess?
- What competencies does the organization need now and in the future to sustain and enhance its competitive position?
- How can the organization develop the full potential of its employees to motivate and attain their commitment and trust?

From the employees' perspective, a training programme must cater for the individuals' development needs. To define the development training requirements, management need to answer the following:

- What are the current competences of the employees?
- What competencies need to be strengthened and developed?
- What is the mismatch between the current employee and organizational competencies requirements?
- What is the best way for an organization and its employees to bridge the competency gap?

The response to the two sets of questions will establish the required project competency development needs for both the organization and its employees to attain the defined strategic goals of the organization.

Defining an Organizational Development Training Process Model

To establish a successful employee development training programme an organization must focus on creating the proper environment by fostering a sense of commitment, motivation and trust in the workplace. However, this is only achieved by having strong leadership. Leaders produce the environment that directly affects the employees' capacity and desires to perform at their highest potential. Research shows that the employees' perception of the organization in terms of how well the organization is being managed has a strong association with individual and organizational performance.

A major objective of an employee development training programme is to develop employees to become the best in their industry and for the employees themselves to act as the best. However, for this to happen, employees need to be in no doubt that the organization knows where it is heading. Figure 11.1 shows an employee development training requirements model.

This model describes the process for defining the employee development training requirements of an organization and is based on five major activities:

1. Defining the competencies that are required by the organization to carry out its strategy;
2. Identifying the competencies that the organization already has;
3. Assessing the organizational competencies gap;
4. Defining an employee development training programme;
5. Implementing the defined employee development training programme.

Competencies Required by the Organization

Competencies are identified behaviours, skills and knowledge that have a direct and positive influence on both the success of employees and the organization. At the same time, these competencies must be compatible with and aligned to the organization's mission and business strategy. From a project management perspective, management

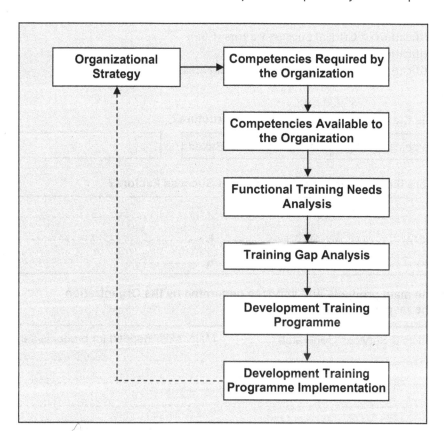

Figure 11.1 Employee development training requirements model

must clearly articulate the type of projects that the organization is qualified to undertake. For instance, being a construction company does not mean that the organization can undertake all types of construction projects.

For example, a company that specializes in housing construction would need to possess competencies to build houses and its projects will be focused on housing projects. However, a housing construction company would not likely be qualified to undertake the construction of roads and bridges, simply because it would not have the skills, experience and the equipment required to conduct such projects. In other words, it would not have the competencies to undertake the construction of roads and bridges.

It is therefore important for an organization to identify and define its business product and service lines by having a comprehensive business strategy. The defined business strategy will outline the current and future direction of the organization. At this stage an organization would need to address an essential question: "What competencies does the organization need now and in the future to achieve its defined strategy and enhance its competitive position?" To answer this question, management will need to make an appraisal of the competencies required by the organization. Figure 11.2 provides a template for an organization to appraise its required competencies. The organizational competencies appraisal template is divided into three major segments:

1. Identification of Critical Success Factors (CSF);
2. Identification of products and services;
3. Identification of organizational functional areas.

What is the Organization's managerial structure?

Hierarchical	Flat	Matrix	Project Based	

What are the main Organizational Critical Success Factors?

1 ------------------------------	4 ------------------------------
2 ------------------------------	5 ------------------------------
3 ------------------------------	6 ------------------------------

List the main products and services generated by the Organization and the respective skills needed.

Products & Services Generated	Major skills needed for products/services
1 ------------------------------	------------------------------
2 ------------------------------	------------------------------
3 ------------------------------	------------------------------
4 ------------------------------	------------------------------
5 ------------------------------	------------------------------
6 ------------------------------	------------------------------

List the main functional areas of the Organization and respective skills needed.

Organization Functional	Major skills needed for functional area
1 [In-bound Logistics]	------------------------------
2 [Operations]	------------------------------
3 [Out-bound Logistics]	------------------------------
4 [Marketing & Sales]	------------------------------
5 [Customer Services]	------------------------------

Figure 11.2 Organizational competencies needs appraisal template

Identification of Critical Success Factors (CSF)

The CSF itemize requirements that are essential and are required to be in place to ensure the successful provision of the products and services that are made available by the organization. For example, collaboration and teamwork may be identified as a critical success factor. Hence, competencies related to team building would help to achieve this particular critical success factor.

Identification of products and services

It is important to itemize the products and services that are currently (and anticipated to be) generated by the organization and the associated skills required. For example, if an organization produces information systems then the essential skills that may be needed include: business process engineering, systems analysis and design, and computer programming. Hence, the identification of the products and services, including the associated skills will allow the organization to define the competencies that it needs for its core activities (the organization's *raison d'être*).

Identification of organizational functional areas

Identifying the organizational functional areas and the related skills required within each functional area will have three primary purposes. First, all core and support functions that are carried out by the organization will be itemized. Second, itemizing the core functions will ensure that functions related to the generation of products and services are analysed to determine the competencies needed to carry out these functions. This will enable a cross check to be made with the competencies identified previously (identification of products and services). Third, the itemization of the support functions will identify all the competencies required to support the generation of the core products and services. For example, although procurement may be viewed as a support function, the organization will still need to ensure that certain employees have the competencies to carry out this function.

Figure 11.3 is produced by assessing the information contained in Figure 11.2, removing all duplicate competencies and presenting the data in a horizontal format. The resultant output from Figure 11.3 is a normalized list of competencies required by the organization.

Competencies Available to the Organization

Once the competencies required by the organization have been identified, it is essential to determine the competencies that are currently available to the organization. Comparing the competencies required with those that are available to the organization will provide the competency gap that needs to be satisfied. Details of the existing organizational competencies may be gathered by the Human Resource (HR) Department for each employee or alternatively the information may be extracted from the HR Management System. An example of the template regarding available competencies is shown at Figure 11.4.

Competencies		CSF							Products							Functional Areas*				
I.D	Description	1	2	3	4	5	6	1	2	3	4	5	6	In Bound	Ops	Out Bound	Sales	Customer Services

Note:

The functional areas shown are functions found in the organization value chain. These include: In-bound logistics, operations, out-bound logistics, marketing and sales, and customer services.

Figure 11.3 Analysis of competencies required by the organization

Note that the Competencies (ID) in Figure 11.4 are similar to those required by the organization (Figure 11.3, left column).

Employee Details				Competencies (ID)													
Functional Area	ID	Name	Current Role	01	02	03	04	05	06	07	08	09	10	11	12	13	14

Figure 11.4 Competencies available to the organization

Before a comparison between the required and available organizational competencies can be made, the information at Figure 11.4 must be sorted by functional area. This would enable management to determine the number of employees that have particular competencies within a functional area. Moreover, the sorted information showing the competencies available to the organization must have a similar format to Figure 11.3 to make the comparison process easier as shown at Figure 11.5.

Competencies		Number of Employees Having Competency per Functional Area				
ID	Description	In-bound Logistics	Operations	Out-bound Logistics	Marketing & Sales	Customer Services

Figure 11.5 Analysis of competencies available to the organization

Assessing the Organizational Competencies Gap

The comparison and combination of Figure 11.3 and Figure 11.5 showing the competencies required by the organization and those available to the organization enables management to determine the magnitude of the competency gap within the organization per functional area as shown by Figure 11.6. The number of employees having the competency for each functional area is obtained from Figure 11.5.

The Human Resources Department must estimate the number of employees that should have the particular competencies. Note that the number of employees (Under or over) is calculated by the subtraction of the number of employees having the competency from the estimated number of employees to have the competency.

Development Training Programme Definition and Implementation

The employee development training programme will consist of three elements, namely. the competencies to be developed, the employees who are to be the recipients of the competency development and the time schedule for the competency development. The employee development training programme is defined by using two inputs:

Employees per Functional Area	Competencies (ID)													
	01	02	03	04	05	06	07	08	09	10	11	12	13	14
In-bound Logistics														
No. of employees having competency														
Estimated number to have competency														
No. of employees (Under or over)														
Operations														
No. of employees having competency														
Estimated number to have competency														
No of employees (Under or over)														
Out-bound Logistics														
No. of employees having competency														
Estimated number to have competency														
No. of employees (Under or over)														
Marketing & Sales														
No. of employees having competency														
Estimated number to have competency														
No. of employees (Under or over)														
Customer Services														
No. of employees having competency														
Estimated number to have competency														
No of employees (Under or over)														

Figure 11.6 Organizational competencies gap analysis

1. Employee competency details (see Figure 11.4). This identifies the competencies possessed by individual employees for their respective role within an organizational functional area. Moreover, by inference, it identifies those employees who do not have particular competencies and need training in specific sectors. The employee competency details answers the question:
   • Who are the employees to be developed and trained in the identified organizational competencies gap?

2. Organizational competencies gap analysis (see Figure 11.6). This identifies the competencies that the organization needs but has encountered a shortfall in the number of employees who possess the identified competencies. Hence, it measures the magnitude and identifies the competency gap in terms of number of employees. The organizational competency gap analysis answers the questions:
   - What competencies does the organization need to develop?
   - How many employees need to be trained for the identified competencies?

Figure 11.7 illustrates a typical employee competencies development training programme template. The employee development training programme provides information about three major elements:

1. *What competencies are to be developed?* These are highlighted by the competencies ID.
2. *Who will take part in the competencies training?* This is provided by the employee details.
3. *When will the competency development take place?* This is the scheduled training date. The scheduled training date would appear within the space provided below the competencies ID and adjacent to the employee details.

Functional Area:_____ **Functional Area Manager:**_____

Employee Details			Scheduled Competencies (ID) Training Date													
ID	Name	Current Role	01	02	03	04	05	06	07	08	09	10	11	12	13	14

Figure 11.7 Employee competencies development training programme

Note that the sample templates provided will need to be formatted with sufficient space to enter the appropriate information.

Conclusion

Employee development training has been identified as one of the critical project management success factors. Employee development training is an essential mode for acquiring the competencies that the organization needs to deliver its strategic products and services. Furthermore, training helps employees to become more effective in carrying out their functions thus increasing organizational performance. In formulating an employee development training programme, management are required to address:

- What competencies does the organization require to implement its strategy?
- What competencies are available to the organization?
- What are the employee development training needs for each organizational functional area?
- What is the scale of the competencies gap or mismatch between the current employee competencies and the organizational competencies requirements?
- What is the best way for the organization and its employees to bridge the identified competency gap?

To address these questions, management must define an organizational employee development training requirement model as a guide for the enhancement of the employees' and the organization's capabilities. Having such a model will allow the organization to have a systematic process in place that will define a competency training programme for the identified employees within an organizational functional area. This chapter has provided the reader with adequate information to implement such a process that includes:

- The appraisal and analysis of the competencies required by the organization (refer to the templates in Figure 11.2 and Figure 11.3);
- The appraisal and analysis of the competencies that are available to the organization (refer to the templates in Figure 11.4 and Figure 11.5);
- Assessing the magnitude of the organizational competency gap by organizational functional area (refer to the template in Figure 11.6);
- Defining the competencies development training programme for the relevant employees within each organizational functional area (refer to the template in Figure 11.7).

This step-by-step process allows an effective employee development training programme to be determined. However, it should be noted that the suggested templates will need to be modified and fine tuned to suit a specific organization. Moreover, in defining an employee development training programme, management may wish to focus specifically on the project management core competencies.

The suggested templates take a holistic view of the organization and are suitable for both the core and support organizational functions. Remember that from an organization's perspective an employee development training programme must cater for the achievement of the strategic objectives while simultaneously taking into account the individual employees' development needs.

References

Frame, J.D. 1999. *Building Project Management Competence.* San Francisco: Jossey-Bass Publishers.

Thamhain, H.J. 1991. Developing project management skills. *Project Management Journal*, 22(3), 39–45.

—— 1992. Developing the skills you need. *Research Technology Management*, 35(2), 42–7.

IV Project Behavioural and Managerial Support Factors

The chapters in Part IV will examine in detail the Project Behavioural and Management Support Factors that consist of the following project success–failure dimensions:

- Management and Leadership;
- Employee Commitment and Participation;
- Internal and External Communication.

The behavioural and management support factors are viewed as influencing project success, with the focus being the project outcomes. These support factors are applicable to all types of projects. For a project to be successful in every aspect there must be strong leadership and the application of suitable management skills. In addition, high commitment and participation is essential. In a project oriented environment, commitment takes a wider meaning. It refers to stakeholder commitment with the major stakeholders being the client, executive management, project team and in some cases the public. Another requirement is right level of internal and external communication.

Project managers must continually maintain communication links with stakeholders, whether they are within or outside the organization. Admittedly, this takes a lot of time and energy but it is essential to the achievement of project success. Internal and external communication would aim to satisfy the behavioural implications, such as, fostering consensus amongst the various stakeholders to achieve their respective requirements and mitigate their concerns. As stated previously, the behavioural and management support factors focus on the project outcomes to ensure project success.

CHAPTER 12 *Management and Leadership*

> *To lead people, walk beside them … As for the best leaders, the people do not notice their existence. The next best, the people honor and praise. The next, the people fear; and the next, the people hate … When the best leader's work is done the people say, "We did it ourselves!"*
>
> Lao Tzu, philosopher (600BC)

Ask project managers about what they think are the most difficult situations encountered in delivering projects and most of the time their answer is related to the people side of project management. It is common knowledge among project managers that technical difficulties, although a concern, are normally resolved without much fuss. However, people problems are often much more troublesome to deal with. What is more, when we refer to people, we are referring to individuals, with each individual having different needs and concerns. Hence, project managers need to adapt their leadership behaviour to match different individuals' needs and circumstances.

Leaders must know and understand the people they are leading. A major concern that project managers face is that often they do not posses the authority to reward or promote their personnel. These project managers lack complete authority over the individuals they manage and find themselves in a position where their responsibility overshadows their authority. Because of this, project managers must find ways of increasing their authority through their ability to influence team members by developing affective and normative measures.

The quotation at the start of this chapter implies that good leaders need to inspire confidence in themselves, but truly great leaders inspire confidence within the people they lead, to exceed their normal performance level. However, a universal attribute in successful leadership is the aptitude of a project manager to portray a strong role model to the project team. For instance, remaining calm in chaotic circumstances and inspiring others with the ability to find the way through difficult conditions. The project manager also needs to exhibit the ability to be flexible in the leadership conduct towards various team members, changing relationship behaviours according to circumstances and individual characteristics.

Concepts of Leadership

Good leaders are made not born. Good leaders acquire their skills by means of continuous self development through experience, education, training and interacting with others. Leadership is a process by which an individual influences others to achieve an objective and directs the organization in a way that makes it more cohesive and coherent. Having authority to conduct the activities of the organization does not make a person a leader. Authority or power simply gives the individual the mandate to carry on with the undertaking, but leadership makes people want to follow the leader to achieve high goals. The research literature identifies six main schools of leadership theory:

1. Trait;
2. Behavioural;
3. Contingency;
4. Visionary;
5. Emotional intelligence;
6. Competency.

Trait leadership theory

The trait theory emerged in the 1900s to 1940s, where leadership is viewed as a personality attribute and its effect on the group, with emphasis on the importance of the leader as an individual, to whom the group is largely submissive. In other words, under this theory, leaders are born and not made. The literature identifies different leadership traits, including:

- Aspiration and energy;
- Communications skills;
- Dependability;
- Honesty and integrity;
- Intelligence and talent;
- Negotiating ability;
- Self-confidence;
- Social activity;
- The desire to lead and influence others.

However, this theory was not well received because of its dubious practical value and inconsistent research results.

Behavioural leadership theory

The behavioural theory evolved in the 1940s to 1960s and focused on the conduct of the leader. This theory had two closely-related streams. The first stream views leadership as having two dimensions, namely initiating-structure and consideration. Under initiating-structure the leader defines the leader–subordinate roles for subordinates, while under leadership consideration the leader is concerned with and respects the subordinates' feelings.

The second stream also has two dimensions; these are employee-oriented and production-oriented. Under the employee-oriented approach, the leader is concerned with the well-being of the subordinates, whereas under production-orientation, the leader focuses on performance. The behavioural leadership theory conceived the concept that leaders are made not born. Under the behavioural leadership theory, the leader must be:

- Concerned for people, relationships and production;
- Encourage employee participation in formulating and taking decisions;
- Flexible in applying rules and regulations.
- Use appropriate authority.

Nonetheless, this theory had a weakness in that it did not take into consideration the complexities of individual behaviour in organizational settings.

Contingency leadership theory

The contingency leadership theory was well received in the 1960s to 1970s. It epitomized leadership in a resourceful manner and conceptualized it as accommodating the complexities of leadership due to the impact of different situations. Contingency leadership theory had five streams:

1. Fiedler's Contingency Model;
2. Normative Decision Model;
3. Situational Leadership Theory;
4. Leader–Member Exchange Theory;
5. Path–Goal Theory.

The path–goal leadership theory developed by House (1971) is the most prevalent of the contingency leadership theories and contributed in recognizing the fact that no single pattern of behaviour will be successful in all situations. All the contingency leadership theories are based on three primary principles:

1. Appraising the attributes of the leader;
2. Assessing the circumstances in terms of major contingency variables;
3. Finding a corresponding match between the leader and the circumstances.

The path–goal leadership theory places importance on how leaders affect their subordinates' perceptions of their work and personal goals, and the direction they take to achieve their goals. Furthermore, this theory posits that leaders become effective because of the impact they make on their subordinates' level of motivation, resulting in the subordinates' ability to perform competently. The path–goal leadership theory attempts to describe the consequences of four specific styles of leadership behaviour on subordinate attitudes. The subordinate attitudes considered by this theory are:

1. Satisfaction of subordinates;
2. Subordinates' acceptance of the leader;
3. Subordinates' expectations that their effort will result in effective performance, which is the route to rewards.

House and Mitchell (1974) conceptualized the path–goal leadership theory by integrating previous leadership research into a multi-dimensional model that depicted four leadership styles:

1. *Instrumental or Directive Leadership.* With this style, the leader informs subordinates what is expected of them; provides subordinates with specific support as to what tasks are to be carried out and how they are to be executed; indicates and explains the role of each subordinate in the group; upholds specific standard of performance; and requests group members to adhere to standard rules and regulations.
2. *Supportive Leadership.* The leader under this style is viewed as being friendly, showing particular interest for the status, well-being and needs of subordinates. A supportive leader is consenting, doing little things to make the tasks more satisfying and considers members as equals.
3. *Participative Leadership.* A participative leader seeks opinions from subordinates and genuinely takes these suggestions into account before making a decision.
4. *Achievement-Oriented Leadership.* This type of leader sets demanding and stimulating goals, where subordinates are expected to perform at their highest level. The leader constantly looks for ways to improve performance and displays a high level of trust that will stimulate subordinates to take on the prerequisite level of responsibility,by exerting the necessary effort to achieve the established goals.

According to House and Mitchell (1974) these four leadership styles must correspond to both environmental and subordinate contingency factors. The environmental attribute which moderates the impact of a leader's behaviours is task structure. Task structure includes the level of repetitiveness, the formal authority system and the work group. Whilst the subordinate attributes that moderate the impact of a leader's behaviours are locus of control, experience and ability.

Visionary or charismatic leadership theory

The visionary or charismatic leadership theory is based on a study conducted by Bass (1990) related to successful business leaders managing their organizations through change. The visionary leadership theory gained acceptance during the 1980s and 1990s. Generally, Bass (1990) posited that there are three basic ways to explain how people become leaders:

1. Some personality traits may lead people naturally into leadership roles;
2. A crisis or important event may cause a person to rise to the occasion, which brings out extraordinary leadership qualities in an ordinary person;
3. People can choose to become leaders by learning leadership skills.

Bass (1990) also identified three types of leadership styles:

1. *Laissez-faire leadership.* This type of leader avoids making decisions, attempts to relinquish responsibility whenever possible and does not exercise authority.
2. *Transactional leadership.* This style places importance on contingent rewards. Transactional leadership gives emphasis to rewarding team members for meeting performance targets and fostering management by exception by means of taking action when activities are not according to schedule.
3. *Transformational leadership.* This leadership style focuses on the attributes of the leader, such as charisma, developing a vision, and rousing self-esteem, respect and trust.

Thus, the transformational leader is seen as providing inspiration, motivating subordinates by initiating high expectations and being a role model for proper behaviour. The transformational leader will also be sensitive to the individuals' needs, paying personal attention to the individuals in the group and showing them respect and dignity. Moreover, the transformational leader will provide intellectual stimulus and provoke group members with fresh ideas and approaches.

In practice, the combination of the latter two leadership types will be suitable in diverse operational conditions. However, transactional leadership assumes that the manager has the authority to reward the team members. This is not always the case. As stated previously, project managers may not posses the authority to reward or promote their team members and therefore they lack complete authority over the individuals they manage. In this situation transformational leadership becomes more important.

Emotional intelligence leadership theory

The emotional intelligence leadership school emerged in the late 1990s. This leadership theory is based on the premise that emotional intelligence will have a far greater impact on being a successful leader in terms of achieving higher team performance than intellectual ability. Goleman, Boyatzis and MeKee (2002) identified four dimensions of emotional intelligence and six leadership styles. The six leadership styles consist of visionary; coaching; affiliative; democratic; pacesetting; and commanding. The four dimensions of emotional intelligence are divided into two major streams, namely:

1. *Personal Competence*. The two dimensions under this stream are self-awareness and self-management. In addition, the self-awareness dimension includes the attributes of self-confidence, emotional state and accuracy, whilst the self-management dimension includes the attributes of emotional self-control, transparency, adaptability, achievement, initiative and optimism.
2. *Social Competence*. The two dimensions under this stream are social awareness and relationship management. The social awareness dimension includes the attributes of compassion and the desire to be of service. Under the relationship management dimension, the leader should be an inspiration to the team members, a change catalyst, foster teamwork and collaboration through building bonds, able to manage conflict and encourage the development of others.

Goleman, Boyatzis and McKee (2002) contend that visionary, coaching, affiliative and democratic leadership styles promote team resonance and under the appropriate conditions facilitate better performance. However, they also conclude that the pacesetting and commanding styles can encourage team dissonance and while recognizing their utility in certain conditions, these styles will need to be applied with care.

Competence leadership theory

Turner and Müller (2005) argue that the current leadership trend is the competence school of leadership. The competence school of leadership embraces all the earlier leadership theories by giving the term competence a wider meaning. Crawford (2003) defines competence as knowledge, skills and personal characteristics that deliver superior results. This leadership theory promotes the concept that different competence profiles are suitable under diverse conditions. This basic concept aligns this leadership theory to the contingency leadership school, whilst the elements that make up the attributes of knowledge, skills and personal characteristics embrace all the other various leadership schools.

The above leadership theories and concepts have evolved over time with the general conclusion, that what constitutes an able leader will depend on the circumstances. The major turning point in the leadership theories without doubt is the contingency school of leadership. The leadership theories that have followed afterwards have tended to fine tune the contingency leadership school concept. Moreover, it may also be concluded that leadership can be learnt, although some individuals are more predisposed to leadership roles than others. Hence, personal characteristics appear to be important, but their level of importance varies according to the circumstances.

Project Management Leadership Models

Both Frame (1987) and Turner (1999) argue that a change in leadership style may be required as a project progresses through its life cycle. In support of this argument, Prabhakar (2005) conducted a study across 28 countries from 12 major industries ranging from healthcare to information technology, regarding switching leadership style in projects. Prabhakar (2005) found a positive relationship between switches in leadership style and a high success level on a project. Furthermore, 86 per cent of the leadership style switches were from the autocratic style to a more consultative form. This finding demonstrates a tendency for project managers to commence a project in an autocratic mode and subsequently switch to a more consultative tactic. Prabhakar (2005) suggests that the reason for switching leadership style may be due to a number of factors, including awareness that the project is not progressing at the right speed; the project is veering in the wrong direction, not moving at all or is slipping backwards; and the project team has lost direction.

Furthermore, Prabhakar's (2005) study showed that the time factor has an impact on the choice of project leadership style. For instance, Pinto and Thoms (1999) emphasized the significance of personal temporal skills as being an essential attribute to a project manager. Prabhakar's (2005) study also demonstrates that the autocratic leadership style seemed to be the most common approach. However, it was highlighted that even when the autocratic style was adopted, there was not a high level of pressure on the project team. It was noted that the majority of project managers using the autocratic style were highly task-oriented. Moreover, it was found that successful project managers tended to switch to or from the autocratic style, but did not remain in the autocratic style through the implementation sub-phases. For instance, Verma (1997) noted that most project team leaders use a shared style of leadership approach that gives importance to participation, empowerment and trust.

Prabhakar's (2005) study also showed that the transformational leadership approach acted as a positive role model for the project team. An important finding suggests that the more experienced project managers achieved a higher level of project success by having a strong relationship leadership orientation, producing the more positive results. Prabhakar's (2005) study illustrated two very important points:

1. Leaders who inspire and motivate others by providing meaning and challenge to their followers' work have more project success. This tends to support the studies by Avolio and Bass (1995, 2002).
2. Projects where leaders arouse team spirit exhibit higher enthusiasm and optimism. This supports the finding of Bass (1998).

Prabhakar (2005) explains that these attributes fit in with the transformational leadership style. In other words, this translates into building relationships with the project team through interactive communication. This forms a cultural bond between the leader and the project team that leads to a shifting of values by both parties towards a common ground.

Thus the leader motivates the project team to be optimistic about the future, while concurrently communicating expectations and displays a commitment to goals and a shared vision. Similarly, Prabhakar (2005) found that project managers who are relationship-oriented generate more successful projects. This finding partially confirms a study by Hersey and Blanchard (1977) where it was suggested that leaders need to display more relationship-oriented behaviour in some instances and more task-oriented behaviour in others. However, in Prabhakar's (2005) study there was no direct relationship between project manager task-orientation and project success.

Moreover, the leadership decision-making approach (autocratic versus democratic style) appeared to be influenced by national culture and type of industry. The analysis of the various leadership theories and research findings suggest the following major leadership attributes:

- Allow employees to partake both in formulating and taking decisions;
- Be production-oriented by upholding a specific standard of performance;
- Be flexible in the application of rules and regulations;
- Be friendly and sociable;
- Be honest, reliable and trustworthy;
- Be sensitive to the needs of the employees;
- Foster teamwork and collaboration;
- Have a vision that stimulates employees;
- Have communications skills and negotiating ability;
- Have drive, energy, aspiration and an optimistic outlook;
- Inform team members what is expected of them by explaining their role;
- Provide support as to what and how tasks are to be conducted.

Nevertheless, while the above attributes are essential, the project manager must keep in mind two general principles:

1. Not to be apprehensive about switching leadership styles. Ensure that the leadership style that is applied is congruent with the circumstances of the project at that particular point in time or particular implementation phase.

2. In choosing a particular leadership style, keep in view national culture differences. This principle is particularly important when undertaking international projects or leading multi-national project teams. Therefore, spend some time assessing the national culture of the project team where the project (or phase of the project) is being executed and switch to the leadership style as appropriate.

In general, the leadership style, apart from reflecting the physical and technical nature of the project itself, must give great importance to the different needs and concerns of the individuals that make up the project team. Hence, project managers need to adopt their leadership behaviour to match different individuals' needs and project circumstances. Project managers must know and understand the people that they are leading.

Project Management Leadership Focus

In highly competitive and turbulent economic environments, management leaders must devise ways of lowering expenditure, building closer customer relationships, providing novel solutions to attract new clients and keep old ones, and seeking new markets. Hence, a tremendous amount of effort in organizations is consumed on seeking and implementing change. It is also important to recognize that project management for many organizations is mainly associated with implementing change.

The previous section focused mainly on leadership styles, with particular emphasis on project managers. This section focuses on the particular sectors that project management leaders should generally concentrate upon to ensure that they contribute to building a competitive organization. The sectors that project management leaders should focus upon include:

- Organizational Business Strategy;
- Project Management Methodology;
- Performance Appraisal;
- Project Priorities;
- Leadership Style;
- Communication Strategy;
- Conflict Resolution;
- Project Outcome Quality;
- Resource Optimization.

Organizational business strategy

This aspect has been dealt with in Chapter 4, (see pp. 49–61). However, it is important to emphasize that project management leaders must comprehend the strategic direction of the organization. They need to be knowledgeable about the outputs of the organization in terms of the services and products that are being offered now and in the future. From this knowledge, these leaders must be in a position to know:

- The core competencies that are required to attain client orders;
- The existing capabilities that must be enhanced;
- The competencies that should be developed to satisfy future outputs;
- How priorities in terms of utilizing resources are to be decided;
- The key performance indicators that are to be implemented to measure success in attaining objectives.

When project management leaders posses this knowledge they are in a position to know which projects are congruent with organizational strategy and hence the projects that should be executed to maximize the corporate success level.

Project management methodology

It is important for organizations to have a standard project management methodology for defining, planning, executing and monitoring projects. The Project Management Institute Book of Knowledge is a comprehensive methodology that is relatively simple to use and may be adapted for both small and large projects. Having a standard methodology will ensure that all projects and respective project teams apply a common approach. This makes it easier to establish the project success levels between projects and also enables team members to switch from one project to another fairly quickly.

Performance appraisal

It is essential that key performance indicators are defined at the outset of any project. These help to create a performance environment that provides an equal chance for all projects to succeed and allow the team members to be rewarded for their effort, not only in financial terms but also in terms of satisfaction, personal development and advancement. Therefore, it is imperative that the project performance environment establishes:

- Clear responsibilities and objectives;
- Allocates adequate resources with the appropriate skills to achieve specific functions;
- Provides sufficient support;
- Imparts ample feedback in relation to their performance and management expectations.

Project priorities

Project priorities are determined by the organizational strategy. Project management leaders must appraise all projects against strict criteria. Basically, the criteria are twofold:

1. The extent projects contribute to the implementation of the organizational strategy;
2. The value that these projects create for the entity in general.

The outcome of the project priorities evaluation is an itemized list of projects that when undertaken and executed in the indicated priority order, achieves the identified key performance indicators and maximizes the return of the strategic objectives.

Leadership style

Project management leaders must recognize that no single leadership style is applicable to all situations. Therefore, project managers must appraise the situation on a continuous basis adopting a suitable style depending on the project environment and particular circumstances. Project managers must be aware of the prevailing circumstances and be able to read the signs and switch the leadership style as necessary. Moreover, project managers must keep their ears to the ground and have sufficient knowledge of the individual project team members and address their individual concerns when necessary.

Communication strategy

There is no excuse for not having sufficient communication between project teams, project team members and stakeholders in general. Modern technology makes it possible to communicate across the globe with little or no difficulty. However, the project manager must ensure that channels of communication (and authority) are explicitly defined to create clear communication links that work without causing confusion.

Conflict resolution

Conflict will always arise when undertaking projects. However, it is vital that conflicts are not allowed to linger on. Conflicts must be resolved absolutely and quickly. Project management leaders must establish procedures for escalating any issue so that it is resolved quickly. Furthermore, conflicts if possible should be resolved at the project team level. Therefore, project team members are to be trained in skills related to basic situation appraisal, problem solving and decision making.

Project outcome quality

It is critical for projects to be closely monitored for quality. Too often project managers tend to focus on time and cost with not enough attention being devoted to quality. It is emphasized that rescheduled (rework) project work is costly and needs to be avoided by defining suitable quality indicators and monitoring them at frequent intervals. These quality indicators should be defined at the planning stage and reviewed during project execution.

Resource optimization

Project management leaders must allocate resources in a way that maximizes the project portfolio outcome. This is never an easy task and it is typically a source of conflict. Project managers must have a system in place that informs them of the resource availability at any one time, in terms of human resource skills, equipment and finance. It is important that any project undertaken is supported by the appropriate resources and that disputes between project teams vying for resources are avoided.

The above provide a general description of certain areas that project management leaders should generally focus upon in a project management environment. It should be noted that some of these aspects are critical in executing successful projects and have a chapter specifically dedicated to them.

Conclusion

Modern leadership theories suggest that good leaders are made not born. Leaders acquire their skills by means of continuous self-development through experience, education, training and interacting with others. Having authority does not make a person a leader. Authority gives the individual the mandate to lead. However, leadership makes people want to follow the leader to attain prescribed goals.

A major turning point in the development of leadership theories is the contingency school of leadership. This leadership school of thought basically contends that no single leadership style is universally applicable to all situations and will depend on the circumstances. The research literature indicates that a change in leadership style may be required as a project progresses through its life cycle. The major reason for switching leadership style may be due to an awareness that the project is not progressing at the right pace towards the desired goals; that the project is veering in the wrong direction or not moving at all or slipping backwards; or that the project team has lost direction. In general, the research findings suggest that:

- Leaders who inspire and motivate others by providing meaning and challenge to the work of those they lead have more project success;
- Projects where leaders arouse team spirit exhibit higher enthusiasm and optimism.

The analysis of the various leadership theories and research findings suggest the following major desirable leadership attributes:

- Allow employee participation in formulating decisions and taking decisions;
- Be production-oriented by upholding a specific standard of performance;
- Be flexible in the application of rules and regulations;
- Be friendly and sociable;
- Be honest, reliable and trustworthy;
- Be sensitive to the needs of employees;
- Foster teamwork and collaboration;
- Have a vision that stimulates employees;
- Have communications skills and negotiating ability;
- Have drive, energy, aspiration and an optimistic outlook;
- Inform subordinates what is expected of them by explaining their role;
- Provide support as to what and how tasks are to be conducted.

Project managers must keep in mind two general principles:

- Not to be apprehensive about switching leadership styles. Ensure that the leadership style applied is congruent with the circumstances of the project at a particular point in time;

- Keep in view national culture differences. This is critical when undertaking international projects or leading multinational project teams. The project manager needs to assess the national cultural of the project team members and switch to the most suitable style.

It is also important to itemize those areas that project management leaders should focus upon. The research literature suggests that project management leaders should generally ensure that they contribute to building a competitive organization by giving particular attention to organizational business strategy; the project management methodology; performance appraisal; project priorities; the appropriate leadership style; defining and implementing a communication strategy; the rapid resolution of conflicts; ensuring an appropriate level of outcome quality; and resource organization.

Project managers generally agree that the people side of project management often creates more difficulties than the technical issues. Therefore, it is important for project managers to know and understand the people they are leading and adopt their leadership behaviour to match different individuals' needs and project circumstances. What is more, they should focus on those areas that are seen as being critical to achieving project success.

References

Avolio, B.J. and Bass, B.M. 1995. Individual consideration viewed at multiple levels of analysis: Multi-level framework for examining the diffusion of transformational leadership. *The Leadership Quarterly*, 6(2), 199–218.

Avolio, B.J. and Bass, B.M. 2002. *Developing Potential Across a Full Range of Leadership Cases on Transactional and Transformational Leadership*. Mahwah, NJ: Lawrence Erlbaum Associates.

Bass, B.M. 1990. From transactional to transformational leadership: Learning to share the vision. *Organizational Dynamics*, 18(3), 19–31.

—— 1998. *Transformational Leadership: Industrial, Military, and Educational Impact*. Mahwah, NJ: Lawrence Erlbaum Associates.

Crawford, L.H. 2003. Assessing and developing the project management competence of individuals. In J.R. Turner (ed.), *People in Project Management*. Aldershot: Gower Publishing Company Limited.

Fielder, F.E. 1967. *A Theory of Leadership Effectiveness*. New York: McGraw-Hill.

Frame, J.D. 1987. *Managing Projects in Organizations*. San Francisco, CA: Jossey Bass.

Goleman, D., Boyatzis, R. and McKee, A. 2002. *The New Leaders*. Boston: Harvard Business School Press.

Hersey, P. and Blanchard, K.H. 1977. *The Management of Organizational Behaviour* (3rd Edition). Englewood Cliffs, NJ: Prentice Hall.

House, R.J. 1971. A path-goal theory of leader effectiveness. *Administrative Science Quarterly*, 16 (September), 321–38.

House, R.J. and Mitchell, T.R. 1974. Path-goal theory of leader. *Contemporary Business*, 3(Fall), 81–98.

Hsu, J., Hsu, J.C., Huang, S.Y., Leong, L. and Li, A.M. 2003. Are leadership styles linked to turnover intention: An Examination in Mainland China? *Journal of American Academy of Business*, 3(September), 37–43.

Pinto, J.K. and Thoms, P. 1999. Project leadership: A question of timing. *Project Management Journal*, 3(1), 19–26.

Prabhakar, G.P. 2005. Switch leadership in projects. An empirical study reflecting the importance of transformational leadership on project success across twenty-eight nations. *Project Management Journal*, 36(4), 53–60.

Turner, J.R. 1999. *The Handbook of Project-Based Management: Improving the Process for Achieving Strategic Objectives*. London, UK: McGraw-Hill.

—— and Müller, R. 2005. The project manager's leadership style as a success factor on projects: A literature review. *Project Management Journal*, 36(2), 49–61.

Verma, V.K. 1997. *Managing the Project Team*. Newtown Square, PA: Project Management Institute.

CHAPTER 13 *Employee Commitment and Participation*

> *People do not follow uncommitted leaders. Commitment can be displayed in a full range of matters to include the work hours you choose to maintain, how you work to improve your abilities, or what you do for your fellow workers at personal sacrifice.*
>
> Stephen Gregg, Company Chairman and CEO

Employee commitment is viewed as being a key prerequisite for the effective execution of projects, operational processes and the successful implementation of organizational change programmes. It has particular significance for the successful accomplishment of all types of projects. Reichheld (1996) stated: "Loyalty is by no means dead. It remains one of the great engines of business success." A committed employee is an individual:

- Who supports the organization through good and bad times;
- Attends work on a regular basis;
- Defends the organization;
- Contributes a full day's effort and more;
- Is supportive of the organization's goals and objectives.

In other words, committed employees are loyal and devoted to the project team and organization they work for. Commitment is generally viewed as the employees' emotional attachment and identification with the organization, and their strong desire to maintain membership with the organization. Research suggests that employee commitment has a favourable impact on job performance by lowering absenteeism, lateness and turnover. Hence, having committed employees assigned to a project team has potentially positive consequences for project and organizational performance.

However, there may be a negative aspect to commitment as well. For example, having employees committed to the organization solely due to financial reasons. Such commitment normally grows fainter and diminishes completely during adverse or declining economic conditions. Equally risky is to have passive or blind commitment, where employees remain silent and do not provide their feedback. In other words, their level of participation is low or non-existent. Such an environment could stifle creativity and result in an organization trailing behind in the innovative process. It is therefore essential for management to identify and develop the proper type of employee commitment.

Employees must therefore be encouraged to participate in the formulation of decisions and in decision taking. An appropriate level of employee participation fosters their understanding of the projects being undertaken and will influence them to increase their commitment to both the projects and the organization in general.

Concepts of Employee Work Commitment

Commitment is viewed as an attitude towards the organization that links the identity of the individual to the entity. According to Meyer and Allen (1991) commitment is a psychological state that characterizes the employee's relationship with the organization and has implications for the decision to continue membership in the organization. Meyer and Allen (1997) extended the meaning of commitment as referring to the employee's emotional attachment to, identification with, and involvement in the organization, and the employee's feeling of obligation to remain with the organization taking into consideration the costs that the employee associates with leaving it.

Although there seems to be little consensus as to the precise meaning of commitment, Meyer and Allen (1997) contend that the various definitions reflect three broad propositions. These propositions indicate that commitment may be viewed as:

• Reflecting an affective orientation toward the organization;
• Recognition of the costs associated with leaving the organization;
• Reflecting a moral obligation to remain with the organization.

The various definitions of commitment share a common proposition, in that commitment is considered to be a bond or linking of the individual to the organization. The definitions differ in terms of how this bond is considered to have developed. For example, some researchers refer to attitudinal commitment. This is defined as the relative strength of a person's identification with and involvement in a particular organization. Conceptually, these researchers characterized commitment by at least three factors:

• Strong belief in and acceptance of the organization's goals and values;
• Willingness to exert considerable effort on behalf of the organization;
• Strong desire to maintain membership in the organization.

A second form of commitment is referred to as calculative commitment. Calculative commitment is defined as a structural event that occurs as a result of individual–organizational transactions and alternatives in side-bets over time. Through calculative commitment, individuals become bonded to an organization because they have invested in the organization (for example, a pension plan) and cannot afford to separate themselves from it. Other types of commitment have emerged, including normative commitment that describes a process whereby organizational actions, such as selection, socialization and procedures, as well as individual predispositions, such as loyalty attitudes, lead to the development of commitment.

According to O'Reilly and Chatman (1986) the psychological bond between an employee and an organization can take three distinct forms, termed as compliance, identification, and internalization. They contend that compliance occurs when attitudes and behaviours are adopted not because of shared beliefs but simply to gain specific rewards. Identification occurs when an individual accepts influence to establish or maintain a satisfying relationship. For instance, an individual may feel proud to be a part of a project team, respecting its values and accomplishments without adopting these values as his or her own. Internalization occurs when influence is accepted because the induced attitudes and behaviour are congruent with one's own values, that is, the values of the individual, project team or organization are the same.

Meyer and Allen (1991) developed an integrated approach, utilizing the concepts put forward by various researchers and have defined commitment as consisting of three components:

1. *An affective component.* This refers to the employee's emotional attachment to, identification with and involvement in the organization. Those with strong affective commitment continue employment with the project team or the organization because they genuinely want to do so. They see the organization or project team as being part of themselves.
2. *A continuance component.* This refers to commitment based on the costs that the employee associates with leaving the project team or organization. Employees whose primary link to the entity is based on continuance commitment remain with a project team or an organization because they need to do so and have no other viable alternative.
3. *A normative component.* This refers to the employee's feeling of obligation to remain with the organization. Employees with high level of normative commitment feel that they ought to remain with the project team or organization because they are grateful to it.

Research findings indicate that employee commitment is very fluid in the early period of employment but quickly begins to stabilize with the passage of time. Moreover, management behaviour can influence an employee's commitment type, in terms of whether an employee is more affectively committed. Employee work commitment is an important issue for all types of organizations, particularly for organizations that undertake projects or are undergoing organizational change programmes. Some of the contributing factors that make employee work commitment imperative include:

- The trend to organizational downsizing;
- Employment mobility;
- Job satisfaction;
- The economic environment.

TREND TO ORGANIZATIONAL DOWNSIZING

Even though organizations are becoming leaner, they must maintain a core of committed individuals who are the source of organizational activity. Those who remain, represent the "heart, brain, and muscle" of the organization (Meyer and Allen, 1997). It is therefore important to retain employees who will provide the greatest benefit to a specific project and the organization in general.

EMPLOYMENT MOBILITY

Workers who become less committed to an organization will route their commitment in other directions (Meyer and Allen, 1997). These employees may start to evaluate their skills and experience in terms of their marketability outside the organization, rather than by their implications for their current or future jobs in the organization. Management must invest in employees who want to remain members of the organization and participate in its projects. It should be noted that employee turnover rates in projects, particularly of specialist staff, affect the eventual success of the project in terms of delivering the defined scope on time, to cost and quality level.

JOB SATISFACTION

Research suggests that employees who develop a high level of work commitment are more inclined to be highly satisfied and fulfilled by their jobs. Therefore, employee work commitment is essential in the development of proactive and innovative project teams and organizations.

ECONOMIC ENVIRONMENT

In the current turbulent global economic scenario, organizational change is a continuous process that requires support of all employees in the hierarchical structure. Having employees with the appropriate levels of commitment facilitates the change management process and ensures its successful implementation.

Furthermore, human resources strategies related to employee recruitment, retention, reward and incentive policies need to be defined in a holistic manner having the primary aim of encouraging employees to posses the appropriate type and level of commitment. It is therefore essential for management to comprehend the dynamics that influence the development of commitment and take proactive initiatives to ensure that employees want to remain members of the project team or the organization, not because they have no other alternative but because they genuinely want to be part of the project team.

Consequences of Organizational Commitment

Figure 13.1 shows the development and consequence of employee work commitment within an organization, particularly a project team. Commitment depends on a number of factors, such as the employees' personal characteristics, level of role conflict and ambiguity, job attributes, relationship between the employees and their supervisor, and the employees' perception of how well an organization is being managed. Moreover, an outcome of commitment is work motivation. However, the level of work motivation will depend on the degree that individuals integrate with their organization and identify themselves with the organization's objectives. Finally, the intensity of the employees' integration with the organization and the magnitude of the work motivation will determine the level of the achieved performance gain.

Research suggests that affective, continuance and normative commitment are all related to employee retention, but in different ways. Given that an employee with strong affective and normative commitment feels an emotional attachment to, identification with and involvement in the organization, and has a feeling of obligation to remain with the organization, then this individual is likely to have a higher motivation level to contribute meaningfully to the project or organization than would an employee with weak affective and normative commitment.

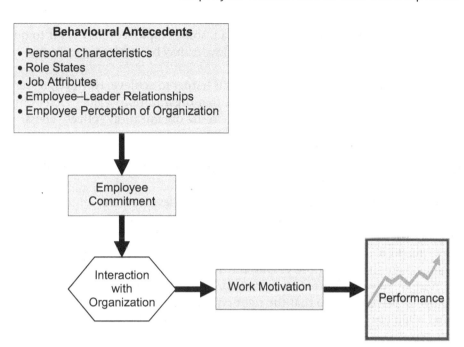

Figure 13.1 Development and consequences of employee commitment

Therefore, it is reasonable to suggest that those employees with strong affective and normative commitment are more likely to be absent less often and motivated to give a higher performance. This is in contrast to individuals who have strong continuance commitment. These individuals appear to become bound to an organization because they have invested in the organization and cannot afford to separate themselves from it. Thus, employees with strong continuance commitment are likely to make a decision to remain with the organization based on the costs that they associate with leaving the organization. Hence, these individuals are likely to abandon the project team or organization if they find an opportunity elsewhere that pays them more.

In practice, management wants more from committed employees than simply membership to the project team or the organization. Various research findings suggest that employees with strong affective and normative commitment are more valuable. When commitment reflects an emotional link to the project team, the project team may benefit through reduced turnover, increased productivity and higher job satisfaction among employees. However, when the commitment by the employee is based primarily upon financial aspects (costs associated with leaving) then the project team and organization may experience higher employee retention at the expense of reduced job satisfaction and self-esteem, and higher employee stress.

It is therefore suggested that organizations should implement Human Resource (HR) policies to develop the right type of commitment. For example, strategies such as rapid promotions and the development of departmental specific skills all tend to increase continuance commitment that may eventually work against the organization. Although continuance commitment measures may contribute to ensuring that an employee stays with the project team or organization, they may not encourage them to contribute to the project team's or organization's benefit. Instead, some employees may want to quit, but may not be able to afford to do so. Some employees may be motivated to do just enough to maintain their jobs.

On the other hand, affective commitment is harder to achieve. However, research has shown that it is strongly related to the results that organizations value, such as high job satisfaction and a strong motive to contribute to the organization's effectiveness.

Developing the Right Type of Organizational Commitment

Perceptions have an important influence in the development of employee work commitment. The literature indicates that employees who perceive their organizations as being supportive tend to become affectively committed. Those who perceive that they have made a substantial investment that would be lost if they leave, develop continuance commitment. Those employees that think that loyalty is expected of them become normatively committed. It is therefore essential for management to influence the employees' perceptions so that the right type and level of commitment is developed. Meyer and Allen (1997) and others contend that management must aim to:

- Directly develop affective commitment;
- Develop HR management policies that encourage affective commitment;
- Manage the change management process.

DEVELOPMENT OF AFFECTIVE COMMITMENT

According to Meyer and Allen (1997), affective commitment develops in various organizational settings, such as:

- Having effective management policies. Empirical research suggests that an organization that is concerned about controlling its costs and increasing productivity is more likely to have employees who identify with it than organizations that are loosely managed. Besides, an organization's decision and resultant action to reduce staff is not likely to affect employee commitment when it is properly implemented.
- Making every effort to treat employees with respect and consideration. Employees must feel that they are valued and appreciated by their supervisors and the division or project team that employs them.
- Project and divisional managers should provide a clear signal to all employees that the organization is highly concerned with quality and customer service.
- Project managers should clearly define employees' jobs and responsibilities. Job clarity refers to how precisely supervisors communicate to their employees what has to be done and what their expectations are.
- Project managers should communicate quality information on project and divisional plans and activities to employees. This is particularly vital during periods of extreme organizational change when employees feel insecure about their future.
- Project managers should design and assign tasks that allow the employees to use their aptitudes, professional knowledge and judgement, offering them job enrichment.

DEVELOPING SUITABLE HR MANAGEMENT POLICIES

HR management policies may greatly influence employee work commitment. Therefore, suitable practices are needed for the following activities:

- *Recruitment and selection.* When recruiting project team members, management should avoid using the conventional approach, but provide practical job previews that describe both the positive and negative aspects of the assignment. Being fully informed about the job allows applicants to become fully aware of the choice they have to make and they are likely to be more committed once the choice is made.
- *Socialization and training.* Those who participate in a development training programme might perceive that the organization values them as individuals and hence they tend to develop stronger affective commitment. However, the same development training programme could lead to the growth of continuance commitment if it is perceived as providing organizational specific skills that contribute to status or economic advantage within the project or division that will not transfer to jobs outside the organization.
- *Employee promotion policy.* A policy of promoting from within may be perceived by employees as an indication that the organization is committed to them. This may lead the employees to reciprocate.
- *Employee appraisal policy.* The perception of fairness in the evaluation and promotion process is very important. Affective commitment is likely to decrease when an employee fails to be promoted. If the decline in affective commitment is accompanied by an increase in continuance commitment, the organization might find that it is retaining employees who perform just enough to keep their jobs. Therefore, it is important to ensure that affective commitment is maintained by providing these employees with assistance in gaining opportunities elsewhere.
- *Compensation policy.* If an employee views a compensation and benefits contract from a purely financial angle, then continuance commitment is likely to increase. However, if an employee perceives that the organization is considerate and is fair in its dealings with the workforce, then affective commitment is likely to develop. Therefore, management must ensure that compensation and benefits packages place emphasis on the non-financial features, even though the end result may be an increase in the employees' financial position.

MANAGEMENT OF CHANGE

Many organizations undergoing extensive change very often lead to organizational downsizing. An outcome of downsizing is uncertainty and the potential for increasing responsibility among the non-managerial grades due to the cutback of management layers. Research indicates that employee turnover is a concern following layoffs and that often, the increasing turnover is among the organization's most valued employees.

Researchers also found that those who were most confident in their abilities were most likely to consider leaving the organization. Hence, it is essential to find ways of maintaining the commitment of employees, when important organizational change is taking place. The following are suggested:

- Redundant employees are to be given adequate support. This may involve generous termination pay or aiding them to relocate inside or outside the organization. It is essential that the redundancy policy is communicated to employees;
- The selection of those employees to be made redundant or relocated must be perceived by all the employees to be fair and that the action taken is seen as a measure to increase the job security of those remaining;
- Management must convince the employees that the implemented changes will lead to job enrichment and greater job satisfaction;
- Management must put in place a comprehensive communication strategy prior, during and after the changes are to take place to mitigate uncertainty among the employees.

All the above measures are intended to increase the level of affective commitment of employees. Finally, it should be emphasized that having a committed workforce will result in project execution effectiveness and will facilitate high levels of cooperation during difficult times when that extra effort is required to tilt the balance towards having a successful project.

Employee Participation

Employee participation reflects a participative style of leadership and encompasses a wide variety of activities that are aimed at:

- Increasing the employees' understanding of the organization and projects undertaken;
- Using the employees' abilities and talents;
- Giving employees the opportunity to influence decisions;
- Nurturing the employees' commitment to the established project and organizational goals.

Employee participation is closely linked to the organization's communication process. It is important to recognize that communication is a two-way process. Employees want guiding principles from their manager and management desire feedback from the team members. This two-way interactive process is likely to encourage employee participation. Most organizations have little difficulty passing information downwards. However, their difficulty stems from obtaining an upwards information flow, since it is viewed as being more demanding.

A lack of employee participation (input) may lead to negative outcomes for the organization and the projects being undertaken, such as missed opportunities, failed initiatives, neglected performance improvement and project delays. Research suggests that benefits generated by employee participation include:

- Improved efficiency and closer collaboration;
- Enhanced quality and competitiveness;
- Increased job satisfaction and work motivation;
- Better employee–leadership relationship.

Management must strive to develop a quality interactive process between the management team and employees through employee participation. There are basically two major methods of encouraging employee participation:

1. Indirect involvement where employees are represented by a delegate or an association, as in collective bargaining or joint consultation;
2. Direct involvement where employees actively participate in making decisions about work practices.

The focus of this section is related to direct employee involvement. There are four basic elements that promote direct employee involvement:

1. Communicating the needs;
2. Skill and knowledge sharing;
3. Creating a communication culture;
4. Creating an employee empowering environment.

COMMUNICATING THE NEEDS

Employees must be told that communication is a two-way process and therefore they have a responsibility to provide their input. Employees should be encouraged to inform management of their concerns and how these concerns may in their view be mitigated by management. Management, on the other hand, must repeatedly reinforce the project and organizational vision and show how the current objectives contribute to this vision. Management must also explain the necessity for the employees' participation by providing input to achieving the defined vision.

SKILL AND KNOWLEDGE SHARING

When employees impart their advice regarding a specific situation, these employees are utilizing their experience to reach a particular conclusion. In reality, this is what employee participation is all about. However, some employees may need to be prompted to provide their input. Hence, having a dialogue session with employees regarding their task process and concerns, reviewing data or discussing a client's needs can stimulate and encourage employees to offer their suggestions. Discussing "what if" situations based on proposals made by the employees may enable them to comprehend their particular role on the project and organizational outcomes and will prompt them to contribute in the process.

CREATING A COMMUNICATION CULTURE

The extent of management input in keeping employees informed is a major contributing factor in motivating employees to provide feedback and making suggestions for improvements. This process achieves an appropriate level of employee participation. However, appropriate techniques must be utilized to make the communication process easier and more effective, such as:

- Organizing team meetings specifically designed to allow employees to share their ideas about a particular project;
- Setting aside a time period to conduct open discussions that specifically address their concerns;
- Providing short one-to-one sessions between managers and employees to discuss particular employee issues.

CREATING AN EMPLOYEE EMPOWERING ENVIRONMENT.

To attain employee participation through empowerment, employee input must be documented and acted upon, once agreement has been reached. Before assigning tasks, managers are required to discuss specific goals and parameters with the project team, so that the team members accept their responsibilities and make any necessary adjustments to ensure success.

Effective employee participation leads to feelings of empowerment for employees. This helps to reduce their feelings of anxiety and uncertainty during periods of organizational change or when a project or organization is encountering difficulties. However, employee empowerment does not occur automatically. Empowerment results when management consciously and actively provide their employees with the knowledge, skills, information and resources, together with the authority to use these elements without always having to seek approval.

These work practices can generate the type of discretionary behaviours that lead to enhanced performance in a wide range of aspects, including increased client satisfaction, profitability and productivity, and reduced employee turnover. One should note that a high employee turnover rate is a frequent factor that contributes to delaying projects. Employee participation motivates employees to identify themselves with the project team and seek to remain members of that project team. In other words, employee participation helps to motivate employees to directly contribute to the project's success.

Conclusion

Employee commitment has implications for the decision of an employee to continue membership in the organization. A committed employee supports the organization through trouble-free and difficult times, attends work on a regular basis, defends the organization at all times, contributes a full day's effort and is supportive of the organization's goals and objectives. Employee commitment has a positive impact on job performance and is likely to decrease absenteeism, lateness and turnover. However, having blind commitment is risky. Blind commitment stifles innovation and vision. It is therefore essential to develop the proper type of employee commitment. According to Meyer and Allen (1997) commitment consists of three components:

1. Affective component. Those with strong affective commitment continue with the project team or organization because they genuinely want to do so.
2. Continuance component. Employees whose primary link is based on financial aspects remain with a project team because they need to and have no other viable alternative.
3. Normative component. Those with a high level of normative commitment feel that they ought to remain with the project team or organization because they are grateful to it.

Employee commitment reflects an emotional link to the project team and organization, thus the project may benefit through reduced turnover, increased productivity and higher job satisfaction among employees. When employee commitment is based on financial aspects then the entity may undergo higher employee retention at the expense of reduced job satisfaction and self-worth, and higher employee stress. On the other hand, affective commitment is advantageous to both the individual and the organization. Project teams by their very nature are receptive to the development of affective commitment, if adequate care is taken. Affective commitment may be nurtured by project managers through the following actions:

- Treating employees with respect and consideration;
- Showing employees that they are valued and appreciated;
- Providing a clear signal that quality and customer service are a priority;
- Clearly defining the employees' job and responsibilities;
- Giving employees an opportunity to use their aptitudes, knowledge, judgement and offering them job enrichment;
- Communicating quality information to employees regarding project plans and activities;
- Controlling costs and increasing productivity rather than having organizations or projects that are loosely managed.

Other measures that encourage affective commitment include:

- When recruiting project team members, provide practical job previews that describe both the positive and negative aspects of the assignment;
- Reinforce the employees' sense of self-worth and providing a supportive environment;
- Promoting from within conveys a commitment on behalf of the organization to the development of employees' careers;
- Ensuring fairness in the assessment and promotion process;
- Ensuring that compensation packages place emphasis on the non-financial aspects, even though the end result may be an increase in the employees' financial position.

Furthermore, measures to foster affective commitment during times of major organizational change include:

- Employees made redundant due to downsizing should be given adequate support, such as adequate termination pay or aid to relocating inside or outside the organization;
- Selection of employees to be made redundant or relocated must be perceived to be fair and is a measure intended to increase the job security of those remaining;
- Convince employees that change will lead to greater job enrichment and satisfaction;
- Lower uncertainty amongst employees by having a comprehensive communication strategy prior, during and after the change is to take place.

The above suggest that having committed employees is important to improving organizational and individual performance. However, employee commitment must not be passive. Active employee commitment is achieved through employee participation.

Similarly, employee participation reflects a participative style of leadership and is closely linked to the organization's communication process.

Employees want guiding principles from their manager and management desire feedback from the team members. This two-way interactive process is likely to encourage employee participation. The benefits generated by employee participation include improved efficiency and closer collaboration; enhanced quality and competitiveness; increased job satisfaction and work motivation; and better employee–leadership relationship.

To attain direct employee participation management must communicate the project and organizational needs by encouraging employees to inform management of their concerns and how these concerns may, in their view, be mitigated by management. Management, on the other hand must repeatedly reinforce the project and organizational vision and show how the current objectives contribute to this vision.

Additionally, employees are to share their skills and knowledge. This may be achieved by encouraging employees to impart their advice regarding specific situations and utilizing their experience to reach a particular conclusion. Management must also create a communication culture. The extent of management input in keeping employees informed is a major contributing factor in motivating employees to provide feedback and making suggestions for improvements, thus fostering employee participation.

Employee participation is thus facilitated when management create an empowering environment. Empowerment results when management consciously and actively provide their employees with the knowledge, skills, information and resources, together with the authority to use these elements without always having to seek approval. Employee participation motivates employees to identify themselves with the project team and seek to remain members of that project team.

Finally, employee participation helps to motivate employees to directly contribute to the project's success. Moreover, it should be emphasized that having a participative and committed workforce is likely to make it easier for organizations to obtain cooperation during difficult times.

References

Camilleri, E. 2002. Some antecedents of organizational commitment: Results from an information systems public service organization. *Bank of Valletta Review*, 25, 1–29.
—— 2006. Towards developing an organizational commitment–public service motivational model for the Maltese public service employees. *Public Policy and Administration*, 21(1), 63–83.
—— and van der Heijden, B. 2007. Organizational commitment, public service motivation, and performance within the public sector. *Public Performance and Management Review*, 31(2), 241–74.
Laabs, J.J. 1996. Employee commitment. *Personnel Journal*, August, 58–66.
Mathieu, J.E. and Hamel, K. 1989. A causal model of the antecedents of organizational commitment among professionals and non-professionals. *Journal of Vocational Behaviour*, 34, 299–317.
Mathieu, J.E. and Zajac, D.M. 1990. A review and meta-analysis of the antecedents, correlates, and consequences of organizational commitment. *Psychological Bulletin*, 108, 171–94.
Meyer, J.P. and Allen, N.J. 1991. A three-component conceptualization of organizational commitment. *Human Resource Management Review*, 1, 61–89.

—— 1997. *Commitment in the Workplace: Theory, Research, and Application.* Thousand Oaks, California: Sage Publications, Inc.

Mottaz, C.J. 1988. Determinants of organizational commitment. *Human Relations*, 41, 467–82.

Mowday, R., Porter, L.W. and Steers, R.M. 1982. *Employee-organization Linkages: The Psychology of Commitment, Absenteeism, and Turnover.* San Diego, CA: Academic Press.

Mowday, R.T., Steers, R.M. and Porter, L.W. 1979. The measurement of orgnizational commitment. *Journal of Vocational Behavior*, 14, 224–47.

O'Reilly, C.A. and Chatman, J. 1986. Organizational commitment and psychological attachment: The effects of compliance, identification, and internalization on prosocial behavior. *Journal of Applied Psychology*, 71, 492–9.

Reichheld, F.F. 1996. *The Loyalty Effect.* Boston: Harvard Business School Press.

14 *Internal and External Communication*

Leaders who make it a practice to draw out the thoughts and ideas of their subordinates and who are receptive even to bad news will be properly informed. Communicate downward to subordinates with at least the same care and attention as you communicate upward to superiors.

L.B. Belker, author

Effective internal and external communications are key factors that contribute to successful projects. Internal communication has the objective of informing employees of developments that are influencing their organization, particularly the projects that they are collectively involved with. The previous chapter has illustrated that internal communication is a vital ingredient for successful employee participation and facilitates the development of affective work commitment. Both these factors were viewed as being essential for increasing individual and organizational performance.

However, in a project environment, external communication becomes extremely important as well, particularly if the project is a controversial one. External communication in a project environment has the objective of facilitating collaboration and cooperation with various stakeholders that are outside the formal structure of the organization. The collaboration and cooperation of these stakeholders is viewed as being essential to project success. Stakeholders may be categorized into five groups, namely clients, contractors, investors and shareholders, employee unions and society in general. Therefore, two critical aspects are essential when tackling the external communications issue. These are the identification of the active and influential stakeholders that may impact a specific project and the formulation of an external communication strategy that specifically targets the concerns of these stakeholders.

This chapter will focus on the internal and external communications aspects. The section on internal communication will concentrate on the underlying principles of employee communication, the importance of leadership involvement in the internal communication strategy and establishing a shared vision to ensure that everyone involved in the organization is pulling in the same and correct direction. The section on external communication will focus on the importance of identifying the active and influential stakeholders that are likely to have an impact on the success of the project and to establishing an adequate external communications strategy that mitigates the concerns of the identified stakeholders.

Internal Employee Communications

Internal communication is viewed as being vital for encouraging employee participation and is seen as being an essential ingredient for high performance project teams. Research suggests that in many organizations, both employees and their managers are not satisfied that their organization's internal communication mechanism is adequate. In a turbulent economic environment, managers have had to live with rapidly changing business conditions that result in a radical change to their business strategies. This radical change to the business strategies has in turn resulted in overloading their internal communication process leading to severe criticism from employees. Employees complain that they were often confused by conflicting messages, were overloaded with information, had difficulty prioritizing their activities and felt there was insufficient leadership.

This scenario suggests that there is a need for management to introduce a communication configuration that enables the management team to formulate and impart clear and consistent messages to all the employees. There is also a need for management to display leadership by having face-to-face meetings with employees and holding regular team briefing sessions. Moreover, a communication strategy only becomes effective when it is a meaningful two-way process. Employees, either as individuals or as a team, must be given the opportunity to provide their feedback. However, the provided feedback is to be perceived as being seriously taken into consideration by management and be visibly seen to be applied in the organization's decision-making process.

Effective communication facilitates and enhances organizational performance. But for this to happen, management must treat its employees as if they were part owners of the organization. Thus, as perceived shareholders, employees through employee–management meetings will be informed about the organization's corporate and functional strategies, and about the organization's results. With suitable impetus, the communications process can develop into a programme for different types of organizational improvements, particularly if the process is linked to the organization's incentive scheme.

Employee–management meetings should be characterized by a non-threatening environment, complete openness and honest spontaneous responses to all types of questions, acceptance of constructive criticism and a request for feedback. The setting for these meetings must be based on mutual trust where all cards are placed on the table. It is through such a process that everyone in the organization is focused on the vision, mission, strategies and objectives of the organization. Hence, the internal communication process provides direction in terms of where the organization is heading, defines clear objectives in terms of expected productivity and quality levels, provides momentum by focusing everyone towards a common goal and offers an opportunity for senior management to demonstrate leadership qualities and further develop their leadership competencies.

UNDERLYING PRINCIPLES OF EMPLOYEE COMMUNICATION

A study of UK organizations by Blue Rubicon and Henley Management College (2002) shows that the methods business leaders use to communicate with their employees considerably influences their profitability. Furthermore, the authors of the study argue that a performance culture stresses goal attainment and the value of effort and quality, while a people culture emphasizes employee involvement, trust and commitment. Both of these cultures are important and largely stem from the top management layers.

However, the study results show that 93 per cent of managers think that the purpose of employee communications is to keep staff well informed, with only 57 per cent thinking that the purpose is to give employees the opportunity to provide input into the organization's business strategy. These results suggest that organizations lack sincerity to the principle of employee communication and are not utilizing it as a means of advancing their business. In a study regarding human capital and financial management, Marshall and Heffes (2006) show that companies with the most effective communication programmes provided a higher return to their shareholders with a resultant substantial increase in market value. What is more, these companies report substantially lower employee turnover rates when compared with similar entities.

It should be recognized that essentially organizations are simply a collective group of individuals who belong to a particular division, unit, department or project team. However, unless a holistic approach is specifically taken, these categories of individuals will develop their own particular culture. An effective internal communication strategy provides a common link between the different groups to promote within the organization a universal set of attitudes, beliefs, values and a common appreciation of the organization's objectives.

In addition, an effective internal communication strategy promotes the formulation and implementation of a shared organizational vision that is supported by the defined corporate strategy. The literature suggests that an effective internal communication strategy will help to:

- Acquire acceptance of the organization's corporate and functional strategies;
- Clarify policies and how these are linked to the overall organizational vision;
- Demonstrate in real terms management commitment;
- Encourage employees to put more effort into tasks that are assigned to them;
- Ensure employees understand their individual roles and expectations;
- Identify potential organizational areas for improvement;
- Monitor and evaluate performance through employee input;
- Motivate the organization's entire workforce.

Although the benefits of effective internal communication are well known, there may be barriers to proper communication. For example, an organization culture where management talk down to employees allows only one-way communication. An effective internal communication process allows two-way communication to take place. This communication process is built on a partnership between management and employees, working together for the mutual good of the organization and ultimately for their own individual mutual benefit.

Moreover, the nature of the organization may be a barrier. For example, in a project environment, the time consumed on communicating may be perceived as lost project production time. However, a proper internal communication process may also provide opportunities for continuous improvements in the way a project is being conducted, that will far outweigh the cost incurred in the so-called lost project time.

The most difficult barrier in the internal communication process is deciding how much to say, when and to whom. On the other hand, in a proper communication environment, openness, honesty, sincerity and trust are essential. If the employees perceive that the purpose of the internal communication strategy is to manipulate them, then only failure will result, with very serious negative performance consequences. There may be other barriers to an effective communications strategy, these include:

- *Biased opinions.* Individuals may be predisposed to certain opinions therefore they hear only what they want to hear. It is vital that information sent is clear and transmitted in a manner that does not distort its meaning;
- *Clarity.* What may be obvious to the one conveying the message may be ambiguous to the receiver of that message. Hence, messages sent must be clear, consistent and meaningful;
- *Dispersion and distance.* Having an organization with numerous projects physically dispersed on a national or global basis will make the internal communication process difficult;
- *Hierarchical position.* Persons occupying a lower post in the organization or project team may feel introverted and find it difficult to communicate their contribution to management. These employees must be encouraged to make their thoughts known;
- *Inadequate communication skills.* There is a need to develop proper communication competencies within the organization by developing the best methods for communicating;
- *Information transmission.* Having an internal communication process that cascades down the organization will tend to distort and omit information;
- *Sincerity.* The communication process must be based on mutual trust.

It is these barriers that make effective employee communication complex and difficult to achieve. Therefore, it is important for organizations to identify the barriers and take the appropriate measures to mitigate them. The study of UK organizations (Blue Rubicon and Henley Management College, 2002) found that the most successful channels of two-way communications were:

- Appraisals and feedback forums;
- Interactive conferencing;
- Intranet site with bulletin board;
- One-to-one staff dialogue;
- Regular team meetings with quality and assurance sessions;
- Talk back sessions with senior management.

The UK study showed that face-to-face meetings are seen as being much more productive than eCommunication methods. For instance, less than 3 per cent of respondents considered interactive conferencing to be effective. The authors of the UK Study make a number of recommendations classified under three categories:

1. Auditing employee perceptions by:
   - Developing actions to increase staff trust and commitment;
   - Identifying employees' future intentions towards the organization;
   - Linking employees' future intentions to employee feelings and work experience;
   - Seeking reliable information using focus groups and questionnaires.
2. Improving communications by:
   - Acting on the feedback and communicating the actions taken;

- Extending the use of face-to-face communications;
- Fulfilling commitments to communicate regularly;
- Requesting feedback, actively listening to it and testing whether the key messages from the feedback have been properly understood.
3. Developing behaviours by using communications as a business tool by:
   - Developing and using a broad range of communications tools;
   - Gradually increase the level of employee involvement in business goals.

Marshall and Heffes (2006) found that the top communication practices that directly contributed to increasing the companies' success in terms of market value included compelling the managers' behaviour to communication; linking employees to the business strategy; and adhering to a formal communication process.

Research consistently indicates that an organization's internal communication strategy coupled with employee involvement has an important influence on organizational strength by supporting business and individual results and performance, building corporate culture and values, and developing individuals.

LEADERSHIP INVOLVEMENT IN AN INTERNAL COMMUNICATION STRATEGY

Research suggests that senior management is the most important element in developing a loyal and committed workforce. Hence, it is essential for management to be greatly involved in the definition and implementation of the internal communication strategy. An internal communication strategy should not be viewed as being a purely Human Resource (HR) function, to be defined and managed by the HR Department. An internal communication strategy is a collective effort embracing all different types of employees performing a variety of job functions and occupying diverse hierarchical levels within the organization or project team.

Shaw (2005) in a world-wide study of communication and HR professionals found four major obstacles that prevent senior leaders from being involved in internal communication time, willingness, skills and behaviours. The major findings from this research are summarized below.

Time

Senior management are very busy people and therefore have little time to think about or develop the appropriate internal communication approach that suits their particular project environment. Although the availability of more time is difficult to resolve, it may be possible to incorporate face-to-face dialogue sessions with project team members as part of their project management meetings. In addition, continually reminding project managers of their obligation to spend more time with project team members and helping them to conduct short face-to-face sessions may assist them to integrate internal communication as part of their normal routine.

Willingness

Senior managers often lack the enthusiasm and the motivation to enhance their communication ability. The difficulty is to change the mind-set of managers. Managers need to view internal communication as an important task that belongs to everyone, including themselves. Senior managers are inevitably results-oriented. Therefore it may be possible to link their participation in the communication process to their established organizational and project goals and objectives. This link will create congruence between the communication strategy and organizational targets thus creating the necessary motivation for project managers to be involved in the communication process.

Skills

There is a need to assess the project management's communication skills and decide which competencies need to be developed, how and when. Hence, leadership communication training should aim to help project managers adhere to four principles:

1. Actively listening to other points of view before stating one's opinion;
2. Communicating clearly and concisely to all organizational levels;
3. Making strategic use of different communication channels;
4. Share information with others in a responsive and timely manner.

Behaviours

Project managers need to understand their own leadership style and acknowledge their responsibility to inspire and motivate the project team members. The difficulty with the concept of behaviour is that every individual has some unique properties making it difficult to generalize. However, it is possible to develop an internal communication strategy that focuses on standard key sectors that every manager may relate to, namely goals, outcomes, key messages and core audiences.

A combination of the project manager's attributes and the standard key communication sectors allow a "tactical plan" to be defined for the project manager, consisting of a list of standard actions, such as:

- A competencies framework, focusing on tasks to provide adequate exposure and visibility;
- A measurement framework to itemize normal intangible cultural and environment outcomes that would be achieved given that the manager meets the established communication goals.

The above illustrate that the issue is not whether project managers become aware of the value of internal communication, but how to change their behaviour so that they are actively involved and take the lead in the internal communication process.

ESTABLISHING A SHARED VISION

Often transforming an organization's vision to reality requires a total change in the established attitudes and culture within an organization. Unfortunately, the bias towards the continuation of past modes of behaviour is powerful in many organizations. Although employee communication is generally acknowledged as the key to effective management, it must also be enduring, coherent and discernible.

Establishing a shared vision requires a well-defined employee communication strategy that disseminates high quality information horizontally and vertically throughout the organization, with the capability of being receptive to the views of the recipients. Establishing a shared vision is an iterative process and consists of a number of stages. First, management defines its vision which is disseminated to all the organizational levels for feedback. Second, when feedback is received from employees, it is processed within a defined mechanism that allows for vision fine tuning. The final stage consists of effectively communicating the fine-tuned vision to all the organizational levels. Research indicates the following key principles to keep in mind to meet the internal communication challenge:

- *Communicate the future.* Communication is not about what happened last week but what is about to happen. An efficient internal communication strategy mitigates employee anxiety and uncertainty;
- *Communication must be made to happen.* It requires planning and support staff to prepare information, answer queries, document and follow up feedback from different sources;
- *Communication requires honesty.* Employee trust will develop with open management. Open management means providing good and bad news, answering embarrassing questions, discussing issues that management may not know the answers to or prefer not to contend with;
- *Communication takes effort.* Deciding and preparing relevant information requires energy. Therefore, adequate time must be devoted to it;
- *Consider various communication approaches.* There are many ways of communicating, such as newsletters, face-to-face sessions, group sessiosn, team briefings, employee forumsand many other approaches. Examine the work environment and use the most appropriate and effective approach;
- *Consistency of message.* The communication strategy should be coordinated and be designed to send a consistent and clear message;
- *Develop communication skill competencies.* Implement a communication skills training programme. The training programme will need to be designed for different levels of employees and not just for managers and supervisors.
- *Ensure the communication strategy is affordable.* Make sure that the internal communication strategy is realistic. An internal communication strategy that is elaborate for the available resources will not work. Therefore, ensure that the internal communication strategy is designed to operate within the allocated resource availability;
- *Establish a communication schedule.* Develop a regular internal communication programme for a specific period, say three or six months. The internal communication programme should incorporate the different approaches to be used, including time allowed for each activity, the scheduled date, agenda, resource requirements and the target audience;
- *Link the internal communication strategy to business goals and management concerns.* The linkage between communication and business success is essential and should be emphasized. Business success is to embrace all issues that are important to the project and the organization, including management concerns and decisions.

It is vital for management to monitor the internal communication strategy and be particularly aware of any employee grievances about communication. Grievances about internal communication may point to a concern that needs to be addressed.

External Communication

As stated previously, external communications in a project environment has the objective of facilitating cooperation and collaboration with the various stakeholders that are outside the formal structure of the organization. A variety of communication channels may be utilized for external communication, including the internet, print and broadcast media, face-to-face meetings and establishing virtual discussion forums.

However, the communication channels utilized will depend on the nature of the relationship with the specific stakeholder. For instance, the contractors and suppliers of an organization are considered as external stakeholders. The main communication channel in this instance could be the management information systems of the respective organizations, to procure supplies, track orders and initiate payments. Furthermore, external communication may support important organizational objectives by:

- Ensuring regular information flow from the various categories of stakeholders to the organization. This may help the organization to define its targets, operational performance and management performance indicators and stakeholder information flow may influence organizational policies, particularly those related to the environment. This is especially critical for those organizations that undertake projects which have environmental consequences, such as,construction projects.
- Ensuring the information flow from the organization to various stakeholders to promote projects and enhance organizational credibility. External communication is also important when organizations want to demonstrate their commitment to citizens' welfare, particularly environmental rights.

External communication should be interactive and bi-directional. In other words, it should be a two-way communication process similar to internal communication. External communication should be sensitive to the requirements of the organization and the stakeholders with whom the organization intends to communicate. The content and form of external communications should be developed in a participatory manner, to foster cooperation and collaboration. External communications should be objective, use accurate and reliable data sources, and be clear and accessible to its intended audiences.

IDENTIFYING EXTERNAL STAKEHOLDERS

External communication is a complex issue because there are various stakeholders involved with entirely different agendas and objectives. Stakeholders may be categorized into five groups, namely:

1. Clients;
2. Investors and shareholders;
3. Contractors and suppliers;

4. Employee unions;
5. Society in general.

Clients

The project manager must keep close contact with the client on a regular basis, throughout the execution of the project. This will ensure that the eventual project outcomes match the requirements and expectations of the client. First, it is important that there is a formal project scope and contract that is unambiguous and defines in a clear manner the project deliverables and outcomes.

Second, there must also be a formal project change management process. If the scope of the project is to be amended, the amendments must be clear and the consequences of the changes be made known to all concerned, particularly the client. The objective of the external communication process at this level is to seek collaboration from the client.

Investors and shareholders

Investors and shareholders must be kept fully informed of the organization's position, in terms of vision and future potential, finance and competitiveness. The investors and shareholders are entitled to accurate and complete information to enable them to make their investment decisions.

Management must seek to be informed by investors and shareholders. Management need to know the financial expectations of the investors and shareholders. They need to know the attitudes and values of the majority of the investors and shareholders towards specific issues. For instance, investors and shareholders may not want to see the organization undertake projects which have military implications or projects that arouse environmental controversy.

This is not an easy task because there may be a mixture of different values and attitudes within the investors and shareholders stakeholder group. However, it is important that management is sensitive to the different opinions and steer a course which will find the middle ground. The objective of the external communication process at this level is to seek collaboration.

Contractors and suppliers

Contractors and suppliers are a specific type of stakeholder because they are considered to be external but at the same time they still an important part of the project team. In other words, contractors and suppliers have dual external–internal stakeholder roles. These stakeholders will likely be linked to the information management systems of the organization and vice versa. The communication process is important because the contractors and suppliers, although independent from the organization, must abide by the organization's production practices and quality levels.

Therefore, the organization must keep these stakeholders informed of its management practices and quality standards. Again, the communication process is two ways. Contractors and suppliers must keep the organization informed about task performance, particularly the specific deliverables.

Moreover, the organization must be careful about selecting its contractors and suppliers. It should be recognized that contractors and suppliers in reality are partners in the project venture. Therefore, the financial stability of these stakeholders is particularly important. There is nothing worse than having a major contractor or supplier experiencing bankruptcy during project execution or entering into legal disputes over questionable deliverables. The objective of the external communication process at this level is also to seek close collaboration.

Employee unions

The objective of the external communication at this level is to avoid industrial disputes due to misunderstandings that may arise from a range of issues. These issues may range from a change in work practices to work safety. Employee unions are also a specific type of stakeholder because they are considered to be external, yet they represent the project team members, who are internal.

Management should aim through its internal communication strategy to resolve employee grievances before they are escalated to the employee unions. Often industrial disputes occur because of a severe breakdown of the internal communication process. Industrial disputes literally destroy project team harmony. In other words, the issue becomes the management versus the employees, hence the sense of cooperation and collaboration turns into confrontation. It is important that management adheres by specific values that are associated with honesty, integrity and trust. This is the reason why management must keep employees informed of both the good and bad news, because the relationship between the employees and management must be built on trust. Once again, the objective of the external communication process at this level is to seek close collaboration.

Society in general

Fortunately, most projects do not have controversial connotations attached to them. Therefore, the general public are not overtly concerned or interested. However, certain projects by their very nature are controversial. This is where the issue of satisfying the "society in general" stakeholder group becomes a complicated issue, because often the concerns may turn emotional. Emotional issues often transform into angry protests that may eventually become violent. For instance, no one would be keen to have a waste management plant erected in their region, even if the plant is seen as having an environmentally friendly objective.

No matter where the waste management plant is located, therefore, protests may follow, unless the people involved see opportunities from the project or their concerns are resolved. Opportunities may result in an increase in permanent employment generated during project execution and during the operational phase. The organization should also provide honest and sincere assurances about the project when possible. For instance, ensuring that the project strictly adheres to the environmental regulations and that waste disposal vehicles are routed well away from residential areas.

The external communication strategy must be aimed at obtaining as much input as possible from the public about the specific concerns, and providing reliable and honest information about the threats and opportunities of the project to mitigate the concerns of the general public of the relevant region. In addition, the external communication strategy should aim at convincing the public that the threats will be addressed and resolved. The objective of the external communication process at this level is to seek cooperation rather than collaboration.

COMMUNICATION STRATEGY FOR EXTERNAL STAKEHOLDERS

The external communication strategy will need to consist of a process definition and product identification. Process definition focuses on the method for formulating and implementing an external communication strategy. The knowledge identification involves providing specific counselling on information products, such as environmental impact studies or information about operating in a carbon constrained economy.

Process definition

The process definition provides details about the main principles and major implementation phases of the external communication strategy. It also provides information about the external communication tasks to be conducted, such as:

- Defining the objectives and the target stakeholders of the external communication strategy;
- Defining the type of information to be communicated. This includes the presentation mode and the method of disseminating the information to be communicated to stakeholders. For example, providing data about the operational performance once the project is implemented, providing environmental impact studies that show the true impact of the project and other details related to how stakeholder concerns are addressed;
- Establishing a mechanism to regularly review the existing situation and making amendments to the external communication strategy when needed;
- Establishing an appropriate mechanism to monitor the quality, performance and effectiveness of external communication;
- Establishing an appropriate organization structure to take on the responsibilities for external communication;
- Identifying existing relevant information that is of interest to the identified stakeholders.

Similarly, key stakeholders, such as the local community, government regulators, environmentalists and other interested parties should be involved in the formulation of the communication strategy.

Knowledge identification

The knowledge identification process will depend on the nature of the project. This phase deals with the content and layout of the specific information products used in external communication process. These may include environmental impact studies, relevant regulations and applicable web-sites. The knowledge provided must be defined in a simple and unambiguous manner so that it may be easily understood by all levels of stakeholders.

The information content and presentation of the external communication strategy must address the specific external communication objectives, particularly the concerns of the key stakeholders. The external communication strategy should provide the following additional details:

- All data sources as well as those who undertook the study must be fully acknowledged to allow stakeholders to scrutinize the expert authorities;
- The external communication strategy should adhere to a standard framework;
- The external communication strategy should be presented in a systematic fashion to enable the reader to acquire and comprehend the presented information promptly;
- The presentation of information is to be in a format that is easily understood by both technical and non-technical individuals;
- The procedure adopted to secure the relevant raw data and the methodology used for making the conclusions.

The external communication strategy should be presented in an objective manner providing a balanced view to the reader. Trust is a key element and is essential for the acceptance of the external communication strategy by the key stakeholders. Acceptance does not mean that the stakeholders will agree to all that is presented. But every attempt should be made to ensure that stakeholders do not perceive the external communication strategy as a tool to manipulate them. The external communication strategy should also give the key stakeholders the opportunity to provide their feedback. The stakeholder feedback should be seriously considered and included in future revisions.

ASSESSING THE PROJECT COMMUNICATION ENVIRONMENT

Assessing the project communication environment is essential to determine the effectiveness of the internal and external communication strategies and whether the strategies provide sufficient opportunity for the involvement of the internal and external stakeholders. Assessing the project communication environment consists answering the following – In your view is the project communication strategy:

- Adequate in addressing key internal and external stakeholder concerns?
- Adequate in allocating adequate time and funds?
- Based on a two-way process?
- Based on adequate training?
- Based on an open and honest approach?
- Based on clear and agreed objectives?
- Based on high quality information?
- Based on top management commitment?
- Consistent, recurring and well timed?
- Explicit and conveys a precise message?
- Flexible and of service to all stakeholders?
- Identifies all the key internal and external stakeholders?
- Of sufficient and manageable capacity?

- Open to feedback from different attitudes, including key stakeholders?
- Organized and methodological?
- Planned and premeditated?
- Provides a mechanism for regular reviews to include stakeholder feedback?
- Relevant to all key internal and external stakeholders?
- Trustworthy and dependable?

Each question is given a score out of ten. Any question that has a score of seven or less may suggest a specific weakness. The indicated weakness area should be reviewed and appropriate action taken to strengthen it.

Conclusion

Effective communication takes into consideration the views of both the internal and external stakeholders. Research suggests employee participation is a key factor in contributing to high performance project teams. However, a communication strategy will only show results when it is a meaningful two-way process. Employees, either as individuals or as a team, must be given the opportunity to provide their feedback and for the feedback to be visibly seen to be applied in the organization's decision-making process. An effective internal communication strategy will help to:

- Acquire acceptance of the organization's corporate and functional strategies;
- Clarify policies and how these are linked to the overall organizational vision;
- Demonstrate in real terms management commitment;
- Encourage employees to put more effort into tasks that are assigned to them;
- Ensure employees understand their individual roles and expectations;
- Identify potential organizational areas for improvement;
- Monitor and evaluate performance through employee input;
- Motivate the organization's entire workforce.

A proper communications strategy helps project managers to send sufficient and unambiguous information to their employees and provide them with an opportunity to give their views, hence achieving two-way communication. It is important too that the provided feedback is visibly seen to be applied in the organization's decision-making process. Such a process will build the required leadership–employee trust for implementing a successful communication strategy.

Another important aspect is external communication. External communications in a project environment has the objective of facilitating cooperation and collaboration with the various stakeholders that are outside the formal structure of the organization. A variety of communication channels may be utilized for external communication, including the internet, print and broadcast media, face-to-face meetings and establishing virtual discussion forums.

However, the external communication channels utilized will depend on the nature of the relationship with the specific stakeholder. It is therefore important to identify carefully the key external stakeholders. External communication should be interactive and bi-directional. In other words, it should be a two-way communication process similar to internal communication. External communication is a complex issue because there are various stakeholders involved with entirely different agendas and objectives. Stakeholders may be categorized into five groups, namely client, investors and shareholders, contractors and suppliers, employee unions and society in general. The general public becomes an important stakeholder particularly when a project has controversial connotations. The objective of the external communication process is to seek cooperation and where possible collaboration.

The external communication strategy should be presented in an objective manner providing a balanced view to the reader. Trust is a key element and is essential for the acceptance of external communication strategy by the key stakeholders. Acceptance does not mean that the stakeholders will agree to all that is presented. But every attempt should be made to ensure that stakeholders do not perceive the external communication strategy as a tool to manipulate them. The external communication strategy should give the key stakeholders the opportunity to provide their feedback. The stakeholder feedback should be seriously considered and included in future revisions.

References

Blue Rubicon and Henley Management College. 2002. Employee Communications and Relationships Report 2002.

Johnson, P.M. 1992. Closing the communication gap. *Training & Development*, 46(12), 19–22.

Marshall, J. and Heffes, E.M. 2006. Communication: employee communication linked to performance. *Financial Executive*, 22(1), 11–12.

Meyer, J. 2002. Strategic communication enhances organizational performance. *Human Resource Planning*, 25(2), 7–9.

Shaw, K. 2005. Getting leaders involved in communication strategy. Breaking down the barriers to effective leadership communication. *Strategic Communication Management*, 9(6), 14–17.

Wadman, L. 2006. Showing leaders the impact of Comms. *Strategic Communication Management*, 10(4), 6–7.

▼ V Organizational Project Diagnostic Model

The objective of Part I of this book was to define a project success model (see Chapter 3, p. 39). This consisted of three major categories of project support factors:

- Project hygiene support factors;
- Project informational support factors;
- Project behavioural and management support factors.

This proposed project success model provided the basis for the following Parts II–IV, where the dimensions of each project success factor category were described, examined and discussed in detail. As one may recall, the project hygiene support factors embrace the traditional project management process that aims for the application of best project management practice. Furthermore, the chapter on project strategic fit (Chapter 4) has the objective of ensuring corporate success, by ascertaining that the undertaken projects have the desired impact on the organizational business strategy.

Moreover, the project informational support factors are mainly applicable to a multi-project environment. Together with a standard project management methodology, these factors aim for repeatable project management success, with the focus being on the deliverables. Finally, the project behavioural and management support factors are viewed as influencing project success, with the focus being the project outcomes.

Part V consists of one chapter. The objective of this concluding chapter is to assess the preparedness of an organization to undertake projects and determine whether it has the mechanisms in place to implement its projects. It addresses the important question: "How prepared is my organization for undertaking and managing its projects?"

15 Diagnosing an Organization's Preparedness for Undertaking and Managing Projects

Thinking is easy, acting is difficult, and to put one's thoughts into action is the most difficult thing in the world.
                    Johann Wolfgang von Goethe, German author (1749–1832)

The previous chapters have examined in detail the individual project success–failure factors. This has provided the reader with ample knowledge to determine what needs to be done correctly in order to have a successful project. However, executive management must address an important question: "How prepared is my organization for undertaking and managing its projects?" In other words, it is important to assess the extent that the principles related to the project success–failure factors are entrenched in the organization's culture so that:

- Undertaken projects produce the desired deliverables, in other words, project outputs (project management success);
- The organization has the ability to consistently execute projects that have produced the desired outputs (repeatable project management success);
- Undertaken projects produce the desired outcomes (project success);
- The outcomes yield the intended impact on the business strategy (corporate success).

This chapter has the objective of developing an effective project diagnostic model to assess the organization's preparedness for undertaking and managing its projects.

Developing an Effective Project Diagnostic Model

An effective project diagnostic model must take a holistic view. There is a tendency to relate projects and project management to the function of the project manager. However, it should be kept in mind that project managers are only responsible for the projects that are under their direct remit. It is the project manager's remit to ensure that a specific project yields the desired outputs (project management success). However, the following objectives are not the remit of the project manager:

1. The organization's ability to consistently execute projects that yield the desired outputs (repeatable project management success);
2. Ensure that projects produce the desired outcomes (project success);
3. Ensure that the project outcomes yield the intended impact on the business strategy (corporate success).

These three objectives are the responsibility of executive management or an individual within the organization who has the holistic responsibility for all undertaken projects within the organization. Figure 15.1 illustrates that there are four success–failure levels, commencing at the corporate level and ending at project management. Each project success–failure level has a different responsibility thrust, objective and focus. Hence, the diagnosis of an organization's preparedness for undertaking and managing projects must collectively address these individual four success–failure levels.

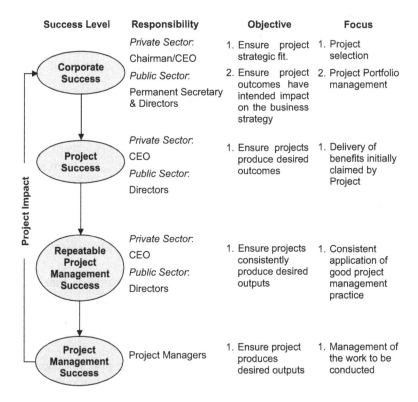

Figure 15.1 Framework for a project diagnostic model

Assessing an Organization's Preparedness for Undertaking and Managing Projects

The basic principle to keep in mind when devising an assessment scheme is that what cannot be measured cannot be managed and what cannot be managed cannot be changed. Therefore, the assessment of an organization's preparedness for undertaking and managing projects requires the development of a balanced set of measures for each of the four project success–failure levels as illustrated by Figure 15.1.

An easy way of conducting this assessment is through a diagnostic questionnaire that may be administered to employees ranging from middle to executive management. The aim of the diagnostic questionnaire is to identify the strengths and weaknesses for each of the four project success–failure levels within the organization, thus allowing one to appraise the organization's preparedness for undertaking and managing projects.

The Diagnostic Questionnaire Administration

The diagnostic questionnaire is divided into four sections, with each section representing one of the four success–failure levels as shown in Figure 15.1. A sample diagnostic questionnaire is found in Figures 15.2 to 15.5.

Statement	1	2	3	4	5	6	7
Strategic Impact of Projects							
1 My organization has a well-defined documented strategy.							
2 The execution periods of projects undertaken by my organization normally reflect the strategy planning horizon.							
3 The projects undertaken by my organization normally support the business span of the organisation.							
4 The projects undertaken by my organization normally support the future strategic positioning of the organisation.							
5 In my view the organization objectives are:							
(a) Specific							
(b) Measurable							
(c) Realistic							
(d) Time bound							
(e) Consistent with mission							
6 The projects undertaken by my organization normally support the objectives of the organisation.							
7 The projects undertaken by my organization normally support the organisation's line of business.							
8 My organization normally makes available the necessary resources to undertake the approved projects.							
9 My organization's project selection criteria ensure that its collective project portfolio effectively contributes to the business strategy.							
10 The projects undertaken by my organization normally do not have resource implications that expose the organisation to economic non-sustainability.							
11 Generally, the outcomes of the projects undertaken by my organization are aligned with stakeholder expectations.							
12 Generally, the projects undertaken by my organization are unlikely to have a negative effect on the organization's future growth.							

Figure 15.2 Questionnaire – corporate success level

Statement	1	2	3	4	5	6	7
Project Outcomes							
1 The deliverables from the projects undertaken by my organization normally produce the desired outcomes (overall project purpose and objectives).							
2 A business case identifying the project benefits is always conducted before a project is approved to be undertaken by my organization.							
3 In my organisation, a business case review is always conducted before a major project change request is approved.							
4 In my organization, management normally assigns ownership for the attainment of the project benefits undertaken by the organization.							
5 My organization has the appropriate mechanism to conduct a rigorous post-implementation project review that holds people accountable for the delivery of the project benefits.							
6 My organization has the appropriate mechanism to assess whether a project undertaken by the organisation delivers the business benefits that were initially identified in the business case.							
7 My organization has the appropriate mechanism to ensure that the project outputs (deliverables) are integrated into the business operations.							
8 My organization has the appropriate mechanism to ensure the concurrent development of process change and people skills during project execution.							
9 My organization has a clear mechanism to capture, document and share the lessons learned from ongoing projects (knowledge management).							
10 My organization has the appropriate mechanism to assign individual responsibility for the attainment of the defined project benefits.							

Figure 15.3 Questionnaire – project success level

Statement	1	2	3	4	5	6	7
Project Outputs							
1 The projects undertaken by my organization consistently produce the desired outputs (project deliverables).							
2 All projects undertaken by my organization are executed according to a recognized standard project management methodology.							
3 My organization has the appropriate mechanism to ensure the consistent application of good project management practice.							
4 A standard project management methodology is used throughout my organization for the undertaking of all projects.							
5 My organization has established learning mechanism to ensure that personnel undertaking projects are trained in the use of the standard project management methodology.							
6 My organization has the appropriate organisational structures that: a. Are designed to share and support project management best practice.							
b. Ensure predictability of outputs (project deliverables).							

Figure 15.4 Questionnaire – repeatable project management success level

Statement	1	2	3	4	5	6	7
Project Outputs							
1 Normally a project undertaken by my organization produces the desired outputs (project deliverables).							
2 My organization has the appropriate mechanism to ensure that there is consensus on the nature of the required output for a particular project.							
3 My organization has the appropriate mechanism to ensure that there is consensus on the quality criteria applied to a particular project.							
4 My organization has the appropriate mechanism to ensure that a project has a clear scope and deliverable definition.							
5 My organization has the appropriate mechanism to ensure that a project is delivered on:							
a. Time.							
b. To budget.							
c. To required specifications.							
6 My organization has the appropriate mechanism to ensure that:							
a. There is a thorough and continuous risk assessment of a project.							
b. A project is planned to an appropriate level of detail.							
c. Good estimating practices are applied when planning a project.							
d. Cost and schedule tracking are continually taking place for projects.							
e. A project is truly under control.							
7 My organization has the appropriate mechanism to ensure the on-time delivery of a project by having the proper risk management practices.							
8 My organization has the appropriate mechanism to:							
a. Monitor a project against business case expectations.							
b. Conduct earned value analysis for a project.							
c. Apply good project reporting practices.							
9 My organization has a rigorous project change control mechanism in place to minimise changes to project scope.							
10 My organization has the appropriate mechanism to identify interim deliverables so that powerful stakeholders benefit early from the project.							

Figure 15.5 Questionnaire – project management success level

First published in paperback 2024

First published 2011 by Gower Publishing

Published 2016 by Routledge
4 Park Square, Milton Park, Abingdon, Oxon OX14 4RN

and by Routledge
605 Third Avenue, New York, NY 10158

Routledge is an imprint of the Taylor & Francis Group, an informa business

© 2011, 2016, 2024 Emanuel Camilleri

Emanuel Camilleri has asserted his moral right under the Copyright, Designs and Patents Act, 1988, to be identified as the author of this work.

Publisher's Note
The publisher has gone to great lengths to ensure the quality of this reprint but points out that some imperfections in the original copies may be apparent.

British Library Cataloguing in Publication Data
Camilleri, Emanuel.
    Project success : critical factors and behaviours.
    1. Project management.
    I. Title
    658.4'04–dc22

Library of Congress Cataloging-in-Publication Data
Camilleri, Emanuel.
    Project success : critical factors and behaviours / Emanuel Camilleri.
        p. cm.
    Includes bibliographical references and index.
    ISBN 978-0-566-09228-2 (hbk. : alk. paper)
    1. Project management –Evaluation. I. Title.

    HD69.P75C362 2010
    658.4'04–dc22

                                                                2010033177

ISBN 13: 978-0-566-09228-2 (hbk)
ISBN 13: 978-1-03-283840-3 (pbk)
ISBN 13: 978-1-315-60249-3 (ebk)

DOI: 10.4324/9781315602493

	Response Score for Each Question															
Response	Q1	Q2	Q3	Q4	Q5a	Q5b	Q5c	Q5d	Q5e	Q6	Q7	Q8	Q9	Q10	Q11	Q12
1																
2																
.																
.																
N																
Total:																
Ave. Score:																
Adj. Score:																

Figure 15.7 Diagnostic questionnaire responses – corporate success

	Response Score for Each Question									
Respondent	Q1	Q2	Q3	Q4	Q5	Q6	Q7	Q8	Q9	Q10
1										
2										
.										
.										
N										
Total:										
Ave. Score:										
Adj. Score:										

Figure 15.8   Diagnostic questionnaire responses – project success

	Response Score for Each Question						
Respondent	Q1	Q2	Q3	Q4	Q5	Q6a	Q6b
1							
2							
.							
.							
N							
Total:							
Ave. Score:							
Adj. Score:							

Figure 15.9   Diagnostic questionnaire responses – repeatable project management success

	Response Score for Each Question																		
Response	1	2	3	4	5a	5b	5c	6a	6b	6c	6d	6e	7	8a	8b	8c	9	10	
1																			
2																			
.																			
.																			
N																			
Total:																			
Ave. Score:																			
Adj. Score:																			

Figure 15.10 Diagnostic questionnaire responses – project management success

Interpreting the Diagnostic Questionnaire

The best way to explain how to interpret the diagnostic questionnaire is through an example.

EXAMPLE – INTERPRETING THE DIAGNOSTIC QUESTIONNAIRE

For simplicity, let us assume that five senior managerial staff completed the diagnostic questionnaire and that their responses have been recorded as shown in Figure 15.11 to Figure 15.14.

	Response Score for Each Question																
Response	Q1	Q2	Q3	Q4	Q5a	Q5b	Q5c	Q5d	Q5e	Q6	Q7	Q8	Q9	Q10	Q11	Q12	
1	6	4	7	4	5	2	3	4	5	5	6	4	4	7	5	6	
2	7	5	6	5	5	4	2	5	5	5	7	3	5	5	4	5	
3	7	5	6	3	6	3	3	3	7	7	6	3	3	6	5	6	
4	6	6	7	5	6	2	4	5	6	7	6	5	4	6	5	6	
5	5	6	7	5	5	2	5	5	6	6	7	3	5	5	5	5	
Total:	31	26	33	23	27	24	22	23	29	30	32	28	25	29	30	32	
Ave. Score:	6.2	5.2	6.6	4.6	5.4	4.8	4.4	4.6	5.8	6.0	6.4	5.6	5.0	5.8	6.0	6.4	5.6
Adj. Score:	8.9	7.4	9.4	6.6	7.7	6.9	6.3	6.6	8.3	8.6	9.1	8.0	7.1	8.3	8.6	9.1	7.9

Figure 15.11 Recorded responses – corporate success

	Response Score for Each Question									
Respondent	Q1	Q2	Q3	Q4	Q5	Q6	Q7	Q8	Q9	Q10
1	6	3	2	1	1	2	6	5	1	2
2	6	3	3	1	1	2	5	6	1	3
3	7	2	1	3	2	1	6	6	2	2
4	6	1	2	2	2	1	5	7	1	4
5	5	3	3	2	2	2	6	5	1	3
Total:	30	12	11	9	8	8	28	29	6	14
Ave. Score:	6.0	2.4	2.2	1.8	1.6	1.6	5.6	5.8	1.2	2.8	3.1
Adj. Score:	8.6	3.4	3.1	2.6	2.3	2.3	8.0	8.3	1.7	4.0	4.4

Figure 15.12   Recorded responses – project success

	Response Score for Each Question						
Respondent	Q1	Q2	Q3	Q4	Q5	Q6a	Q6b
1	5	2	1	1	1	2	4
2	5	1	1	1	1	2	5
3	7	1	2	1	1	2	5
4	6	2	2	2	2	1	4
5	5	1	1	1	1	2	5
Total:	28	7	7	6	6	9	23
Ave. Score:	5.6	1.4	1.4	1.2	1.2	1.8	4.6	2.5
Adj. Score:	8.0	2.0	2.0	1.7	1.7	2.6	6.6	3.5

Figure 15.13   Recorded responses – repeatable project management success

	Response Score for Each Question																	
Response	1	2	3	4	5a	5b	5c	6a	6b	6c	6d	6e	7	8a	8b	8c	9	10
1	5	6	4	5	2	4	5	2	5	2	2	2	2	1	1	2	1	5
2	7	5	3	4	3	3	4	1	5	2	1	2	2	1	1	3	2	4
3	6	5	5	5	3	3	4	3	6	1	1	1	2	2	2	2	2	5
4	6	6	5	6	4	3	6	2	4	2	2	2	1	1	1	3	1	6
5	7	6	3	6	3	3	5	2	5	1	1	1	2	2	1	3	2	5
Total:	31	28	20	26	15	16	24	10	25	8	7	8	9	7	6	13	8	25
Ave. Score:	6.2	5.6	4.0	5.2	3.0	3.2	4.8	2.0	5.0	1.6	1.4	1.6	1.8	1.4	1.2	2.6	1.6	5.0	3.2
Adj. Score:	8.9	8.0	5.7	7.4	4.3	4.6	6.9	2.9	7.1	2.3	2.0	2.3	2.6	2.0	1.7	3.7	2.3	7.1	4.5

Figure 15.14   Recorded responses – project management success

Figure 15.15 provides a summary of the overall adjusted average scores from the diagnostic questionnaire for each of the four success levels (Figures 15.11 to 15.14). These overall scores are plotted as shown in Figure 15.16 to provide a graphical view of the overall appraisal of whether an organization is adequately prepared for undertaking and managing projects. The overall assessment (see Figure 15.16) indicates that while projects undertaken by the organization are generally aligned with the organization's strategy (score 7.9) there appears to be a serious weakness regarding the ability to consistently achieve repeatable project management success (score 3.5).

Similarly, the success–failure levels related to project success (project outcomes) and project management success (project outputs) also needed substantial improvements. Therefore, in this particular example, the organization needs to sustain and aim to improve its project success–failure position for the corporate success facet, and requires immediate and urgent action to significantly improve the repeatable project management aspect. This would in turn improve the project management success and project success aspects.

Choice	Overall Adjusted Score
Level 1. Corporate Success	7.9
Level 2. Project Success	4.4
Level 3. Repeatable Project Management Success	3.5
Level 4. Project Management Success	4.5

Figure 15.15   Overall adjusted average scores from diagnostic questionnaire

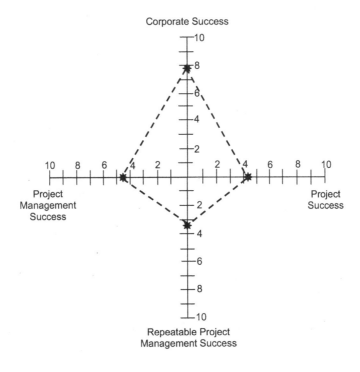

Figure 15.16   Diagnostic questionnaire – overall assessment

Figures 15.17 to 15.20 give a more detailed appraisal of the organization's ability to undertake and manage its projects, highlighting particular areas where an improvement is necessary. This detailed appraisal is carried out by examining the scores for each individual question within the diagnosis category. The corporate success diagnosis (Figure 15.17) suggests that generally, the organization has the mechanism necessary to ensure that undertaken projects are aligned with the organization's business strategy and that they will have a positive impact on the strategic direction.

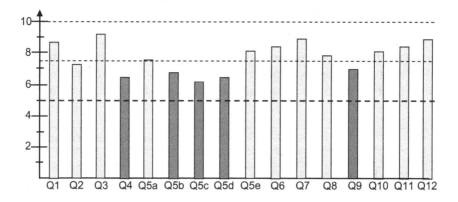

Generally, the projects being undertaken are aligned to the business strategy of the organization and appear to have a positive impact on the strategic direction. However, the organization must:

o   Make further efforts to ensure that collectively the project portfolio contributes to the business strategy and support the future strategic positioning of the organization.

o   Have measurable, realistic and time-bound organizational objectives to facilitate project selection.

Figure 15.17   Diagnosis – corporate success

However, the diagnosis also indicates that the organization is to have measurable, realistic and time-bound organizational objectives to facilitate project selection. At the same time, the organization is to make further efforts to improve its ability to ensure that collectively the project portfolio contributes to the business strategy and that undertaken projects support the future strategic positioning of the organization.

The project success diagnosis (Figure 15.18) suggests that the organization does not prepare a business case before undertaking its projects. This has serious consequences in that there is no way of ensuring that:

• Benefits which are normally identified in the business case are achieved;
• Individuals are assigned responsibility for the attainment of the identified project benefits and held accountable for their delivery.

The organization also lacks a knowledge management system to capture, document and share lessons learnt from projects undertaken (post-project review regarding what went right and wrong with a project).

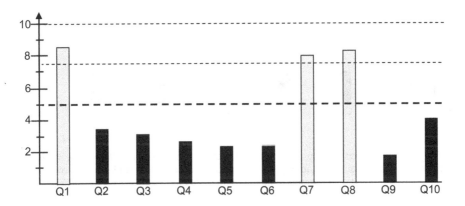

The organization has three major areas of weaknesses related to:

○ Preparation of the project business case and subsequent continuous monitoring of the business case with the project to ensure that the benefits identified are achieved.

○ Ensuring that individuals are assigned responsibility for the attainment of the identified project benefits and holding them accountable for the delivery of the benefits.

○ Having a knowledge management system to capture, document and share lessons learnt from projects undertaken (post-project review regarding what went right and wrong with a project).

Figure 15.18   Diagnosis – project success

The repeatable project management success diagnosis (see Figure 15.19) shows that the organization lacks a standard project management methodology which is applied across the whole organization and supported by personnel that are adequately trained in its use.

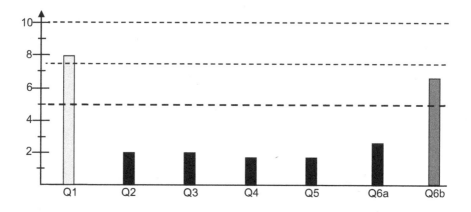

The major weakness being experienced by the organization is a lack of a standard project management methodology that is applied across the whole organization and ensuring that personnel are adequately trained in its use.

Figure 15.19   Diagnosis – repeatable project management success

Finally, the project management success diagnosis (Figure 15.20) shows that the organization has a serious lack of project control practices related to the time and cost elements. Although quality does not appear to be an issue, it is likely that quality is being attained through higher expenditure and an associated delay in delivery time (possible rework). Moreover, the project management success diagnosis reveals that the organization needs to improve its processes by:

- Having good estimating practices;
- Conducting regular and continuous project cost and schedule activity tracking;
- Minimizing project scope amendments during project execution through rigorous project change control;
- Conducting regular project earned value analysis and matching the end result with the business case expectations.

Moreover, the organization needs to introduce risk management practices to ensure that project managers regularly conduct risk management analysis of the project under their responsibility. All of these recommendations are to be supported with the appropriate project reporting practices.

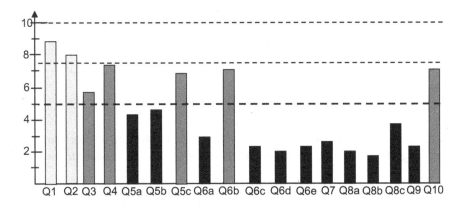

The major weakness being experienced by the organization is a serious lack of project control practices regarding the time and cost elements. Although quality does not appear to be an issue, this is likely being attained through higher expenditure and an associated delay in delivery time. Hence, the organization needs to improve its processes related to:

○ Having good estimating practices and continuous project cost and schedule activity tracking.

○ Minimizing project scope amendments during project execution (rigorous project change control).

○ Conducting regular project earned value analysis and matching with business case expectations.

Furthermore, the organization needs to introduce risk management practices and ensuring that all of the above recommendations are supported by the appropriate project reporting practices.

Figure 15.20   Diagnosis – project management success

Conclusion

This chapter has provided a simple but effective method of ascertaining an organization's preparedness for undertaking and managing projects. The suggested project diagnostic model takes a holistic view in the way projects influence the organization. Hence, the illustrated appraisal method is based on the four project success–failure levels, namely:

- Corporate success;
- Project success;
- Repeatable project management success;
- Project management success.

It is important to note that fundamentally, the project manager is responsible for only one project success–failure level, that is, project management success. The remit for the other three project success–failure levels is beyond the individual project manager and rests with executive management or someone within the organization who has holistic responsibility for all undertaken projects. It is this management level that has the remit for ensuring that an organization has suitable methods in place so that:

- Projects undertaken by the organization support and have a positive impact on the corporate strategy;
- Resultant project outcomes reflect the business case that was originally formulated to justify undertaking the project in the first place;
- Projects are executed through the application of a standard project management methodology that is applied homogeneously across the whole organization.

An alternative method of administrating the diagnostic questionnaire is by holding a focus group meeting managed by a trained facilitator. The facilitator would discuss each individual question with the focus group members and record the group's response. Therefore, instead of having each individual completing the diagnostic questionnaire, the focus group would discuss each item (question) in detail and document a single group (consensus) response. If this method is used, the facilitator must be careful to ensure that each member of the focus group participates in the discussion and the final response decision (for every question) and that not just one or two people dominate the discussion and resultant responses.

The careful application of the suggested diagnostic questionnaire will provide a simple but effective assessment method for determining how prepared the organization is for undertaking and managing projects. The diagnostic questionnaire will reveal the strengths and weakness within each particular project success–failure level so appropriate action may be taken to maintain the strengths and transform the identified weaknesses into sustainable strengths.

Index

knowledge process cycle 182

leadership 24, 28, 30–35, 37, 39, 40–41, 44,
80–81, 87–92, 95–6, 106, 111–12,
239–52, 262, 266, 269–70, 273–4,
281 attributes 87, 247, 251
transactional 244–5
transformational 245–7, 252–3
see also management
learning organization 89, 153
legal risks 201–2

management 32, 34, 37, 39, 40, 44, 239,
241; *see also* leadership
management constraints 116, 148–9
management decision making stratum 52
management of change 261
Material Requirement Planning (MRP) 8
matrix project organization 79, 84–8
matrix teams 97
McGregor, D. 92
milestones 15, 25, 31, 33, 36, 54, 69, 115,
149, 152, 155, 159, 191, 200, 210
Mintzberg 76
monte carlo simulation 204, 206, 208, 210,
214, 217
MRP, *see* Material Requirement Planning 8
multi-project environment 23, 40–41, 144,
157, 200

network diagram 116, 126, 129, 137, 139,
148, 154
normalized project success and failure
factors 32, 36
normative commitment 256–9, 264

operations management 1, 4, 5, 17
organizational
commitment 258, 260, 266
performance 21, 45, 53, 77, 228, 236,
255, 269–70
risks 201
strategic framework 49
structure theory and models 76–7
output information 160, 162, 175, 177,
180, 182, 191–2

PERT, *see* Project Evaluation Review
Technique
physical constraints 123–4, 154
physical value chain 159–60
Planning division 160–64, 166–7, 170–73,
175, 182, 191
PPS, *see* Project Planning and Scheduling
precedence network 126–30
product (or service) project organization
79, 83, 85, 87
project
behavioural and management support
factors 40, 44, 239, 283
chemistry 89, 94–6, 112
competency development 32, 36, 39–41,
44, 157, 227–36
components 67, 85, 116, 118–21, 126, 154
control 20, 26–7, 34, 43, 114, 149–52,
155, 298–9
critical data set 191
deliverables 31, 39, 42, 66, 69, 72, 75,
100, 113, 118, 150, 154, 162, 164,
277, 289–90
diagnostic model 283–300
hygiene support factors 40–42, 47, 157,
283
information flow 160–61, 180
information repository 182–4
informational support factors 7, 41, 152,
157, 283
life cycle 41, 98, 222
management 1–10, 13–21
risks 201–2
success 4, 17–20, 39–42, 47, 70, 75,
116, 157, 192, 236, 283–99
modelling 209–10
network 43, 116, 126, 137, 142, 145,
148–51, 154–5, 162, 166, 172, 182,
185, 187–8, 192, 209–10, 217
organization structure 27, 32–3, 37–43,
47, 75–88
outcomes 17, 20, 35, 39, 41, 59, 63–4,
209, 239, 277, 283, 286, 295, 300
outputs 18–21, 23, 39, 41, 64, 72, 78,
285, 289–90, 295
performance 26, 35, 78, 80, 87–90, 96,
161–4, 173, 249